Ethics and Social Responsibility

Kurt Mosser
University of Dayton
Ashford University

Bridgepoint Education, Inc.

VP of Learning Resources: Beth Aguiar

Associate Vice President, Editor in Chief: Erik Evans

Sponsoring Editor: Steven Wainwright

Development Editor: Dan Moneypenny

Assistant Editor: Nick Devine

Editorial Assistant: Rebecca Paynter

Printing Services: Bordeaux

Composition/Illustration: Lachina Publishing Services

Cover Image: © Jaromir Lasota/age footstock/Photolibrary

ISBN 10: 1-9359660-3-0

ISBN 13: 978-1-9359660-3-6

Published by Bridgepoint Education, Inc., 13500 Evening Creek Drive North, Suite 600, San Diego, CA 92128.

www.bridgepointeducation.com | content.ashford.edu

Brief Contents

Contents

chapter 2
Individual Rights and Responsibilities   *33*

chapter 3
Social Rights and Responsibilities 77

chapter 4
Rights and Responsibilities—Individual and Social 121

chapter 5
What Can Ethics Teach Us? *163*

Preface

We all encounter questions of right and wrong every day. Sometimes these questions can be relatively minor: Should I drive over the speed limit? Should I "pad" an expense account? Did I tell the government that I gave more to charity than I actually did? But some questions can also affect a great number of people: Should there be a right to assisted suicide? When is going to war justified? What kind of environmental responsibilities do we have to the next generation?

The systematic study of right and wrong is called ethics, or moral philosophy. In this text, we look at some of the theories that philosophers have developed to help guide us in making our own decisions and evaluating the decisions made by others. We consider ethical problems that arise for individuals, as well as ethical problems that arise for society as a whole. We also examine the relationship between the individual and society, in order to determine how that relationship affects our moral decisions.

The approach adopted here identifies specific ethical issues, beginning with those that immediately affect individuals, including gun control, school prayer, and pornography. We then look at broader social questions such as the death penalty and the role religion plays in society. We conclude by looking at questions that arise from the relationship between the individual and society, such as the tension between the right to privacy and national security, as well as examining the responsibility corporations have to consumers.

A number of features are included to help you engage with the material, such as questions about what you would do when confronted by specific ethical issues. This offers you the chance to apply some of the material you have learned to the kinds of moral problems we continue to confront: you will see these indicated by the phrase "What Would You Do?" We also look at a few examples of ethical issues from the past, which demonstrate that genuine progress often can be made in struggling with moral problems.

Each of the specific ethical issues we examine begins by describing the problem itself and then looking at opposing perspectives relative to that problem. We then see how ethical theory can deepen our understanding of those perspectives. We conclude each discussion by looking at some of the results of the discussion, as well as some of its implications.

All of us make moral decisions every day. The study of ethics, and a close examination of the theories and arguments we learn here, won't guarantee that we will always make the right decision. But it will help us better understand what is at stake in making those decisions, clarify our responses to ethical issues, and improve our ability to examine critically our own moral principles and defend our reasons for being committed to these principles.

About the Author

Kurt Mosser has a B.A. in English, history, and philosophy from Southern Methodist University, and an M.A. and Ph.D. in philosophy from the University of Chicago. His *Necessity and Possibility: The Logical Strategy of Kant's Critique of Pure Reason* was published by the Catholic University Press of America in 2008. He has published on the philosophy of logic, language, and music and, in addition to a number of scholarly papers on Immanuel Kant, written about Friedrich Nietzsche and Ludwig Wittgenstein. His other interests include playing the guitar, banjo, and mandolin, and learning Mandarin Chinese.

1

Ethics and
Social Responsibility

Chapter Outline

- **Introduction**
- **Why Study Ethics?**
- **Argument and Emotion in Ethics**
- **A Brief Look at Logic**
    Sentences
    Arguments
- **Application of Theory in Practice**
- **The Individual and Society**

- **Classical Theories**
    Utilitarianism
    Deontology
    Virtue Ethics
    Differences in Virtue Ethics
    Application of the
       Three Theories

- **Alternative Perspectives**
    Relativism
    Emotivism
    Ethical Egoism

1.1 Introduction

People have worried about ethical questions—most simply stated, what is right and wrong—since people have worried about anything. From the most basic, everyday concerns to the most important challenges a society can face, we confront these basic ethical questions all the time. In the following pages, we will look at many such moral problems, as well as some of the ethical theories philosophers have offered to solve them.

The study of ethics can be frustrating at times, largely because the problems ethics deals with rarely lead to a result with which everyone is satisfied. Hence, the arguments continue, new points are raised, old views are discarded, and we seem to be going nowhere. But some of this frustration can be alleviated when we realize that as long as people debate questions of right and wrong, these disagreements will persist. At the same time, however, we will discover that our understanding of those disagreements can be deepened and our abilities to reason about them improved. We may not solve all the ethical problems we confront, but we can make progress by solving some of them, and making clearer what is at stake in the problems themselves.

1.2 Why Study Ethics?

You are standing in line at the movies, and someone cuts in front of you. Your child is sent home from school because what is written on her T-shirt is considered "inappropriate." You discover that your best friend is cheating on his wife. You are forced to pay taxes to support behavior you think is wrong. Your commanding officer punishes you for something you didn't do. Your boss promotes a co-worker who took credit for work that was, in fact, done by you. You have a little extra money and, on your way to play the lottery, pass a homeless woman with her child.

Radius Images/Photolibrary

Your co-worker took credit for your work and was promoted as a result. What should you do?

These situations illustrate some of the ethical questions we regularly confront that force us to consider what we should do, and whether our response is good or bad, right or wrong, moral or immoral. The study of those problems constitutes the discipline of philosophy known as ethics. The study of ethics is ancient and can be found in all cultures and at all times humans have lived in social groups. That people consider what is right and wrong, and what they ought to do is fundamental to living in communities. Thus, another way of thinking about ethics is that it is the study of "oughts" and "shoulds"—what ought I do, what should others do, what ought society do. Even though our focus here will be on ethics, we will also see that the long history of ethics has important relationships with religious traditions and legal and political doctrines. Recognizing how our philosophical concepts—particularly ethical concepts—inform and clarify our understanding of religion, the law, and politics is important.

At the same time, we all have what philosophers call moral **intuitions**. Intuitions, in the philosophical sense, are views that we hold, and share with others, without any specific argument or reasoning involved: they tend to be immediate and spontaneous. Perhaps you see an animal being treated with great cruelty, and you immediately and spontaneously object to that treatment. This reflects your intuition that such cruelty is wrong; you don't hesitate to consider the evidence and arguments involved; you simply react. Such intuitions are often correct, and the study of ethics can help support them by providing deeper reflection on the issues involved and developing sophisticated arguments that support these intuitions. It is also possible that such intuitions may be wrong, or at least may be considered by many others to be wrong. A person's intuitions may tell him that women or people of other races or religions are inferior. Many of us may object to these intuitions. The study of ethics puts us in a stronger position to be able not just to say that we disapprove, but to explain why we disapprove and why such intuitions may both be wrong and lead to other immoral results.

Corbis/Photolibrary

Moral intuition tells you that stealing is wrong. Some intuitions are less commonly held.

Most ethical debates revolve around questions where the correct answer isn't always obvious. If it were obvious, of course, there wouldn't be much room for debate. This can be frustrating, for ethical arguments seem never to end, and rarely is a serious moral problem solved in a way that everyone accepts. At the same time, we shouldn't be terribly surprised that this happens in ethics, for several reasons. Ethical questions are often the most important, but most difficult, problems we ever deal with. We might like it if we had an "ethical calculator." We can enter a couple of numbers into a standard calculator, press the "multiply" button, and be guaranteed of the answer. Ethics doesn't work this way: first, there is rarely an agreed-upon set of rules to follow (presumably most of us, in contrast, agree on the basic rules of multiplication). Second, we may not even agree on how to describe the moral question itself. If two people are debating the morality of physician-assisted suicide, and one person insists on the existence of an eternal human soul while the other denies its existence, they almost certainly will disagree over how to describe the problem itself.

As we will also see, however, ethics can lead to solutions that seem to indicate actual "progress." We will look at some historical debates that are based on certain assumptions about people, assumptions that have changed and led to corresponding changes in our moral understanding of human beings and in our laws. This is a reminder that much can be gained by looking more closely at moral challenges, examining the arguments that arise relative to these challenges, and considering what assumptions are made in constructing these arguments. Studying ethics allows us to do this more carefully and with more sophistication. Although studying ethics will not solve all our problems, it does offer a great deal in terms of understanding those problems and determining what is involved in the solutions to those problems that have been offered. That is why we study ethics!

1.3 Argument and Emotion in Ethics

People often disagree, and express that disagreement with arguments. Two people may disagree about which is better, football or baseball. They may see a movie together and not agree about whether it was a good movie. They can debate the merits of two presidential candidates, or to which restaurant they should go. A parent and young child may have a serious disagreement about what time that child has to go to bed. All these disputes can, and often do, lead to arguments, with each participant trying to establish his or her claim on the basis of evidence, reasons, and logic. Sometimes these arguments can become very heated, and some arguments have been known to lead to violence. Presumably, an argument that is settled violently is one where evidence, reasons, and logic don't play much of a role. Other arguments are settled by one person simply saying "this is what is going to happen." Thus, a parent who may (legitimately) say "this is when you are going to bed!" isn't providing so much of an argument as imposing his or her will on the situation.

Philosophers use the word **argument** in a somewhat different way, one that emphasizes the idea that arguments put forth reasons to accept a conclusion. A philosopher or mathematician would call this the argument for the transitive property in arithmetic, even though there is probably little passion or a threat of violence involved here:

$10 < 20$

$5 < 10$

THEREFORE

$5 < 20$

For philosophers, the term "argument" doesn't imply the idea it often does when we use the term to suggest anger, emotion, and hurt feelings. Rather, in this context, arguments simply present a conclusion and suggest why certain reasons indicate that conclusion is true, or probable.

Visions LLC/Photolibrary

For philosophers, the term "argument" is a dispassionate one. But for some ethical questions, such as abortion, it can be difficult to keep emotion out of the discussion.

At the same time, arguments about ethical questions tend to generate quite a bit more passion, and it can be difficult to keep emotion out of the discussion. Whether it be abortion, taxes, guns, gay rights, race, spanking children, or a whole host of other issues, we have a bit more at stake personally than we may have, for instance, in the transitive property in arithmetic. These are issues that we seem to care about a great deal, and it is difficult to keep our emotions out of the debate. Indeed, it isn't clear that we should keep all emotion out of it; we may be motivated to construct better arguments, weigh the evidence more carefully, and examine the logic more meticulously if we care a great deal about the issue over which we are arguing.

In arguing about ethical issues, most of which are very controversial and involve some of our most deeply held beliefs, it will be important to try to make sure the arguments focus on the evidence, the reasons, the logic, and the argument. This doesn't eliminate the emotional element, if such a thing is possible; rather, it is to try to focus on the arguments themselves, and to not let the conclusions be driven by emotion. Unlike parents with young children, we can't "settle" arguments by dictating the conclusion. Nor, of course, is it legitimate to establish a conclusion on the basis of violence or even an implied threat of violence. Rather, we have to stick to the arguments themselves, and see if we can support our conclusions on the basis of good evidence and solid reasoning. As some philosophers have insisted, it is only by submitting our most cherished beliefs to such critical scrutiny that we determine which of our beliefs can really sustain this kind of examination.

Will Datene/First Light Associated Photographers/Photolibrary

In arguing about ethical issues, it is important to scrutinize our cherished beliefs and focus our arguments on evidence, reason, and logic.

In evaluating arguments, we've mentioned evidence and reason as crucial elements of that evaluation. One of the most useful tools philosophers have to examine arguments is logic, the discipline that investigates the rules of reasoning. It is to logic that we now turn, if only briefly, so that we can have some of its apparatus at our disposal.

1.4 A Brief Look at Logic

Logic is the study of arguments and how they are put together. The study of logic is one of the oldest parts of philosophy—possibly as old as ethics!—and is a rich and vast field of inquiry. Here, we will look at only some of the basics of logic, in order to have some of its technical language available when we want to talk about arguments, and to get an overview of what "good" arguments look like. If you want to see more complete discussions of these topics, they are easily found on the Web, and most libraries have dozens of introductory logic textbooks.

Sentences

Arguments are constructed out of **sentences**, but not just any string of words qualifies as a "sentence" in the sense we will be using the term. On the following list, the sentences are underlined:

Shut the door!

The door is shut.

It is not the case that the door is shut.

Is the door shut?

The door is shut or the door is not shut.

As you can see from this list, commands or imperatives (such as "Shut the door!") and questions are not treated as sentences. For our purposes, sentences are strings of words that can have the values of true or false applied to them. Here we can assume that all sentences will be either true or false—these are called truth values—and we will also assume that sentences cannot have any truth value other than true or false. This assumes what logicians call bivalence, the two values of true and false.

We will call sentences that provide reasons to accept a claim **premises**; the claim that is supported by those premises we will call the **conclusion**. For our purposes, all arguments will have premises and conclusions. Premises will be true or false, and conclusions will be true or false (for premises and conclusions are sentences). However, only the components of the argument—the individual sentences that constitute the premises and conclusion—are said to be true or false; the arguments as a whole are themselves characterized in a different way.

Arguments

Logicians generally distinguish two basic kinds of arguments, deductive and inductive. A **deductive argument** is an argument that draws a conclusion solely on the basis of the premises provided; that is, the information in the conclusion is (or should be) contained entirely within the premises. Deductive arguments are characterized as valid or invalid; a valid deductive argument supports the conclusion in a specific way, and an invalid deductive argument fails to support the conclusion. We want to be able to show whether an argument is valid or not, for if we can show an argument is not valid, we can reject it. If we determine that an argument is valid, then we can go on to worry about whether the premises are, in fact, true.

Validity is a structural feature of arguments. Here are two valid deductive arguments, beginning with what is perhaps the most famous argument in the history of logic:

1. Socrates is a man.

   All men are mortal.

   THEREFORE

   Socrates is mortal.

2. Socrates is a trombone.

   All trombones are made of peanut butter.

   THEREFORE

   Socrates is made of peanut butter.

As noted previously, both of these arguments are valid; this is because the premises support the conclusion in the appropriate way, and if the premises are taken as true, the conclusion must be taken as true: that's what "validity" means. Both arguments have the same structure (just different words), so we can see that the "if" is an absolutely crucial aspect of validity. The premises are actually true only in the first argument; I think we can agree that the premises in the second argument are (in fact) false (not true). Thus, even though both arguments are valid, only the first argument is said to be **sound**. A sound argument is thus a deductive argument that is valid, and its premises are, in fact, accepted as true. In general, when we are looking at deductive arguments, we have two tests: Is it valid? If it is valid, are the premises true? If the argument is not valid, we can reject it; if the argument is valid, we then have to determine if the premises are actually true. That, of course, is where a great deal of work has to be done. In other words, when considering validity, the logician doesn't have to worry about the "real world." So in considering whether an argument is valid, we must keep in mind the "big if": if the premises are true, we must accept the conclusion as true. But it is a different question, usually ignored by the logician, if the premises are "in fact," or "actually," or "in the real world," true.

Robin Bartholick/Uppercut Images RF/Photolibrary

All monkeys are primates. All primates are mammals. Therefore, all monkeys are mammals. This is an example of a sound deductive argument.

Inductive arguments are different than deductive arguments in a couple of crucial ways. First, the information in the conclusion of an inductive argument is not completely contained within the premises; the conclusion introduces new information that can't be found in the premises. Thus, we often see inductive arguments used to make predictions about the future, based on our current evidence. However, we can also construct inductive arguments about the past, by looking at the evidence we have in seeing what kind of conclusions that evidence might support.

This leads to the second way inductive arguments are distinct from deductive arguments: no matter how much support the premises may provide for the conclusion, the conclusion can still be false. That is, even if we have premises that are true and provide good reasons for the conclusion, the conclusion of the inductive argument may not be true. These arguments can be regarded as establishing, on the basis of reasons given in the premises, a probability that the conclusion is true. Here are a couple of examples to indicate how we evaluate inductive arguments.

1. Every morning in the past the sun has risen.

   The sun rose this morning.

   THEREFORE

   The sun will rise tomorrow morning.

2. Every time I've washed my car in the past it has then rained.

I will wash my car tomorrow.

THEREFORE

It will rain tomorrow.

The first inductive argument here is said to be very, very strong; so strong we are tempted to think that its conclusion is necessary. But since we know that the sun—as do all stars—will explode, collapse, or burn out at some point in the future, then it will not do what we call "rising." It is, however, such a strongly supported conclusion that we don't think twice about whether the sun will rise tomorrow. In contrast, the second inductive argument is relatively weak; we probably think we just have bad luck, and that it is just a coincidence that it rains after we wash the car. For, otherwise, if we thought this was a strong argument, we might be tempted to think that by washing the car we cause it to rain.

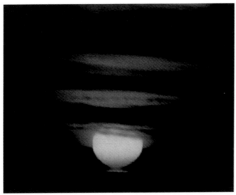

MIXA Co. Ltd./MIXA RF/Photolibrary

Assuming the sun will rise tomorrow because it has risen in the past is an example of an inductive argument. However, not all inductive arguments are as strong.

In general, deductive arguments are evaluated using one of two sets of terms: deductive arguments are either valid or not valid, and if valid, they are either true or not true. In contrast, inductive arguments are evaluated in terms of a continuous scale of strength, from very, very strong (establishing a conclusion we rarely, if ever, doubt) to very, very weak (so its conclusion is seen to be purely accidental).

In the arguments we will examine in our study of ethics, we will see a mix of both deductive and inductive arguments. This shouldn't come as much of a surprise, in that this is what we already do in our everyday reasoning. I may argue, for instance, that aspirin stops headaches, and that I have a headache; I conclude that to stop my headache, it would make sense to take some aspirin. But the claim "aspirin stops headaches" may be the conclusion of an inductive argument. Many times in the past, aspirin has stopped my headache; I thus have a fairly strong inductive argument that aspirin will do so again. On the other hand, you may not have had such good luck, and so the claim "aspirin stops headaches" isn't well supported. Here, and in most of our reasoning, we see a mix of deductive and inductive arguments, and in evaluating ethical arguments in general we will have to keep this distinction in mind. In understanding the structure of arguments, and seeing how well premises support their conclusions, these terms will be very useful in our examination of the specific arguments we will encounter.

Corbis/Photolibrary

Your conclusion that a certain medicine will work can be based on deductive or inductive reasoning—perhaps both.

1.5 Application of Theory in Practice

Our actual, everyday lives are pretty messy, and they can be at their messiest in dealing with questions of morality. Often, when confronting an ethical problem, we may see various solutions, as well as all sorts of different factors that need to be considered. We may need to take into account our perspective and the view of others, often many others, and all of these perspectives can involve vast amounts of information. We may need to factor in our religious and moral perspectives while trying to keep out, to the extent that we can, our biases and emotions. But the others who may be affected by our decision probably have their own biases, emotions, and perspectives that will influence the way they understand the ethical problem and how they evaluate its proposed solution. Thus, when we stop to think about it, actually putting ethical decisions into practice can seem to become complicated, possibly even overwhelming in the complexity involved.

Zero Creatives/Cultura/Photolibrary

Confronting ethical problems in real life isn't always so simple. Sometimes, you need to take others' perspectives into account.

That may seem to be a recipe for seeking to avoid making ethical decisions, but, of course, refusing to make such a decision is, in its own way, to make that decision. If I see something that I regard as deeply immoral, and do nothing about it, I have thereby decided that I won't try to prevent it. Many of us will regard this result as itself objectionable, and ethicists have consequently developed various theories to try to make clearer what is at stake in making ethical decisions and to offer useful and productive guidance in making them.

The ethical theories we will be looking at, and applying to specific moral problems, have enormous advantages to offer in analyzing these problems, and suggesting solutions to them. The three main theories we will be looking at—utilitarianism, deontology, and virtue ethics—offer sophisticated and rigorous ways of both describing and resolving the ethical challenges we confront. They help clarify how those problems arise, provide specific ways of thinking about right and wrong, and make explicit the tools we can use in evaluating the various solutions put forth. At the same time, however, they may oversimplify and generalize ethical issues, and it is a good idea to remember that what we gain in terms of argumentative strength and analytical clarity may, at least on occasion, require us to sacrifice some of the specific details involved in a particular case.

Thus, the relationship between ethical theory and ethical practice tends to be a two-way street. We may apply a specific ethical theory to a specific ethical problem and discover that, in the particular case involved, important details in the case require some adjustment in applying the theory. Or, perhaps, the theory offers us a way to describe the problem itself and allows us to see it in a different way. In general, ethical theory can

Oleksiy Maksymenko/Imagebroker.net/Photolibrary

It is often important to find a balance between theory and practice in ethics.

be developed by looking at ethical practice, but at the same time, ethical practice can utilize ethical theory; each informs the other. Engineers might refer to this as a feedback mechanism, where two things are in a mutually dependent relationship and have to be adjusted in terms of how one component is affected by the other. Philosophers tend to describe such a relationship as **dialectical**. The important point, in any case, is to see that theory and practice in ethics are in this kind of relationship: a theory that cannot be applied is not very helpful, but trying to understand ethical problems without some sort of theoretical apparatus is to risk proceeding without any guidance at all.

1.6 The Individual and Society

When we are asked to describe ourselves, we probably do so in terms of the various relationships we have to other people. We may characterize ourselves as a daughter, a father, a brother, or a grandparent; that is, we may think of ourselves as part of a family, and those relationships are crucial to how we think of ourselves. There are many other such relationships, of course: a person might consider herself part of a religious group, or identify herself as a member of a specific ethnicity or culture, or claim to be a resident of a town, a community, a state, or a nation. These are all social conceptions; that is, we often think of ourselves in terms of our relationships to other people, and other groups of people. Many philosophers have argued that our self-conception is fundamentally described in terms of these relationships, and that we cannot think of ourselves without thinking of the many interdependent relationships we have with other people. Try to describe yourself without using such "social" terms and see how important those terms are in describing who, and what, you are.

Momentimages/Photolibrary

Many of our decisions have effects on others, directly and indirectly. What relationships help define who you are? How do your decisions affect those around you?

If this is the case, then who we are cannot be separated from all those others to whom we are somehow related, whether directly or indirectly. This means that many—perhaps most, or even all—of our decisions will have an effect on others, and those effects must often be taken into account in making ethical decisions. Sometimes this idea is expressed as an implied "social contract"—we all agree to obey certain rules simply in order to be able to live together in a society. Sometimes these rules—such as those against murder and theft—are so important that they become part of a society's legal code. Other rules are more informal and are simply the kinds of things we agree to do to get along with each other. There might not be a law against cutting in front of someone waiting in line, but we have probably experienced line jumping so that we have a pretty good idea of why we object to such behavior. This may be how our first ethical intuitions begin to develop: someone does something wrong that affects us, and we come to see that our understanding of it as wrong tells us that we shouldn't do such a thing. It is a quick step to the Golden Rule: treat others as you would like to be treated.

As noted, many of our decisions have effects on others. Evaluating these effects, and our responsibilities involved, can be difficult. The effects may be fairly obvious if I live with someone who never does the dishes or takes out the trash. But do I have any responsibilities if I buy clothes that I discover are so inexpensive because those who make them are paid very low wages and treated badly? If I continue to purchase such clothing, do I help support such a system? If our decisions affect others, how we determine what others we include in our moral evaluations can therefore make an important difference. Indeed, some philosophers have even argued that in evaluating questions about, for instance, the environment or the increased national debt, we must consider the effects on generations to come.

In what follows, we will look at a number of ethical problems, some of which seem to be individual decisions; often such problems involve "victimless crimes" such as not wearing one's seatbelt or doing drugs. We will also look at issues that clearly have an effect on many others, including those who live and work far away. We will see our ethical intuitions challenged, and we will confront a number of different ways of thinking

Angela Drury/Fancy/Photolibrary

A woman shops for lettuce at a local farmers' market. Deciding where to purchase our food is another ethical choice that could be affected by the others we include in our moral evaluations.

about those challenges. But a crucial feature of many ethical arguments will be the realization that we often cannot isolate our behavior, and its evaluation, from the effects it has on others. It will be important for what follows to keep in mind the nature of the relationship between an individual and the society in which that individual lives and the difficulty inherent in understanding individuals and their behavior apart from the other members—and their values—who make up that society.

Even though our focus will be on utilitarianism, deontology, and virtue ethics, we will also examine three meta-ethical approaches to ethics: relativism, emotivism, and ethical egoism. They are sometimes referred to as meta-ethical perspectives because they aren't so much specific ethical theories as ways of looking at ethics itself. Many find such approaches, particularly relativism, quite attractive. Ethical relativism insists that there is no right or wrong, but that such evaluative terms must be understood relative to a culture, a society, or even an individual. This approach seems to allow us to avoid having to defend ethical claims that can be difficult to defend; however, others maintain that relativism has certain crippling problems. First, many want to say something stronger that what relativism allows. Returning to an earlier example, if we see an animal being treated with extreme cruelty, are our moral intuitions satisfied by simply saying, "in my view that is wrong"? Or do we want to be able to say "that is wrong," even though that may be more difficult to defend? In addition, when we try to draft laws that reflect our moral values, if all such values are relative to one view or another, is it even possible to offer such laws? Even if a majority of a given community insists on a particular legal code being morally correct, others may not, and it isn't clear how relativism can address that problem. Finally, some philosophers have insisted that relativism is conceptually incoherent, and that when pushed to its extreme, one person may not, on the relativist's view, even understand another person—including another person arguing for relativism. This objection is a sophisticated philosophical point based on the idea that since we do understand each other to a great extent, we actually agree on much more than what we disagree about, even though we tend to focus on the disagreements.

When we look at specific ethical issues, beginning with gun control and ending with immigration, we will, for the most part, be applying the three classical ethical theories of utilitarianism, deontology, and virtue ethics. But the meta-ethical perspectives are also important to keep in mind, and we will have occasion to apply them. Those perspectives will also be very useful to remind us that it can sometimes be difficult to provide a satisfactory analysis of a given moral problem and that we may be shirking our moral responsibility if we try to avoid doing so.

1.7 Classical Theories

Every day we are confronted with questions of right and wrong. These questions can appear to be very simple—is it always wrong to lie?—as well as very complicated—is it ever right to go to war? Ethics is the study of those questions and suggests various ways we might solve them. Here we will look at three traditional theories that have a long history and that provide a great deal of guidance in struggling with moral problems; we will also see that each theory has its own difficulties. Ethics can offer a great deal of insight into the issues of right and wrong; however, we will also discover that ethics generally won't provide a simple solution on which everyone can agree.

Utilitarianism

A natural way to see if an act is the right thing to do (or the wrong thing to do), is to look at its results, or consequences. Utilitarianism argues that, given a set of choices, the act we should choose is that which produces the best results for the greatest number affected by that choice.

Definition of Utilitarianism

After helping their mother clean the attic, John and Mary are told they can each have a cookie. When they open the cookie jar only one is left. What do you think would be the fairest solution for John and Mary?

Those who follow **utilitarianism** suggest that there is an obvious solution that is fair, and it may be one that appeals to common sense as well: John and Mary should share the cookie. Since each has an equal right to it, they should split it in half. They may not get what they want—each wants the entire cookie—but both are better off with half a cookie than with no cookie. Dividing the cookie produces the greatest good for the greatest number. This is the fundamental principle of utilitarianism: one should choose to do that which produces a better outcome for the largest number of people.

The cookie example is, of course, a very simple case, but it allows us to introduce some of the terminology philosophers use to examine ethical choices. Here, for instance, we might call the pleasure John and Mary get from the cookie their "utility"; a standard assumption among ethicists, economists, and many others is that people seek to maximize their utility. Thus, Mary would like to maximize her utility by having the entire cookie, but that conflicts with John's desire to maximize his utility (by also having the entire cookie). We should also see that part of this calculation is to minimize pain or suffering; a choice that maximizes utility may often be one that produces the least harm, given the options available. Utilitarianism is the theory that people should choose that which maximizes the utility of all those who are affected by a given act.

Unfortunately, many ethical problems aren't as easy to solve as the cookie example. At this point, however, we see the basic utilitarian principle and how to apply it. Now we can start to make it a bit more precise. According to utilitarianism, one should always act in a way that produces the greatest good for the greatest number of people relative to any other way one might act, or act in a way that maximizes the utility of all affected by an act, relative to any alternative to that act.

Example of Utilitarianism

A couple of examples should make clear how one might go about applying this utilitarian principle. One of the most common ways is to adopt a rule—a law, in this case—against shoplifting. While the shoplifter may maximize his utility by shoplifting, the utility of the store owner is obviously not maximized, and if rules against shoplifting weren't enforced, prices would go up for all the other customers. So here the greatest number of people (the shop owner and the customers) achieve the greatest amount of good by preventing as much shoplifting as possible. This seems like common sense, and that is one thing that makes utilitarianism very attractive. Consider a tax that people in a given community pay for their very good public schools. No one likes to pay taxes, and any tax will decrease an individual's happiness. But the school system in question not only provides the students with a high-quality education (thus increasing the utility of the students and their parents), but the school system makes the housing in that community more valuable, and thus increases the utility of all those who own houses there, not just parents with children. The utilitarian might argue that a relatively small decrease in happiness brought about by the tax creates an increase in happiness for a very large number of people, and thus is the correct thing to do.

Tetra Images/Photolibrary

Paying taxes decreases an individual's happiness, but a utilitarian might argue that taxes are good because they can create an increase in happiness for a very large number of people.

Act Utilitarianism and Rule Utilitarianism

We will see some more details that affect how one applies this utilitarian principle when we look at specific examples. It may already be clear that there can be problems in applying it; some make technical distinctions within utilitarianism, such as differentiating between **act utilitarianism** and **rule utilitarianism**. Generally speaking, an act utilitarian looks at a specific act: Does this act produce the greatest good for the greatest number, given the various options available? If so, the act utilitarian says that this act is what should be done. The rule utilitarian may, in some cases, disagree, contending that one should do things that, as a rule, generate the greatest good for the greatest number. It may, for instance, turn out that cheating on a specific exam will produce, in this specific case, the greatest good for the greatest number. But, in general, cheating will not have that result, so the rule utilitarian will say cheating is wrong in this case, while an act utilitarian may say this specific act is okay. As we will see, many others will challenge, for different reasons, the very idea of using the principle of utility as a guide for making moral and ethical decisions. We can look at one of them here.

Challenges to Utilitarianism

One famous problem for utilitarianism was put forth by the philosopher Bernard Williams (1929–2003). An explorer accidentally walks into a small village just as 20 natives are about to be shot. She is told by the village chief that it is a great honor for a visitor to shoot one of these natives, and because of that, if she shoots one native, the other 19 will be set free. If she declines, however, all 20 will be shot. It seems, as Williams points out, that the utilitarian principle makes pretty clear that the greatest good for the greatest number is produced by the explorer shooting one native, and that any other alternative will not produce as good a result. She has profound objections to taking another person's life; thus, we might wonder about an ethical theory that insists that doing so in this case is not just an option but is in fact the right thing to do. Although we aren't often in the situation of this explorer, it is easy to imagine situations where one might confront this problem. For instance, should you do something that your boss tells you to do but that you think is morally wrong, even though it will produce good results for the company?

Utilitarianism gives us what seems to be a clear and fairly easy principle to apply to ethical problems and so determine the right thing to do in specific cases. It also seems to be an idea that appeals to common sense and is often regarded, therefore, as one that most people use even when they don't realize they are applying a specific ethical theory. As we go along, we will see in many cases that utilitarianism does do this, providing clear solutions to ethical challenges that are simple, easy to explain, easy to justify; it seems to be an obvious, commonsense response to those challenges. Unfortunately, we will also see that it can produce—as it may do in the case of the explorer—results that conflict with our sense of right and wrong. We will also recognize that it isn't always easy to determine what, exactly, is the "greatest good," or how we can decide what the relevant group is when we consider the good for the "greatest number." We may also discover conflicts between short-term and long-term goods when applying utilitarianism. As we will continue to discover, ethical principles frequently can give us guidance and clarify ethical problems, but they usually don't guarantee a result on which everyone will agree.

What Would You Do?

You are the president of a major oil company. A very expensive safeguard, if installed, will almost certainly prevent an explosion of a well you are drilling offshore. You aren't required, legally, to install this safeguard, but if you don't, the risk of an explosion, while still small, is much greater than if you do not install it. You are asked to weigh the costs, or risks, of installing the safeguard against the benefits of not installing it. How do you go about making this calculation? Whose interests should you consider:

- Your company's?

- Your stockholders'?

- The people who might be harmed in such an explosion?

- The larger population that might be affected by the explosion?

- All those affected by the pollution such an explosion might cause?

As the number of interests you consider increases, so does the cost to your company. How do you determine where to draw the line, maintaining a reasonable balance between your company's profits and your company's ethical responsibilities?

Would you have the safeguard installed, or not?

After deciding what you would do, reflect on the kinds of reasons you used to make your decision. For instance, did you weigh the costs and benefits here? Did you focus on the outcome or a general moral rule? Did you ask yourself what an ethical person might do in these circumstances?

Jim Olive/Peter Arnold Images/Photolibrary

Would you install a very expensive safeguard to prevent an offshore oil well explosion if you didn't have to?

Deontology

Rather than looking at the consequences of an act, deontology looks at the reason for which an act is done, and the rule according to which one chooses to act. Deontology doesn't deny that acts have consequences; rather, it insists that those consequences should not play a role in our moral evaluation of such acts.

What Is Deontology?

Utilitarianism is sometimes called a consequentialist theory because it evaluates whether an act is right or wrong in terms of the act's consequences. In contrast to consequentialist theories, a number of different approaches suggest distinct ways of evaluating the morality of an act. Perhaps the most famous of these is **deontology**. Coming from the Greek *deon,* which means "duty," deontology focuses on what we are obligated to do as rational moral agents. It is particularly important to see that the deontologist does not say that actions do not have consequences; rather, the deontologist insists that actions should not be evaluated on the basis of the action's consequences. Again, we can try to bring out the idea of this theory with a simple example; later on, we will apply it to considerably more complex situations.

A computer hacker accesses your on-line banking account and proceeds to drain your account. Clearly, when you discover this, you think what the hacker has done is wrong.

But is it due to the consequences of his act? After all, his utility is increased by exactly the same amount as yours is decreased. The amount the hacker gets is precisely the amount you lose, so this is what would be called a zero-sum game. We may feel that what the hacker has done is immoral, but the consequences don't necessarily show that. Is there another way of looking at his act and seeing why it is immoral?

The deontologist argues that we have a duty, or an obligation, to treat other people with respect; human beings have dignity, and we must take that dignity into consideration when dealing with them. (We also expect others to respect our dignity when they deal with us.) As the most famous deontologist, Immanuel Kant (1724–1804), put the point, we should never treat another person only as a means to our ends, or goals, but should regard them as ends in themselves. In other words, I can't simply use a person to get what I want nor can someone use me to get what he or she wants. We have to consider that other person's needs and desires, respect them, and try to avoid violating them. To give a very simple example: if I'm late to an appointment, I can't run over the pedestrians who are in my way simply to achieve my goal of being on time. (We probably already knew that.)

Comstock/Photolibrary

A deontologist would not consider whether a computer hacker needs to feed his family or pay off debt.

What does the deontologist say about the case of the computer hacker? His goal, evidently, was to steal your money. He used you to achieve that goal and failed to respect your human dignity. This is why the deontologist says that doing what he did is wrong. Notice that the deontologist didn't take into consideration the results of the act. Perhaps the hacker needed to feed his family, spend a weekend in Las Vegas, or donate to a local charity. What he needed (or wanted) the money for is irrelevant to the evaluation of his act; the only relevant thing here for the deontologist is that the computer hacker violated the general rule that you don't steal from others.

Universal Rule Test

We can also say that the hacker's actions failed what is called the universalization test. One way to know if an act is the right thing to do is to ask: Would this act always be the right thing to do, for everyone, in the same circumstances? It seems pretty obvious that we do not want everyone to be allowed to empty out others' bank accounts, so this act can't be universalized.

Another simple example will clarify this idea but also start to reveal why some critics of deontology regard it as conflicting with common sense or as being too rigid. Traditionally, people are taught from an early age to tell the truth. The deontologist might, therefore, put forth this rule: "Never Lie." This will show respect for other people by telling them the truth and can be universalized in that one should always tell the truth. In other words, if I lie to a person, I am failing to respect that person's right to be told the truth; such an act, as a violation of the rule "Never Lie," would therefore be wrong. One may see in the example of lying why the Golden Rule—treat others as you would want to be treated—is similar to deontological thinking. We don't want to be lied to, so we should not lie to others. We expect people to tell the truth, and we can be very dismayed, and even harmed, when they do not. The Golden Rule gives us a pretty good idea of how deontology proceeds, but it has its limitations. The Golden Rule asserts that I should treat others as I wish to be treated. But what if I only have sardine sandwiches and blueberry juice every night for supper; would that make it a good idea to insist that anyone who comes to my house for supper only be given sardine sandwiches and blueberry juice? Should I treat them as I would wish to be treated?

Ghislain & Marie David de Lossy/Cultura/Photolibrary

What would you tell your child about Santa Claus? Would you violate a deontologist's rule of "never lie"?

Imagine a young girl sees a Santa Claus in the mall and asks her mother if Santa really exists and delivers presents to girls and boys who have been good. Should the mother tell the truth, or should she lie to her daughter? Some might say that the daughter is so young—perhaps not having reached the traditional "age of reason"—that in this case it is okay to lie (or at least not tell the truth). On that view, the principle "Never Lie" isn't violated. But what if I've been planning a surprise party for my wife and have had to go to great lengths in order to bring her friends in from all across the United States? If my wife asks, "Are you throwing a surprise party for me?" should I tell her the truth? That ruins the surprise for everyone involved, but I have treated her with the respect she deserves. If I lie to her, to maintain the surprise, don't I violate our rule, fail to treat her as a person— fail to treat her as an end-in-herself—and thus do something wrong? We may be tempted to say, "It is okay to lie in some situations, but not others," but then we have the problem of trying to figure out which situations do allow lying and which do not. In addition, we must justify violating our original rule that seemed, at first, to make sense. We might try to include in our ethical rules "Don't ask questions you don't want answered truthfully," but, then again, we add another complication. One of the attractive features of deontology is the clarity of its rules. But changing the simple rule "Never Lie" to the rule "Never lie except in certain situations or where the other person, who is sufficiently mature, has asked you a question that may not be the kind of question one should ask expecting a truthful answer" makes things quite a bit more difficult in applying the rule to specific situations.

Challenges to Deontology

We saw that utilitarianism has a certain advantage, in seeming to appeal to common sense. Clearly, deontology can claim that same advantage, in that one of its most famous versions is the Golden Rule. The Golden Rule is ancient and can be found in such different civilizations as Egypt, India, and ancient Greece, as well as in many religions including Buddhism, Christianity, Hinduism, Judaism, and Islam. What is probably the best-known version comes from the Christian Bible: "Do unto others as you would have them do unto you." In other words, if you don't like being stolen from, you shouldn't steal from others; if you don't like being a victim of violence, don't act violently toward others. You don't want to be treated by others as simply some kind of "thing," so you yourself shouldn't treat

What Would You Do?

You are the governor of a state with a large Hispanic population. The legislature has recently presented you with a new law that allows police and other officials to ask anyone for documents if they suspect the person is in the United States illegally. What questions might you ask yourself, when deciding whether to make this a law in your state?

- Is this fair to all the people of my state?

- Who will benefit from this law?

- Who might be harmed by this law?

- Would I like to be asked for my documents on the basis of my appearance?

- Is there a presumption that some people are guilty based on their looks?

- Would you sign the legislation, or not?

What are the crucial issues you needed to consider in deciding whether to sign or not? Did you consider, for instance, the interests of everyone affected by your decision, or a smaller group of people? If a smaller group, which group has the most compelling interest you need to consider here?

others that way. The appeal of this approach may be clear from the fact that parents often use this as one of the easiest ways to explain to children, even very young children, the difference between right and wrong. Just consider how many times parents ask their children, "How would you like it if someone did that to you?"

But, as we have already noticed, and will continue to see, deontology can lead to results that conflict with common sense and what we might regard as our ordinary conceptions of right and wrong. Yet again, we discover that an ethical view may have many things going for it, but it can also confront ethical challenges that are difficult to solve. As we saw with utilitarianism, deontology may provide very useful guidance and be quite helpful in clarifying the ethical issues we have to deal with, but we may be expecting too much from it—or any ethical theory—if we think it will solve all such ethical problems, and solve them in a way satisfactory to everyone involved.

Virtue Ethics

Virtue ethics is distinct from both utilitarianism and deontology. Rather than focusing on the consequences of the act we wish to evaluate, or the reason or rule that guides the action, we look at the character of the person performing the act. Virtue ethics, thus, seeks to determine not what makes an act good but what makes a person virtuous.

What Is Virtue Ethics?

Emma is a senior in college; she makes excellent grades, is popular, pretty, funny, and a talented athlete. She has a reputation for being very honest and very generous. Once, when some gang members were threatening one of her friends, Emma stepped in, calmed the situation down, and got her friend out of trouble. She knows how to have a good time, but she never drinks too much or gets out of control. She does, however, sometimes seem to brag a little too much about her accomplishments and seems a bit arrogant about her looks, her achievements, and her popularity.

Emma is an example of a person who is close to the ideal person according to **virtue ethics**, possessing all the characteristics of a virtuous person and having all (but one) in the proper proportion. Virtue ethics emphasizes that the moral, or virtuous, person exemplifies moral behavior.

Emma, of course, has a character flaw: she lacks modesty and is a bit vain. Nevertheless, she does demonstrate the other virtues that virtue ethics identifies as the characteristics of the noble person. These characteristics include courage, temperance, generosity, pride, amiability, honesty, wittiness, friendship, and modesty. While lists of such virtues may vary from philosopher to philosopher, the general idea is pretty clear. The virtuous, or ethical, person, will possess a certain set of characteristics in the correct amount and in harmony with each other.

Emma offers a specific example of the way virtue ethics thinks about right and wrong. Virtue ethics focuses on the person's character and what makes, in general, a person a good (virtuous) person. Aristotle, who is given credit for the first systematic account of virtue ethics in the West (it is a very prominent and old theme in Chinese philosophy), emphasizes specific virtues. Those who possess them in an appropriate way, and in harmony with each other, will be regarded as moral, and serve as examples of morality to others.

What kind of virtues does Aristotle have in mind? He specifies a number of virtues, some of which have already been mentioned, including courage, generosity, honesty, pride, and modesty. He also mentions one that is perhaps less common, temperance, or being moderate in one's appetites and desires. For example, one should neither indulge in overeating nor deprive oneself entirely of the enjoyment food can bring. Temperance illustrates Aristotle's general approach, that these virtues should be reflected in a person's character but should never be taken to an extreme. Thus, one who has too little courage is a coward, whereas one who has too much courage is foolhardy. The virtuous person will have courage in the proper amount. On this view, we should see what is known as the **Golden Mean**, possessing virtue but never having too little or too much of it. The truly virtuous person will have all the Aristotelian virtues and possess them in the appropriate amount and in balance or harmony with each other. In our example, while Emma is close to becoming truly moral or virtuous, she lacks modesty and thus needs to find its Golden Mean in order to become truly moral or virtuous.

Challenges to Virtue Ethics

Aristotle's view, as found particularly in his Nichomachean Ethics, was for centuries a key text in ethics. It became less influential in the 18th and 19th centuries, in part because of the development of the other ethical theories we have looked at, utilitarianism and deontology. There were other reasons that it seemed less satisfactory as a rigorous treatment of ethical ideas. Two particular problems have been identified as generating problems for virtue ethics.

First, it is not clear that it is possible to identify a complete list of virtues, or that everyone would even agree on such a list if it were possible to provide one. Would we all agree on what precisely constituted a given virtue and its appropriate degree? Is, for instance, generosity always a virtue? One might suggest that it is, but how do we determine what its Golden Mean is? Will everyone agree on when one is too generous or too stingy? A soldier in war may sacrifice his life to save others; is that being appropriately courageous, and thus to be praised, or is it being foolhardy and leading to the loss of a valuable soldier whose important contributions are now lost? Can we really be too honest? Is there a Golden Mean for being truthful, and thus a clearly identifiable setting where one should not tell the truth, or lie?

What Would You Do?

You are the parent of a thirteen-year-old boy who recently has been coming home from school with cuts and with his clothes torn. He, reluctantly, has admitted he has been fighting, but it turns out he has been fighting to protect some of the younger kids at school from some well-known bullies. However, after talking with his sister, you discover that your son himself has started to gain the reputation for being a bully. He is, apparently, protecting some kids while bothering others, and it is not entirely clear why he is doing so.

• What would you tell your son?

• If your son asks you how you made your decision, what would you tell him? In explaining your decision, would you emphasize the idea of fairness? Or would you explain it in terms of the kind of person you would like him to be? Would these two explanations contradict or support each other?

m3 m3/Imagebroker.net/Photolibrary
What would you tell your son?

Some of these complaints might be offered by relativism, a view we will examine in more detail later. Here, we can see the relativist's objection as simply noting that one person's courage may be another person's recklessness; if we cannot determine what an appropriate amount of courage really is, the relativist will suggest that this virtue specifically, and all the virtues in general, must be understood not in an absolute way, but relative to a given culture, society, or individual. The relativist is not the only one who will raise this kind of objection. Those who reject relativism, and want to find objective and generally agreed on moral guidance, criticize virtue ethics as not providing it. Very briefly, this criticism recognizes that virtue ethics provides a catalog of virtues but offers little or no indication of how one should act. I may understand that I should be appropriately honest, courageous, temperate, and so on, but does this really tell me what I should do in a specific situation? Does it give me a general set of principles to follow to qualify as a moral person? Many philosophers have suggested that this is a crippling weakness of Aristotle's ethical view. In turn, those who have sought to revive virtue ethics in contemporary philosophy have addressed these kinds of objections, indicating that these criticisms either misrepresent virtue ethics or don't understand how it can be applied to actual situations.

Differences in Virtue Ethics

A couple of things emerge from this example that are significant for ethics in general, and for virtue ethics specifically. First, all three theories draw the same conclusion. They all seem to regard acting generously as the right thing to do, but they come to that conclusion from different directions. This won't always be the case—and the conflicts among these three theories is where things get interesting—nevertheless, we shouldn't be surprised when acts that are traditionally regarded in most, or all, cultures as good are also regarded by our three theories as good. Second, virtue ethics requires that one not just be virtuous but be virtuous in an appropriate way. As we saw, the idea of the "Golden Mean" indicates one can go to an extreme in either direction; one might, for instance, be too vain or too modest. Some critics have pointed out that saying one should achieve the appropriate degree of each virtue seems not to say very much. It may seem here that the virtue ethicist is saying that one must be appropriately virtuous to be moral. But "appropriate," apparently, means being moral in the way one should be. And to tell someone that the way to be moral is to be moral doesn't, again, offer much in the way of guidance.

In general, virtue ethics focuses on the person—the moral agent—and evaluates the character of that person in terms of the specific virtues he or she exemplifies. Ideally, the most virtuous person—sometimes called a person with a "noble soul"—will have all the virtues in their appropriate amount, and they will all be in harmony with each other. As our example with Emma indicates, however, this seems to be a goal for most of us; a person who has all the virtues appropriately ordered seems to be a very rare kind of person. It might also be noted that virtue ethics could be seen as a complement to one of the other theories we have studied. That is, we may want to be a virtuous person, but may find more guidance in becoming that kind of person by looking to utilitarianism or deontology as a way of solving ethical problems. If we are satisfied that, in general, we come to a satisfactory solution to those problems—in other words, we generally do the right thing—then we may well be the kind of person virtue ethics promotes. Some have argued that utilitarianism and deontology may give us more help in figuring out ethical challenges, whereas virtue ethics gives us a goal to aim for and a reason for figuring them out. In this way, virtue ethics might be part of a more general approach to ethics that can be paired with deontology or utilitarianism, rather than an alternative to utilitarianism or deontology.

Virtue ethics was for many years neglected (although a few philosophers endorsed it). It experienced a resurgence in the latter part of the 20th century and received a great deal of attention, through such influential works as **Alasdair MacIntyre**'s 1981 book *After Virtue*, which in many ways sought to update the basics of Aristotle's account of virtue for the present era. It is interesting to ponder why, after so many years, virtue ethics has returned to a place of prominence in the field of ethical study.

Application of the Three Theories

We saw that utilitarianism evaluates a moral act on the basis of whether it produces the greatest amount of good for the greatest number, given the available options. Deontology, on the other hand, employs rules—whether a guideline like the Golden Rule or more complex directives about respecting others and being able to universalize the act in question—to determine whether an act is moral or not. In contrast, virtue ethics focuses on the character of the person in evaluating morality. If we call that person the moral agent, then virtue ethics concerns itself with that agent and his character, rather than consequences or rules. We can use a simple example to see the difference in approach among the three theories we have in front of us.

Laurent Hamels/Photoalto/Photolibrary

What would motivate you to give money to a homeless person? Do you identify more with the utilitarian, the deontologist, or the virtue ethicist?

Imagine you see a mother and child sitting on the sidewalk with what appears to be all their possessions. Presumably, they are homeless and could use some help, and you decide to give them $10. The utilitarian observes that by giving $10, you make yourself a bit less well-off, but make the mother and her child much better-off; thus, giving the $10 produces the greatest good for the greatest number and is the right thing to do. The deontologist, on the other hand, adopts the rule that you should, when possible, help those who are worse off than you. (Or, in terms of the Golden Rule, if you were in the position of the mother, you might well want someone to give you some help.) Thus, in accordance with this rule, the deontologist claims that giving the $10 is the right thing to do. The virtue ethicist, on the other hand, considers your character. You can spare, without too much sacrifice, $10, and the generous person should do so. Since generosity is a virtue, the virtuous person will regard giving the $10 as the right thing to do.

Here we see that all three theories come to very similar conclusions (although for different reasons). This won't always be the case, of course; there are significant disagreements among utilitarians themselves as well as, naturally, among utilitarians, deontologists, and virtue ethicists. As we will now begin to see, there are significant responses to ethical questions that reject these theories as a whole, and offer a different way of thinking about ethics and about doing the right thing.

1.8 Alternative Perspectives

Because of some of the problems we have seen that arise for classical theories in ethics, other approaches to moral questions have been developed to try to solve them. Here we will look specifically at three of these different approaches: relativism, emotivism, and ethical egoism. These views offer certain advantages, but, as we saw with traditional ethical theories, they also have certain drawbacks. It will be helpful to see which of the three theories you find most appealing, and how you think they can overcome the difficulties we will be looking at.

Relativism

The view of ethical relativism regards values as determined by one's own ethical standards, often those provided by one's own culture and background. Rather than insisting that there are moral absolutes, moral claims must be interpreted in terms of how they reflect a person's viewpoint; moral claims are then said to be "right in a given culture" or "wrong for a given society."

What Is Relativism?

Have you ever ended an argument by simply agreeing to disagree? Relativism is the idea that one's beliefs and values are understood in terms of one's society, culture, or even one's own individual values. You may disagree with someone and believe your view is superior, relative to you as an individual; more often, relativism is described in terms of the values of the community in which one lives. Perhaps my culture thinks soccer is the most entertaining sport to watch, and your culture thinks basketball is the most entertaining sport to watch. My view is true, relative to my culture, and your view is true, relative to yours; there isn't some objective "fact" to point to that we would agree on, that would allow us to say one of us is correct (and thus that the other is incorrect). You probably have encountered examples of relativism in discussion with others about music, food, movies, and other issues that involve personal taste: these are said to be subjective and really can't be treated as the kinds of issues that one can treat objectively or as if there is a single, correct answer everyone should accept.

Jorgen Schytte/Still Pictures/Photolibrary

This village chief in Northern Ghana has 11 wives, which is acceptable in his culture.

The relativist in ethics extends this kind of approach to ethical values. Perhaps one person lives in a culture where having a sexual relationship outside of marriage is regarded as one of the worst things a person can do; in this culture a person engaging in extramarital sex may be punished or even forced to leave. But another culture might have a considerably different view of what the first culture calls adultery, and sharing one's spouses in a general way is not only thought not to be wrong but is actively encouraged. Which culture is right? The relativist insists that this question can't really be answered, without taking into consideration the values of the society: adultery is wrong in one, right in the other, and there isn't a lot more to say beyond that.

Application of Relativism

Traditional ethical views, as well as religious views, condemn a number of things as unethical, such as killing another person, rape, and theft. The relativist identifies a culture, or society, which we can call "society 1." So rather than saying "killing is wrong," the relativist claims "killing is wrong in society 1." But, presumably, there might be another culture, call it "society 2," and one might then claim "killing is not wrong in society 2." Since we can't simply assert that society 1's values are right and society 2's values are wrong, we relativize the moral claim involved to the culture in question. Given the many cultures and societies around the world, the ethical relativist then concludes that all moral claims must be relativized in this way. Of course, we also know that many cultural values conflict with each other, over many different issues. The relativist's solution to these conflicts seems to be a recommendation of tolerance and the suggestion that understanding the values of other cultures will help us better appreciate, and respect, those cultures. What we might object to is based on a view relative to our own culture; respect for another culture requires that we respect the moral evaluations of that culture, which are, of course, relative to that culture.

Many people find relativism extremely attractive. After all, determining what is right and wrong is frequently very difficult. It may also be difficult to defend—rather than just assert—that a given culture's (usually one's own) values are the correct ones, and that those values that are different are somehow wrong. Relativism also seems to decrease the kinds of conflicts that arise over such issues. After all, many of us feel uncomfortable judging another society's moral standards, particularly if that society, or culture, is one we aren't familiar with. Indeed, the very term "judgmental" is used to indicate that one fails to understand the perspective of the other person, or the other culture, in making such claims. It is not unusual to hear someone criticized for being judgmental, or too judgmental, a criticism that really amounts to the suggestion that one doesn't sufficiently appreciate the perspective of the other person. Presumably, were we to understand other people's cultural values, we wouldn't be so quick to judge them; we would, that is, avoid being judgmental and thereby be more tolerant of others.

Challenges to Relativism

Relativism seems to offer a plausible, if not easy, way out of confronting ethical dilemmas. Many argue, however, that it may be an easy way out. It may, for instance, commit us to accepting practices that we might ("deep down") regard not as wrong relative to a culture, but simply wrong. One might consider some of the customs cultures have practiced, and may continue to practice, that one might object to: persecuting and killing ethnic minorities, genocide, mass executions of people from a minority religion, infanticide, torture, slavery, systematic oppression of women (and, sadly, the list may go on). Although one may feel uncomfortable judging those in another society, others feel considerably more uncomfortable with an ethical view that seems unable to say that murdering hundreds of thousands, or millions, of people simply on the basis of their religious beliefs is wrong. In other words, stating that "Genocide is wrong for my culture, but might be right for another culture" seems inadequate to express a sufficiently strong condemnation of genocide. We may be happy to embrace relativism when comparing one fast-food restaurant to another; we may be considerably less enthusiastic about regarding mass murder as only wrong relative to a given set of cultural values.

Christopher R. Harris/Photolibrary

One of the problems with relativism is that some more objectionable attitudes and actions—like those of the Ku Klux Klan—might not be considered wrong because they are merely part of the group's culture.

Further difficulties arise for relativism, as well, when one considers that few people come from a single, specifiable "culture." There may be general notions that guide one's society, but one may also consider oneself part of many different groups, each of which can inform one's moral values. Relativism seems fairly clear, until we start trying to decide what provides our moral sense. You have a given country, language, gender, religion or lack of religion, race, ethnicity, class, and so on, but does only one of these determine your values? Or do they all contribute to what you consider your ethical viewpoint? Of course, things may get worse if one claims to be a relativist but subscribes to a view that regards relativism as wrong. Many religious viewpoints are like this: Does one who adopts a specific religious viewpoint really regard it as just a choice, relative to one's culture, or don't most religions put forth their doctrines as true, or right, in a way stronger than relativism can support?

Relativism, as we have seen and will continue to see, has many attractive features, particularly in its recommendation that we try to understand a different culture before criticizing it. Nevertheless, we have also seen (and will continue to see) that it may have substantial problems; for instance, relativism prevents us from registering our objections to practices that seem not just wrong relative to a society's values, but simply wrong. It may be difficult to determine what, precisely, one's culture actually is in the relevant ethical sense to make relativism work. And, finally, it may be difficult for a society to recognize that it might be doing something immoral, if the very idea of immoral policies cannot be raised within that society. Relativism may help us get some perspective on some issues, but it seems to fall short when we consider what some cultures and societies have done in the past—for example slavery—and how they were able to reject such practices. Again, we see this view informing some of our understanding of ethical challenges, but perhaps not providing a way of solving them in a satisfactory way.

Emotivism

Emotivism offers a perspective on our ethical claims that eliminates much of the traditional kind of argument based on reason. Emotivism, instead, sees our moral evaluations as simply the expression of whether we respond to a given act by liking it, or not liking it. Something is good, on this view, if it is something about which we feel good; something is wrong if it is something about which we feel bad.

What Is Emotivism?

Emotivism is a non-cognitive theory of ethics, because it denies, among other things, that moral claims can appeal to "facts." Rather, emotivism, as the name indicates, simply says that moral claims express an emotional response, or an attitude, we may have toward a given kind of behavior. If I see someone stealing candy from a baby, I may have an emotional response that indicates that I regard it as wrong. Of course, I may have a different response: I may not care, or I might think stealing candy from a baby is a good thing. In all these responses, however, there isn't any fact or objective cognitive claim involved. I simply have the response I have, and my emotional response expresses whether I think it is a good or a bad thing or I am indifferent.

Blue Jean Images LLC/Photolibrary
Emotivism dictates that your ethical decisions are made based on how you feel about them.

Sometimes this theory is referred to as a "Boo Hurrah" theory of ethics: if I think something is wrong, about all I can do is say "Boo," indicating that I regard it as wrong. If, on the other hand, I approve of the act, I can say "Hurrah" to indicate that approval. One advantage of this theory is its simplicity: to evaluate an act as moral or immoral I just give a thumbs-up or a thumbs-down. The simplicity is gained by seeing that there isn't a whole lot more to say here, for the moral evaluation simply is my emotional response.

Emotivists insist that there is a significant difference that we should recognize between moral claims and other kinds of claims. We can, it seems, appeal to "facts" in talking about the color of a table; there is, in this case, a public, objective kind of standard we can discuss. If we are talking about what appears to most of us as a brown table, and someone insists that it is, in fact, green, that person seems to us to be wrong. Of course, we can't rule out the idea that we are wrong, and we can continue to discuss the claim among ourselves, doing measurements, comparing other things that we think are brown to see if this person calls them green, and so forth. We may discover she is color-blind or learned her color words in a unique way; we may also discover she is mistaken. But the emotivist thinks this kind of procedure would not work when considering moral claims because moral claims are fundamentally different.

Why Is Emotivism Appealing?

David Hume (1711–1776), in a very famous argument, claimed that it was a basic mistake in reasoning to go from an "is" statement—a claim about some property something has—to an "ought" statement—a claim about some moral conception of right or wrong. Actually, most of us make this distinction on a pretty regular basis. Imagine you live in a country where women are not allowed to work outside the home or have salaried jobs. This way of life is very old, and many people regard it as "natural." So one might offer, as an "is" statement, "women not working outside the home is natural." The corresponding argument, though, concludes (on the assumption that "natural" means "correct") with an "ought" statement, that women ought not, or should not, work outside the home. But just because something is the case, and has been for a long time, doesn't mean it ought to be the case. So Hume and others have argued that one can never go from an "is" statement to an "ought" statement, making a bit more explicit the idea that just because something can be described in a certain way doesn't mean that certain moral obligations follow from that description.

We can see why the emotivist finds Hume's argument attractive. We are happy to talk about properties that objects have. We can examine such claims as the table is brown, the rectangle has four sides, and people who live in Hawaii have suntans ("is" statements), and we can determine, or at least meaningfully argue about, whether they are true or false. The emotivist argues that emotional reactions cannot be examined or argued about in the same way; they involve "ought" statements (such as "one ought not cheat"); by those reactions, we register our moral evaluation of them. Imagine a friend who cried when he saw a movie that he found very moving. Would we say he was "wrong" to have that reaction? It seems to be the case that we would regard the friend's reaction as his emotional response to the movie. The emotivist argues that we could no more say that one's moral evaluation of something is "wrong" (or "right") than we could judge our friend's reaction to the movie.

Challenges to Emotivism

Just as the theory of emotivism is pretty clear, the objections to it are also not very difficult to figure out. For instance, if emotivism really reduces our moral evaluations to simple, almost involuntary emotional responses, does it eliminate our ability to disagree about ethical evaluations? To return to an earlier example, are we satisfied by simply saying "thumbs down" to genocide and recognizing that we don't have any way of refuting someone who says "thumbs up" to genocide? Does this conflict with our moral intuitions? Do we want to be able to say something more or something stronger?

As we can probably tell, some of objections to emotivism are similar to those of relativism. Note, however, that the two theories are distinct. The relativist seems to be saying that it is true (or false) that a given act is wrong; but that truth is relative to the person making the moral evaluation. I may think it is a good thing to lie, and you may think it a bad thing. A relativist will say the claim "Lying is good" is true, but just true for me (or my culture); she will also say that it is false, but just false for you (or your culture).

The emotivist disagrees, insisting that "true" and "false" don't really have any role to play here; the emotional response, in other words, exhausts all one can say about whether one finds something right or wrong. The relativist and the emotivist have different views about the content of moral claims, whether those claims can be true, and how we might evaluate them; on the other hand, many have argued that there ultimately isn't a lot of difference between the two. It is interesting to consider what those differences may be.

Ethical Egoism

Egoism—specifically ethical egoism—argues that our moral evaluations should be made in terms of our desires and goals. Something that promotes what I want is regarded as right; something that interferes with what I want, or prevents me from reaching my goals, is regarded as wrong.

What Is Ethical Egoism?

A position that contrasts sharply with the classic ethical theories of utilitarianism, deontology, and virtue ethics—and most religions—is called **ethical egoism**. The literal meaning of "ego" comes from the Greek word for "self," or "I," and that notion is at the center of egoism: I do what I want to do in order to increase my own happiness, my own pleasure. Simply put, I know what I want, and something is good, or right, if it helps me to obtain that desire (and bad, or wrong, if it interferes with my doing so). If doing something promotes my own happiness or helps me reach my desired goals, I should do it. That is the fundamental principle of ethical egoism.

Psychological Egoism

Ethical egoism, obviously enough, is an approach to ethics, but it should be noted that another kind of egoism, psychological egoism, needs to be kept distinct from ethical egoism. **Psychological egoism** is the view that people in fact do whatever it is that maximizes their utility. (In the language just introduced, this is an "is" statement that describes people as self-interested.) Ethical egoism is the view that people should do what maximizes their utility (so this an "ought" statement about what people ought to do or should do.) If Hume is right, we shouldn't argue that because people are self-interested, or, literally, selfish, that they should be selfish; that would be to go from an "is" statement to an "ought" statement. For our purposes, we can simply stick to ethical egoism as the view that one ought to act in a way that maximizes his or her self-interest, and all moral evaluations should be made on that basis. We will use the shorter term "egoism" to refer to this particular view of morality, and how we make moral decisions.

Application of Ethical Egoism

Here is a standard kind of example that illustrates what egoism argues in terms of ethics. You work very hard, and put in a lot of overtime, not just to take care of your family but also to enjoy the occasional luxury. One day you decide to take in a professional basketball game, and after parking, you walk past a homeless man. You have some extra money in your pocket, but you had also intended to use that money to treat yourself during the game. The egoist simply says that you should do what makes you happiest, or, again, maximizes your utility. It is up to you: perhaps you would feel better if you gave the homeless man some money; perhaps you would feel worse because you think giving out such money encourages people to be homeless and thus not work hard. Perhaps you weigh how much pleasure you get out a snack at the game as opposed to how much pleasure you get from helping someone out. Perhaps you think being charitable, and giving, makes you a better person, and thus that maximizes your pleasure. Perhaps, for religious reasons, you decide to give the man some money. The point is that you determine what makes you better off; you do what maximizes your own utility or increases your own happiness. Some might call that being selfish, and, interestingly enough, the egoist might also call it selfish. But there is a crucial difference here: the egoist doesn't regard being selfish as a bad thing. We may often use the term "selfish" to describe behavior we wish to criticize, but that is not the way the ethical egoist uses the term. "Selfishness," for the egoist, is simply used to recognize that people act, or should act, in their own self-interest. The egoist thinks being selfish can be a good thing; a famous defender of this view, Ayn Rand, even wrote a book called *The Virtue of Selfishness*.

Rubberball/Photolibrary

Ethical egoists act in their own self-interest. They don't see selfishness as a bad thing.

Some economists have suggested that acting in one's self-interest is the basic mechanism through which capitalism operates. If I want to sell something, I want to obtain the highest price possible for that thing; if I want to buy something, I want to obtain that thing for the lowest price possible. In both cases, I'm being selfish, in that I'm trying to maximize my utility by giving up the least and getting the most. And that, more or less, is how the free market is supposed to work. The person who sells me a pizza will want to produce the pizza for the least amount necessary, and sell it to me for the highest amount he can get me to pay. Of course, there are other pizza makers and other pizza buyers out there. Eventually, on this theory, consumers of pizzas will get the most pizza for the least amount of money, while the best pizza makers will be rewarded by selling more pizzas than their competitors. People will cheat, of course; some pizza makers may use inferior ingredients, but, in theory, when this kind of thing is discovered, that pizza maker will sell fewer pizzas or even go out of business. Multiply this kind of free exchange billions of times, and you have what is known in economics as a robust free-market economy. In these cases, we generally don't think those who want to pay the least, or are able to charge the most, are being selfish, rather we see them as acting rationally as economic agents. The egoist in ethics claims that this is the way people, in general, should act.

Challenges to Ethical Egoism

This is an attractive theory for many people; indeed, many seem to be both psychological and ethical egoists, arguing that not only do we act out of self-interest but we also should act out of self-interest. You may already be able to see some of the problems with this view: it seems to challenge many ethical and religious traditions that insist we ought to help each other, contribute to charity, and be concerned with the interests of other people. The egoist doesn't deny that we might do these things or say that we should not do these things; the egoist simply argues that we should do these things if we regard them as increasing, or maximizing, our utility.

One particularly interesting criticism suggests that the positions taken based on ethical egoism can never be shown to be false. If all acts should be done out of self-interest, then it could always be shown that whatever one did was done out of self-interest, and that what we should do is in fact what we actually do. A standard, traditional view is that any claim that could never be shown to be false—which is sometimes called being "unfalsifiable"—is a claim that has no explanatory value. That is, if some explanation or prediction can always be shown to come out to be true, it isn't much of an explanation.

For instance, one might consider two horoscopes. One claims "you will eat three cheeseburgers in the next two weeks," while the other claims "you will meet someone interesting." We can easily determine if the first prediction is true or false; we keep track, and see if, after two weeks, we have eaten three cheeseburgers. While it might not be a particularly bold or provocative prediction, we at least know what would be involved in showing it to be true or false. But what about the second claim? Does it have any predictive or explanatory power? How would it ever be false, if all it says is that someday—next week, next year, or the next decade—you will meet someone interesting (whatever that means)? Could you ever tell the person who presents you with this horoscope that it was wrong? (And isn't this why horoscopes are often written in such a way that they cannot be shown to be incorrect?)

The same objection has been leveled at ethical egoism. Consider a person walking by a burning building; in a second-story window is a baby crying. Should this person risk her life to save the baby? Should the person go get help? Should the person sit down and watch? Should the person call some friends and ask them to come over and watch? Whatever this person does, it will "fit" the prediction, or explanation, of ethical egoism. If this objection is right, and everything and anything one does can be interpreted as maximizing one's utility, then it doesn't seem to ever be false. One might remember that ethical egoism argues not that people act out of their own self-interest, but that they should do so. But is not entirely clear what such a view amounts to. If everyone does act out of his or her self-interest, or if any act can be interpreted that way, then one might ask what additional information is offered by saying one should do so. Some have suggested, for this reason, that ethical egoism "collapses" into a mere description of what people actually do, which seems to eliminate much of any genuine ethical guidance ethical egoism intends to offer.

1.9 Summary

We've now looked at three classical, or traditional theories of ethics, and three alternatives to those theories. As we saw, each has its own advantages as well as certain disadvantages.

Utilitarianism seems very appealing in that it looks at the consequences of an act to see if it results in the greatest good for the greatest number. But, sometimes, even when the results of an act seem to lead to the greatest good for the greatest number, we may be hesitant to regard that outcome as moral.

Deontology also has a certain appeal, as one sees with the Golden Rule. We don't want people to act badly toward us, so we shouldn't act badly toward them. But, again, deontology may have certain drawbacks: some believe it as too rigid, and thus not always the kind of thing that can be easily applied to real-life situations.

Virtue ethics promotes a particular kind of person—a virtuous or noble person—who provides a role model for those who wish to be moral. Determining what the specific virtues are, and what the appropriate balance among those virtues should be, can be difficult. For this reason, some have suggested that virtue ethics is really complementary to other ethical theories so that we may analyze ethical problems from the perspective of another ethical theory, but if done correctly, what will emerge is a virtuous person.

These traditional ethical theories can offer a great deal of insight into ethical issues. But some regard them as either a bit too inflexible or not sufficient to address realistically the kinds of problems people face every day. In contrast to these classical theories, alternative views have been developed.

Relativism argues that moral claims must be evaluated relative to a person, a culture, or a society: rather than something being right or wrong, it is right or wrong relative to the values of a specific community. This seems to eliminate a number of disagreements, but it may prevent us from insisting that something really is, simply, wrong.

Emotivism rejects the idea that we can appeal to any sort of objective moral "facts." Rather, we identify something as being wrong by our attitude that it is wrong and express our disapproval in the same way we would with any other thing we don't like. As with relativism, this seems to eliminate a lot of disagreement, but even more than relativism, emotivism seems to remove the possibility of our being able to insist that something really is the right thing to do, or really is the wrong thing to do.

Ethical egoism adopts the perspective that we should do whatever is in our own self-interest. I determine what is the right thing, or wrong thing, to do by seeing how it satisfies my own desires. This approach seems to capture a good deal of normal human behavior. But, in addition to it conflicting with the traditional idea that it is wrong to be selfish, we also saw that it may offer the kind of explanation that could never be false, and an unfalsifiable claim—such as an astrologer's—isn't much of an explanation.

Theories in ethics are a lot like theories in chemistry, economics, and other disciplines. They can be a bit abstract, a bit dry, and sometimes a bit confusing, but they give us excellent tools to evaluate situations. We will apply these key theories in the chapters that follow.

Some Final Questions

1. You may have an argument with someone, and conclude by saying, "Let's agree to disagree." Think of a moral issue that is so important that it cannot be resolved in this way.
2. A seven-year-old asks you to explain why stealing is wrong. (We will assume here that it is wrong.) How would you go about explaining it?
3. Ethics doesn't seem to provide results that everyone will accept. What are some good reasons for studying ethics?

Weblinks

Some useful links have been provided for you at

http://tellerprimer.ucdavis.edu/pdf/

http://www.themathpage.com/abooki/logic.htm

These would be good sites to start with if a certain logical concept isn't yet clear or if you want more information.

Martin Barraud/OJO Images/Photolibrary

2

Individual Rights and Responsibilities

Chapter Outline

2.1 Introduction

Now that we have discussed the basics of ethical theory, we can apply them to actual situations, and see what they have to say about moral issues in the "real world." This approach has two practical advantages. First, by seeing how a specific ethical theory can be applied to an actual issue, we will see how the theory helps us understand better what the real problems are. We may not solve these problems in a way that will satisfy everyone, but we will have a much better grasp of the problems themselves. This will help us focus our ability to think about these questions more critically and eliminate some of the detours, side issues, and irrelevant parts of the debate that may interfere with our understanding of the questions.

Second, by applying the various theories to actual moral problems, we will also come to understand the theories themselves better. It is one thing to see what a basic ethical position is, but it can be very helpful to see how that ethical position works in dealing with difficult ethical questions.

In this chapter, we will look at questions that arise when individual rights are threatened, or violated, and when one person's rights may infringe upon another person's rights. Here we will look specifically at gun ownership, school prayer, employer-employee conflicts, and pornography. We will also look at a historical debate, over a woman's right to vote. This historical discussion should help us realize that some ethical questions can be resolved, and that talking, and arguing, about them may lead to significant changes in people's lives.

Each discussion will present a debate on a specific topic. For example, we will give an argument for why restrictions on gun ownership should be kept to a minimum, and then look at the counterargument for why those restrictions should be much greater. After presenting the debate, we will show how these positions relate to the ethical theories in Chapter 1—in this case, utilitarianism and relativism. On other occasions, we may apply the same theory in two different ways, to demonstrate that a specific ethical theory may give quite different results in some cases. This will help remind us that although ethics provides guidance and insight, very rarely does it offer solutions to moral issues that everyone accepts. We will then look at some of the results of the debate and the theories involved, and some of the implications that may emerge from those results. After each specific issue is treated in this way, we will briefly discuss a different, but related question that will make clear some of the larger issues involved.

2.2 Gun Ownership and the Second Amendment

The Second Amendment to the Constitution of the United States affirms "A well regulated Militia, being necessary to the security of a free State, the right of the people to keep and bear Arms, shall not be infringed." This amendment has generated enormous controversy, in terms of what rights are really specified here, and what limitations, if any, should be placed on gun ownership. Here we will examine the gun control argument, and then see the perspectives brought to this issue by the utilitarian and the ethical relativist.

The Issue: There Should Be Few Restrictions on Gun Ownership

Gun ownership has been regarded as a right, guaranteed by the Bill of Rights, since the founding of the United States. Here we look at a traditional interpretation of that right, as stated in the Second Amendment.

The argument against restrictions

The Constitution of the United States—specifically the Second Amendment, which outlines the specific right for the people to "keep and bear arms"—is quite clear. That right simply cannot be infringed, or taken away. Just as the other rights enumerated in the Bill of Rights are guaranteed by the Constitution—freedom of speech, freedom of religion, freedom of assembly—the right to keep and bear arms cannot be taken away from the people who live under the Constitution and its amendments (which includes, of course, the Bill of Rights). Fundamentally, there is no further argument needed: the right to keep and bear arms is a constitutionally protected right, and that is sufficient to establish that there should be few restrictions on gun ownership. Any such restrictions on gun ownership would have to meet the kind of requirements one might put on free speech: an overriding public interest, where the good of the vast majority of the public requires some restrictions. But those restrictions must be absolutely minimal and must be shown to be absolutely necessary. Both the law and common morality have found, in very few cases, a need to limit free speech: generally in order to guarantee public safety. In the same way, any restrictions on gun possession must be shown to meet that very high standard,and to be an unavoidable threat to the general public without those restrictions.

This constitutional protection is in itself sufficient to show that gun ownership is a right that should have few, if any, restrictions. But the history of the United States also gives substantial support for the right of private citizens to own guns without interference from local, state, or federal agencies. Americans have long owned guns, and regarded possession of guns to be a right as well as a necessity. After all, the Revolutionary War was won by those who were comfortable and qualified to use guns. Americans enjoy target shooting, skeet shooting, and other types of sport shooting. Many Americans hunt for sport, while others depend upon hunting as an important source of food. Americans should be allowed to own weapons to protect themselves and their families. The Founding Fathers recognized that gun ownership was one part of the very idea of America: self-defense against the kind of tyranny the American Revolution overthrew. Since that time, the right of Americans to defend themselves, their families, and their homes has been recognized as legitimate and justified. Americans are estimated to own some 250 million guns, and more than 25 percent of Americans live in a household that possesses a firearm.

FogStock LLC/Photolibrary

Many Americans own guns for legitimate, legal reasons, including for sport and/or protection.

Reasonable people may disagree with what restrictions can be placed on gun ownership. For instance, it seems reasonable to prevent those with a documented history of criminal violence, such as those convicted of committing violent felonies, from possessing firearms. It may also be reasonable to prevent those with a documented history of substantial mental illness to possess deadly weapons. But it must be recognized, given the historical expectation of Americans to have the right to possess firearms, and the constitutional protection of that right, that any such restrictions must be minimal and shown to be necessary for public safety. Otherwise, small restrictions lead to a "slippery slope" situation where, in the end, the meaning of the Second Amendment is ignored and unjust restrictions are imposed on law-abiding citizens.

To impose such restrictions is not only unconstitutional but also seems to disarm precisely those citizens who have a legitimate interest in, and need for, gun ownership. After all, criminals are not going to be worried about whether their guns are possessed legally. To require the law-abiding to conform to onerous and time-consuming gun laws, or even to prevent in some cases gun ownership at all, is to produce the indefensible situation where guns are more likely to be possessed by criminals than by the citizens who need to protect themselves from those criminals.

The argument for restrictions

In 2005, 14,860 people were murdered in America, 10,100 of them (68 percent) with guns (Department of Justice, 2006). Some of the history of gun-related violence in America is well-known. Two students at Columbine High School killed 12 students and one teacher. At Virginia Tech University, a single gunman killed 32 and injured many more. In the area around Washington D.C., two men killed 10 and injured many others. While these tragedies are remembered, many others, such as mass killings in Dover, Arkansas (16 people killed), in Wilkes-Barre, Pennsylvania (13 killed), and Geneva County, Alabama (11 killed, includ-ing the murderer) are forgotten. The United States has one of the highest rates of violent crime in the developed world; thus, the rate of death by firearm for those younger than 14 is nearly 12 times higher in the United States than in 25 other industrialized countries combined. The New York Times *writer Bob Herbert summarizes the issue: "Since the assassinations of Senator Robert Kennedy and Martin Luther King Jr. in 1968, more than a million Americans have been killed by guns in the U.S. That's more than the total number of U.S. combat deaths in all the wars in American his-tory" (Herbert, 2007).*

OJO Images/Photolibrary

Some worry that lax gun control laws result in more gun-related violence.

Not only are there many guns in the United States, but they are easy to get. Gun shows and private sales may be carried out with minimal or no background checks; in some states a person can buy a rifle or shotgun every month at the age of 12. Even though some minimal background checks and waiting peri-ods have been put in force, some organizations have objected to these restrictions as imposing an undue burden on gun ownership. Those who argue for minimal or no restrictions insist that the public is safer if anyone, at any time, can decide to buy a gun and do so at that time. Lax gun laws and an increasing demand for being able to carry concealed weapons means that it is easy for law-abiding citizens and criminals to obtain such weapons. This has led to a culture in the United States that leads—by a wide margin—the developed world in violent crime and murder. To prevent this growth, reasonable restrictions—requiring substantial background checks, waiting periods, and trigger locks, as well as limits on the kinds of weapons and ammunition that can be sold—are necessary. It should be noted that the

David Doody/Index Stock Imagery/Photolibrary

It has been argued that the Second Amendment extends the right to bear arms to "well-regulated militias" rather than to individuals.

1980s and 1990s saw an increase in controls put on gun ownership, which coincided with a drop in violent crime.

Finally, constitutional scholars have argued, and to a degree the Supreme Court has agreed, in Miller v. United States *(1939), that the Second Amendment clearly intends that the right to bear arms is a right extended to "well-regulated militias," not to individuals. Thus, the Second Amendment, on this interpretation, does not provide for virtually unrestricted gun ownership for private citizens. Even though a later Supreme Court decision seems to conflict with this decision, there is substantial support for the idea that the Second Amendment should not be interpreted as referring to individuals.*

Supporting substantial restrictions should not be regarded as an illegitimate attempt by an oppressive government to seize all guns. As the Founding Fathers recognized, a "well-regulated militia" is sufficient to prevent the kind of tyranny they fought against. Background checks, trigger locks, and limits on some kinds of weapons and ammunition do not prevent the law-abiding citizen from possessing the appropriate kinds of guns for sport shooting, hunting, and home protection. They do, however, minimize the possibility of criminals, the insane, and others who should not have access to deadly weapons from obtaining them. They also indicate that a civilized society should have much less violence, and many fewer murders, than does the United States. This is why many police organizations and police chiefs support such restrictions.

The Theories

As we may already realize, two ethicists may adopt the same ethical theory, yet disagree about how that theory is to be applied or what result that theory indicates as morally correct. Here, we will look at one way to apply a utilitarian argument to see how it supports the view that only the most minimal restrictions of gun ownership should be supported. However, it should be clear that not all utilitarians—just because they are utilitarians— would accept this result. We will contrast the utilitarian view with the perspective put forth by the relativist.

For any community, one of the fundamental requirements of the government that runs that community is to maintain the security and safety of its citizens. Both potentially violent intruders and oppressive governments that arise from within the community or threaten it from outside, pose dangers to the security every citizen rightfully expects. The utilitarian argument against restrictive gun laws is simply to point out that most people see the greatest happiness, or utility, by being more confident that they are safe. Having weapons that one can use to defend oneself, against an individual or a tyrannical form of government, helps ensure that safety. A simple example makes this clear: if an intruder considers robbing your home, and possibly hurting you or your family, this action brings with it certain benefits (whatever money and goods the robber steals) and certain risks (the danger the robber may confront). This cost-benefit analysis changes, dramatically, if the robber considers that you might be armed. The benefits remain the same, but the risks increase quite a bit. If the robber believes, or even thinks it possible, that you are armed and pose a sufficient risk to him, he may well not rob you, either going to another house (one he is more confident does not have such weapons) or just giving up his robbery lifestyle entirely. Generalized, then, people with weapons—and who, of course, are skilled at using them—will feel safer in their homes. The added advantage is that if potential criminals are not sure who does, and who doesn't, have such weapons, then it becomes less likely that the crime will occur, assuming one doesn't want to risk being shot or killed. If the assumption, in other words, is that people can defend themselves—even though it may not be clear who does and who doesn't have the weapons in question—then the entire community increases its level of security, thus increasing its level of happiness. Restricting the possession of weapons thus leads to greater insecurity, decreasing the security of the citizens (and so decreasing the happiness of those citizens). Therefore, utility will be maximized by having the fewest restrictions put on gun ownership. Minimizing the restrictions on gun ownership generates the greatest good for the greatest number and is, therefore, the correct thing to do. From this it follows that any such restrictions must be shown to be required to increase public safety and security; thus, one might argue that such a standard is met by preventing those with histories of violence, or serious mental disorders, from possessing deadly weapons. While we haven't included here the additional utility, or happiness, gained by allowing relative unrestricted access to guns for hunting and sport shooting, including those considerations simply increases the utility of gun ownership, and thus strengthens the argument against restrictive gun controls.

The relativist recognizes that different societies have different histories, different notions of rights, and different approaches to gun ownership. It may be quite rare to know someone in Nigeria, or the Philippines, who owns a gun; the per capita gun ownership rate in Nigeria is approximately 1 percent (one gun for every 100 people), and approximately 4.5 percent in the Philippines. In contrast, Switzerland has a gun ownership rate of about 50 percent (one gun for every two Swiss). The United States has, by far, the highest rate, with 90 guns for every 100 people. Some countries, or cultures, may have very few guns because guns haven't played a particularly important part in that culture's history; some may have very few guns because the government prohibits private ownership of firearms. In contrast, some cultures

Radius Images/Photolibrary

A father teaches his son how to handle a rifle. The relativist recognizes that individuals and cultures have different perspectives and backgrounds on guns.

may have a long tradition of hunting and a history in which guns played a significant role, as in the westward expansion of the United States (Graduate Institute of International and Development Studies, 2007).

The relativist simply sees these values as relative to a given culture. One society may have a lot of guns; another may have very few: neither is "right" (or "wrong"), but a community standard has emerged within that society. The United States can't really object to a country like England, where few people own guns, gun control laws are very extensive, and, traditionally, even the police (called "Bobbies") didn't carry such weapons. In the same way, the English can't object to the approach adopted currently in the United States, where gun ownership is very high.

Within a given society, however, it is more difficult to see what the relativist position offers. Consider Theresa and Bill: Theresa has a number of guns and thinks there should be few if any restrictions on gun ownership. Bill has no guns and thinks private citizens should not be able to possess guns for any reason. Theresa sometimes wonders what Bill would do were he attacked in his home, whereas Bill is unwilling to let his children play with Theresa's children because of the number of guns in her house. Is there anything the relativist can say, beyond identifying the views of Theresa and Bill?

This does not, of course, prevent the relativist from arguing for better enforcement of gun laws or, from his or her own perspective, for more (or less) restrictions on gun ownership. But it isn't clear how disagreements, such as that between Theresa and Bill, can be resolved from the perspective of relativism.

Some Conclusions

Ethics can be frustrating—like much of philosophy—because it doesn't give us the kinds of answers that are clear, obvious, and acceptable to everyone. This doesn't mean that ethics isn't important; indeed, many regard the questions ethics deals with as the most important of all. It does mean, however, that disagreements will continue, and that it is probably too much to expect that an ethical theory will provide the kind of result a formula in chemistry might, or the kind of straightforward answer that an accountant might provide. But getting clearer on the issues, and how ethicists treat those issues, can certainly help provide a better answer, if not a single, correct answer.

We see here, for instance, that one way of treating the issue of gun control, using utilitarianism, can support the idea that restrictions on gun ownership should be as few as possible, and that any restrictions we do put in place must meet a very strict standard to be justified. This follows from a specific conception of what the happiness, or utility, of a community, consists in. If guns make people feel secure, and that security is essential to happiness, then the utilitarian might well argue for minimal gun control. But another utilitarian might take this same conception—the need for security—and argue that this could be better achieved by an absolute ban on all guns; after all, an extremely oppressive society may well be able to guarantee the security of its citizens. This utilitarian, then, might argue that if security is the most important thing for citizens, then this might end up being an argument against a free society, and some utilitarians have argued that an overemphasis on security may lead to a totalitarian government that exercises complete control over its citizens. In any case, it is clear that in applying utilitarianism to a specific issue, it is important—but often very difficult—to determine the happiness, or utility, of the citizens who are affected by that issue. Clarifying the goals of a given society can, however, help define what policies are just and what policies might be unjust.

Our discussion may also show that even though relativism may be attractive at first, it is a difficult theory to apply when making laws. In our example, Theresa would be happiest with no gun laws, and Bill would be happiest with no guns. The relativist can't really help us decide which position, if either, is correct; according to the relativist, each is correct relative to his or her own perspective. Taking both perspectives into consideration when trying to determine what a society's laws should be is difficult. Perhaps, in this case, relativism at least provides us some reasons to think we should listen to the perspective of others—particularly of those with whom we disagree—and to try to come to some kind of compromise that respects the views of all those affected.

Where Do We Go from Here?

The debate over gun control is one of the many ethical issues that involves the question of individual rights. It can be a challenge to determine the extent of those rights, as well as their limits: Where does one person's rights start to interfere with another person's? Does my right to possess weapons infringe on your right to keep your children safe? Does the government have any right to impose restrictions on gun ownership? What exactly does the Second Amendment mean, and, for that matter, what did the Founding Fathers mean by a "well-regulated militia" when they wrote it? These, and many other disputes, continue at the heart of the debate over gun control and the kinds of laws—if any—that should be enacted relative to what kinds of guns one can own and who can own them.

Brand X Pictures/Photolibrary
Both sides of the gun control debate can agree on certain areas. For example, there is more support for restrictions on fully automatic weapons than on limiting gun access for sport shooting and self-defense.

There also seems to be some room for compromise, and in the political arena, there has been a good bit of give and take. Various restrictions, such as those on fully automatic weapons and "cop-killer" or armor-piercing ammunition, are relatively popular. On the other hand, there seems to be little support for depriving citizens of the right to own rifles for hunting, as well as weapons for sport shooting and for legitimate self-defense needs. The study of this particular issue, then, from the perspective of ethics, indicates that the conversation will continue, and will probably be more satisfying if everyone taking part in it spends a little time listening to views that are different from, and even oppose, their own.

Can Ethical Principles Conflict with the Law?

Laws, for a given society, are designed to guarantee those rights recognized in a society, as well as guarantee the security of those who live in it. Debate has raged for thousands of years about what specific rights and responsibilities are involved here. Some argue for a minimal state that does little but guarantee contracts and protect the safety of citizens, by providing secure borders and such minimal services as police and fire departments. Others argue for a much bigger role for the state, insisting that the state function

to provide health care, education, parks, libraries, unemployment support, and many other social services to support a well-functioning and productive society. Of course, there are also many positions in between these two.

Often an individual's, or a group's, ethical principles conflict with the laws that govern the state in which the person or group lives. As we know from history, one might be a member of a religious minority in a society where virtually all the other members of the society follow a distinct religious tradition, or even in a country that has an official state religion. But even in a society that is diverse and places a high value on tolerance, this issue can arise. Whenever a society enacts laws, there is the potential that those laws will conflict with the views of some of the individuals in that society. For instance, a state may outlaw a drug, or ritual, that a group living in that state regards as sacred and fundamental to its religious practice. Obviously enough, a state may pass a law that sanctions a specific kind of marriage. Thus, gay men and women may be prohibited from marrying if a law that defines marriage as a union of one man with one woman is passed. Numerous such instances can be found not just in the United States but throughout the world. The issue this raises for ethics is how one deals with the confrontation between one's morals and the laws of one's state when the two conflict? A state cannot survive if people choose to ignore its laws, but does that mean a person must either leave the state—if that is even possible—or accept laws that are fundamentally at odds with his or her most profound ethical (and possibly religious) views? Traditionally, in a democratic society, citizens have the right to organize, express their opinions, and use the democratic process to change, eliminate, or enact laws. But while that seems to be a theory with many attractive features, it may be a daunting thing to accomplish. Ethics helps us

Mike Kemp/Rubberball/Photolibrary

Many have different views on what the government's role should be. What do you think?

Gulliver Gulliver/Cusp/Photolibrary

Gay marriage is one issue where some individuals' ethical principles have come into conflict with state law.

clarify our ethical choices, but can it help us with having our ethical choices respected? Can it show us how we can guarantee that our moral views aren't violated? And can it give us any guidance when there is a harsh contradiction between one's moral viewpoint and the laws of one's society? These are difficult questions that arise within ethics, and particularly when ethics is combined with an examination of the political process. They may be difficult to answer, but they are good questions to keep in mind when thinking about ethics and the moral values one's state chooses to enforce as its rules and its laws.

2.3 Prayer in Public Schools

Prayer is a particularly personal topic, and thus the role of prayer for an individual has led to some of the most divisive arguments over religious practice: specifically prayer in public schools. Here will we look at this debate, and then apply the theory of utilitarianism, in two different ways, to clarify the issues involved.

The Issue: Prayer Should Be Allowed in Public Schools

Here we will examine some of the arguments over whether organized prayer should be allowed in public schools and try to clarify the issues involved by distinguishing between "allowing" prayer and "promoting" prayer, as well noting the difference between an individual praying privately and a group participating in an organized, coordinated prayer.

The argument for allowing prayer in public schools

The relationship between a person and God is the most precious relationship of all. Society must respect that relationship, and, recognizing this, the First Amendment to the Constitution of the United States prohibits any interference with religion. Because prayer can be considered the most sacred right a religious person possesses, the government absolutely cannot, and should not, interfere with that right by preventing someone from praying. As the First Amendment states, "Congress shall make no law respecting an establishment of religion, or prohibiting the free exercise thereof." To prohibit school prayer is to prohibit the free exercise of one's religion. Thus, not only is eliminating prayer from public schools wrong, it is also unconstitutional. Moral and legal reasons demonstrate that prayer in public school should, therefore, be allowed.

Paul Thuysbaert/GraphEast RM/Photolibrary

An Arab father and son pray together. Some would argue that prohibiting school prayer limits free exercise of one's religion.

Clearly, one's right to prayer is protected by the Constitution; however, there are many other benefits to allowing prayer in public schools. Religious values, such as honesty, charity, and non-violent problem solving are important to a well-functioning society. Few places are more important than public schools to emphasize these values; indeed, public schools provide a tragic example of how these values have been neglected. Teenage pregnancy, STDs, gang violence, and drug and alcohol abuse are common in many public schools. Reminding students that these are wrong and that there are ways of avoiding them are valuable moral lessons students need now more than ever.

This is not an argument for a specific religion's view to be imposed on public school students; that would, indeed, violate the language of the First Amendment and what is known as the Establishment Clause. Rather, the argument here is for voluntary prayer for students who wish to participate. This allows these students to exercise their religious rights and to promote important moral values. Furthermore, most religions promote the same kinds of moral values. The Golden Rule, for instance, can be found in many different religions and in many different cultures. To remind students to treat others as they would want to be treated establishes no specific religion and reinforces a valued fundamental to a well-ordered and moral society.

History and current practice also supports allowing prayer in school. From the founding of the United States, and for almost 200 years, public schools allowed voluntary prayer. Thomas Jefferson refers to the unalienable rights of American citizens as having been granted by their "Creator" in the Declaration of Independence. Both the Senate and the House of Representatives maintain a chaplain, who begins each legislative session with a prayer; legal tender (money) in the United States reads "In God We Trust"; the Pledge of Allegiance includes the phrase "One Nation Under God," and presidents of both political parties frequently end speeches by saying "God Bless America." Few people have seen these practices as violations of the First Amendment.

Jamie Grill/Tetra Images/Photolibrary

Some would note that fewer people have objected to saying the Pledge of Allegiance and singing the national anthem; thus, history and practice support allowing prayer in school.

To prevent students from the exercise of their religion is to require students to obey the dictates of a non-religious minority. A short prayer at commencement exercise, at a football game, or at a school assembly not only reminds students of the importance of religious and moral values but is generally regarded to reflect the wishes of a large part of the student body in most public schools. Thus, to prevent it violates the Constitution and distorts the wishes of the students themselves, as well as their parents. To deny one the right to have prayer in public school, therefore, is immoral and unconstitutional, prevents important moral lessons from being made and reinforced for a large group of students who may need those lessons, neglects the history of the United States, and conflicts with the desires of the majority of students and their parents. Therefore, prayer should be allowed in public schools.

The argument against allowing prayer in public schools

The United States is a remarkably diverse country, particularly in terms of its citizens' religious affiliations. In addition to the numerous Christian denominations, there are Jews, Muslims, Hindus, Buddhists, Taoists, Zoroastrians, Wiccans, Sikhs, and Native Americans with their varied spiritual practices. There are also many who do not identify with any religious affiliation, including agnostics and atheists. All Americans have the right to religious expression, or no expression, and to impose state-sanctioned prayer on them is to violate their constitutional rights. Parents have the right, as well, to have their views respected, and a student whose religious views (or lack of religious views) are at odds with those of a school prayer may not only be offended, but that student's constitutional rights are being violated.

Rob Crandall/Photolibrary

The Yorktown Patriots high school football team kneels for a moment of silence before a game. Some would argue that even something as innocent as prayer before a football game could be seen as involuntary, as a student might not want to be singled out for not participating.

A prayer at a school assembly or football game may seem innocent enough, but if one's religious views are fundamental to that person, then a prayer that specifies a particular conception of God, or a particular relationship between a person and God, may well make that student feel singled out. On the other hand, if the prayer is so vague and general that it really offers very little specific content, it is not clear what purpose it serves; in addition, it will still impose a religious viewpoint on those students who do not share that viewpoint. A student can be required to attend certain school functions; if a prayer is part of that function, the student is not participating in that prayer voluntarily. In addition to having his or her views possibly contradicted, the role of peer pressure and embarrassment should not be underestimated. Many students may prefer to stay in a setting where a prayer is being offered instead of leaving and thus identifying themselves even further as, somehow, not "belonging." Combining a school-sanctioned prayer with such peer pressure makes clear that such an activity is not in any genuine sense voluntary.

Furthermore, it is not the role of public schools to impose specific religious values on its students. Schools are quite free to teach about religion, its history, and its role in society; schools are not permitted to do anything that could be interpreted as endorsing a particular religious viewpoint. Schools have important obligations to see that their students receive a quality education in such subjects as English, mathematics, natural sciences, history, and foreign languages. Given the relatively low achievements in these areas, relative to other countries in the developed world, the public schools clearly need to do a better job in carrying out their educational mission. Spending such valuable time on prayer and imposing specific religious viewpoints on students is neither part of the mission of public schools, nor is it an efficient use of time. Moreover, many parents prefer that specific religious and moral teachings not be part of the school curriculum.

For this last reason, many religious parents demand that religious material be excluded from school curricula. These parents argue that religious values are, indeed, extremely important. For that very reason they insist that the public schools should not interfere with the parents' desire to teach these values at home, and at places of worship: precisely those places where it is appropriate to focus on religious teachings.

Corbis/Photlibrary

Some would argue that parents may prefer that religious values be taught at home rather than at school.

The Constitution does not allow public schools to promote any specific religion or religious viewpoint. Any school-sanctioned prayer would either violate this constitutional requirement or be so vague as to be meaningless. Given a diverse student body, no prayer can respect all the religious views of those students, particularly if one considers that some of those students may have no religious values or even reject religion entirely. Public schools have more important things to devote their time to as part of their legitimate mission. Many parents do not want the values they teach their children contradicted in the public schools and prefer that the religious and moral teachings be provided by the parents, not the schools. School-sanctioned prayer, due to its setting and to peer pressure, cannot be regarded as voluntary. Therefore, due to both constitutional issues and other compelling moral and social challenges, prayer in public schools should be prohibited.

Applying the Theories

One of the difficulties in studying ethics is determining the appropriate way to apply a given theory. A basic utilitarian principle is to do that which will produce the greatest good for the greatest number. But one of the difficulties with applying utilitarianism is identifying the group in question: in other words, "the greatest number of whom?" We will demonstrate this problem by examining the arguments for and against school prayer from the perspective of utilitarianism. As we will see, different conclusions follow from how we describe and apply our use of the utilitarian principle. This doesn't mean the principle is wrong, however. But it does mean that in applying the principle, we need to be careful, and precise, in that application.

Design Pics Inc./Photolibrary

A college student prays during class. Individual students can pray on their own. The courts have ruled that the difference is between allowing prayer and promoting it.

There's an old saying "As long as there are math tests, there will be prayer in school." The idea here, of course, is that individual students cannot be prevented from engaging in prayer on their own, as individuals. Such prayer is voluntary and engaged in only by the individual. Furthermore, the Supreme Court has ruled that students are allowed to organize, voluntarily, religious clubs—which can include prayer and Bible study—at public schools, just as they might any other kind of club.

As we noted earlier, it is important to differentiate between allowing prayer and promoting it. The legal challenges that have been brought have often objected to a school officially endorsing a prayer at recognized school-wide events. On some views, this moves from permitting individuals to pray—a protected right—to endorsing prayer by officially recognizing it, which may well violate a person's rights.

Act Utilitarianism

A utilitarian might well argue that in a given school or school district, or community, the majority (and even a vast majority) of its members belongs to a specific faith tradition. The greatest good for the greatest number, in this case, would seem to allow that majority to pray and participate in religious activities in the way they desire. This might include prayers at football games, school assemblies, and graduation ceremonies. To prevent the majority from expressing its religious views this way is to bend to the dictates of a minority. But even if it could be shown that the minority may maximize its utility by eliminating such prayers, it is clear that allowing those prayers produces the greatest good. Some might regard this as an application, specifically, of act utilitarianism: the act of allowing prayers for the majority of a given community creates the greatest good for the greatest number; therefore, prayer should be allowed.

Rule Utilitarianism

A contrasting approach to utilitarianism, which might be regarded as rule utilitarianism, argues otherwise. Again applying the principle of the "greatest good for the greatest number," the rule utilitarian will argue that allowing the majority's religious views to be imposed on a minority does not create the greatest good for the greatest number. In addition to the minority's rights being ignored (which decreases the happiness of those in the minority), many in the majority may also recognize that ignoring legitimate rights of a minority is harmful, both to those suffering the harm and to those doing the harm. Participating in something that causes harm (harm, here, to the rights of the minority) decreases the happiness of those who participate, even passively, in that harm. Therefore, in general, the rule utilitarian will see simply applying the "greatest good greatest number" principle in a situation that ignores or violates the legitimate rights of members of the community does not lead to allowing prayer in school in general. Rather, it leads to preventing school prayer in situations, such as school assemblies and graduation ceremonies, that cannot be regarded as voluntary in any genuine sense.

Here, then, we see two distinct applications of the utilitarian principle: one leading to the result that school prayer, in a very general way, should be allowed; the other leading the result that school prayer, in a very general way, should not be allowed. What this seems to tell us is that the rights of the individuals involved must be looked at very carefully, to determine where one person's rights begin to conflict with another person's. It also seems to indicate that when we look at the happiness, or utility, of a given group, we need to be aware that how we specify the community makes a difference. Within a public school, is the community we are concerned with everyone who attends the school? Those who are religious who attend the school? Those members of the dominant religious tradition, if any, of those who attend the school? Do we include, for that matter, those who might end up attending this school, or who graduated from this school, and thus are part of its extended community? These questions aren't always easy to answer, but the issues they raise need to be factored in when evaluating the overall set of questions involved.

Some Conclusions

Religion is an extraordinarily personal experience for many people and is often fundamental to a person's understanding of who he or she is. Because religion is such a basic part of a person's self-conception, someone may feel his or her right to the free expression of religious beliefs is restricted by not being allowed to state them when and where he or she wishes. At the same time, two people's religious views may conflict, whether they are of distinct religious traditions or one is religious and the other is not. It is unlikely that any ethical result will satisfy everyone, and that these conflicts will be resolved in a way that makes everyone happy. But ethics can provide valuable insight into clarifying these issues and offer very helpful ways of thinking about such conflicts in a way that can address them.

Photos India RF/Photolibrary

Religion can be fundamental to a person's understanding of who he is.

With respect to both the legal results and a more general way of regarding religion, increasing attention has been paid to the idea of prayer in the public schools being voluntary. An individual cannot be prevented from praying in public school; religious student organizations are permitted the same opportunities as other student organizations. These activities are regarded as voluntary. In contrast, school-sanctioned events, whether football games or graduation exercises, tend to be recognized by the courts as the kinds of events where it is inappropriate to have prayer, in that a prayer at such an event automatically brings with it an official or unofficial school endorsement. Of course, attendance at a high school football game isn't something we regard as mandatory, but, as the courts recognized, such a game is an official school function and also may involve an element of peer pressure. Fundamentally, the argument is that one should be able to attend the football games of one's public school without having to participate in a prayer that contradicts one's beliefs, whether one follows a different religious faith or is not religious at all. And, as many religious people have argued, to insist on a prayer that is so general that it doesn't conflict with another's beliefs (religious or otherwise) seems to make pointless the very notion of "prayer."

Of course, exceptions to what an ethicist might argue, or what the courts have ruled, can be found; often these cases receive a great deal of publicity and seem to indicate either that a "war on religion" is being waged by the public schools, or that minorities are having their own religious rights "violated and trampled." It may be the case that the publicity these cases receive implies that these issues arise more frequently than they actually do. To be sure, a teacher who prevents a Christian student from carrying the Bible violates that student's rights, just as a teacher violates the rights of a Jewish student by insisting that he write an essay on the topic "Why Jesus Loves Me." (These are both actual cases.)

The goal of ethics not only allows us to see that these actions violate an individual's religious rights but also provides us with a way of arguing why they violate them.

Where Do We Go from Here?

As noted earlier, the United States is a diverse society and is particularly diverse in terms of both the faith traditions followed by Americans as well as an increasing number of Americans who have no religion. Even though the diversity in the United States has increased dramatically, Christianity has been and continues to be the dominant faith tradition in the United States.

Somos Images/Photolibrary

Religious values are important to many people. In such debates, there will be a need for some give and take, sensitivity, and tolerance.

The implication of these characteristics seems to indicate that we recognize how important religious values are to many people. But that importance also makes it compelling to recognize others' religious beliefs, as well as the beliefs of those who have no religion. It seems likely that one result is that there will continue to be a good bit of give and take over this issue, with some substantial conflicts arising between those who don't think religion in public schools is given sufficient recognition and those who think otherwise. Some will think a specific religious tradition is too specifically identified, which may be unconstitutional; others may think any mention of religion should be omitted entirely from the public schools; still others may think that religion is too important to allow the public schools to interfere with it at all.

So perhaps the implications of this debate are to recognize that diversity can lead to such conflicts, and that those in the majority may need to be particularly sensitive to the beliefs of others, religious or otherwise. Such sensitivity is, of course, a two-way street, and so this sensitivity may also increase the need for tolerance. No solution will satisfy everyone, but insisting that prayer in public school always be voluntary, and that religion be treated in public schools in a way that recognizes a diversity of beliefs and tolerance for those beliefs, may go a long way to minimizing these conflicts, although it may be too much to ask for these conflicts to be eliminated entirely.

What Would You Do?

You are a high school principal, and some students want to organize a school club devoted to studying and discussing atheism. You are concerned that they may spend some of their time mocking the beliefs of other students. Some of the students in your school have already expressed to you their concern that such an officially recognized student group represents a view that many find offensive.

• Do you allow the students to organize the atheist club?

• What restrictions, if any, do you impose on what they can do and say?

• What do you say to parents who call to protest the existence of such a club?

What Role Does Conscience Play?

People identify themselves in many different ways: through their ethnicity, race, country of origin, class, gender, sexual orientation, religion, among many others. Often people regard themselves as members of a relatively cohesive group because of one or more of these factors: thus, a person might consider herself an African American Roman Catholic, while another may consider himself a member of a Spanish-speaking Protestant community. Belonging to such a community brings certain commitments: perhaps one insists on a particular interpretation of "marriage" or "science"; perhaps one's religious or cultural community requires that women and men act in specific and different ways, in terms of dress, occupation, worship, and so on. Clearly enough, the values of these communities may differ, and even sharply conflict. If the values of your culture or community conflict too much with that of the surrounding community, one is confronted with a difficult problem. As a simple example, if one's community accepts polygyny (a husband having more than one wife), while the larger community rejects it, how does one resolve this conflict?

These kinds of conflicts occur with some frequency, of course, but most people learn to adjust: perhaps they aren't entirely satisfied with the values of the larger community, but the advantages of participating in that community make it more practical to tolerate that dissatisfaction. For instance, a parent may be suspicious about the science behind climate change but otherwise be quite pleased with the education offered by the school; the parent accepts it, and perhaps offers an alternative view to that presented in the school. In the case of religion in public school, some parents find it a better solution to send their children to private, parochial, or religious schools or to homeschool their children. These parents, of course, don't withdraw from the community entirely; they simply leave part of it.

When more serious conflicts do arise, some find it impossible to remain within the community. Although these cases are relatively rare, they provide a way of examining the role an individual's conscience plays when evaluating one's membership in a larger community. If one's values compel one to reject the values of that larger community, one has to confront the choice between somehow tolerating something consistently offensive, or withdrawing entirely from that community in order to live, in a different way, with people who share those values. There may also be serious ethical concerns relative to those shared values that conflict with those of the larger community. Some have chosen to form separate communities, in part, to avoid living among African Americans, or Roman Catholics, or Jews, or members of other groups defined as not sharing the values of that community. Other separate communities have been formed on the basis of economic complaints—specifically tax laws—and on the basis of specific religious values. An ethical investigation here might ask if the dictates of conscience, in this case, should be respected, or critically scrutinized.

Most of us live between the two extremes of our values never being challenged by something in society and our values being so consistently violated that we decide to leave the community entirely. But this raises a number of important ethical questions about living in a community with others who may not share one's values. At what point should we object, when we find our values being violated? How can we make sure our rights are respected? Can our values be preserved without infringing on the rights of others? In our desire to protect our own moral values, do we forget to consider the moral values of others? Ethics offers some insight into these questions, although, again, without offering a solution that will be satisfactory to everyone. In a society that is increasingly pluralistic and diverse, it is very likely that conflicts among the values of the members of a society will persist (if not increase), and we will continue to need to address these questions.

2.4 An Historical Debate: A Woman's Right to Vote

It is a good thing to remember that ethics can make a difference; not all ethical arguments are abstract discussions of hypothetical cases, but they can be seen as having brought about significant change. In this case, we will look at the arguments over giving women the right to vote in the United States, known as the question of "Women's Suffrage." As we will see, something we may now take as obvious and "common sense" wasn't always regarded that way, and ethical considerations were important in making it possible for women to vote. It is probably worth noting that some of the arguments may sound pretty dubious as this point, but when made they were found by many to be extremely persuasive. Here we will look at the issue from the perspective of virtue ethics and from the perspective of deontology, as they might have been presented when this issue was still an issue.

The Issue: Women Should Be Allowed to Vote

Here we look at the kinds of arguments that were involved over a woman's right to vote. This issue is a good example of how moral and ethical arguments can both provide clarity to our understanding of the issues and produce a genuine difference.

The argument against women's suffrage

It is unquestionable that men and women are fundamentally distinct. This is obviously the case in terms of biology; the very differences can be immediately observed, and they are even more obvious in reproduction, where men and women play radically distinct roles. Because of the role women play in carrying, delivering, and raising children, they have a specific approach to things, in terms of their compassion, their abilities to nurture, and their willingness to compromise and avoid conflict. These differences, both physiological and psychological, have long been noted. Aristotle, 400 years before the birth of Christ, noted that

> The female is softer in disposition than the male, is more mischievous, less simple, more impulsive, and more attentive to the nurture of the young; the male, on the other hand, is more spirited than the female, more savage, more simple and less cunning. The traces of these differentiated characteristics are more or less visible everywhere, but they are especially visible where character is the more developed, and most of all in man.
>
> Aristotle, *History of Animals*

This is also reflected in our very language: the word "hysterical" comes from the Latin term referring to the womb, and gives us the English word "uterus." Perhaps less well known is that the term "lady" originally comes from the Old English term for "one who kneads, or makes, bread" and that the very term "feminine" originates from a term for breast feeding. Terms associated with women have, in English and in other languages, always emphasized softness and delicacy, and their importance as wives and mothers. This is also reinforced by the Bible; not just Eve, but Delilah, Jezebel, and Salome are all examples of women who behave immorally, whereas Mary represents the virtues of women.

The British Library/Photolibrary

Prior to the mid-20th century, women were often thought to be best suited for rearing children and running the home.

It is clear from the way the term "woman" developed in English that the virtues of a woman are to be praised; for a well-functioning society, women are indispensable to keep the home running well, to ensure that children are raised appropriately, and to take care of, efficiently and effectively, all those things that fall within a woman's many areas of expertise. But politics is an entirely distinct realm, where women lack the temperament, the attitude, the understanding, and the experience to function effectively. Thus, women are not suited to participate in politics, either as elected officials or as voters.

In addition to these somewhat abstract and philosophical reasons, we can add a few specific points and summarize the position as follows. Women have a crucial role in society, to take care of the home; politics is a separate sphere and is really only suitable for men. Only by keeping these spheres separate can women play their important role in maintaining the values and civility of society. The need for this separation is clearly seen in the distinct physiological and psychological makeup of women, as opposed to men. Women, by their very temperament, are not suited to the unpleasant and sometimes violent confrontations required by politics. In any case, many women do not want the vote, believing it will dilute the very real power they in fact have over their husbands already. Furthermore, it will give the vote to an enormous number of people who have neither the background nor the understanding to make good political decisions. For all of these reasons, women neither need, nor should they be given, the right to vote.

The argument for women's suffrage

Women are human beings. They are expected to care for themselves, their families, their husbands, their children, and their homes. As such, they have some of the most significant responsibilities that can be entrusted to anyone. Yet, while shouldering these responsibilities and others, a woman is deprived of the fundamental right of political representation. She works hard, often for no salary, and often harder than any man, and helps make the society in which she lives function; indeed, women make that society possible. Yet that same society prevents her from the rights any man has, simply by accident of his being born a man: the right to vote. A woman's contributions to society are absolutely indispensable. In addition to being a human being, with certain rights that cannot morally be violated—such as the right to vote—women deserve to have an equal say in how that society is organized and how its politics should be structured. As Susan B. Antony stated, "There never will be complete equality until women themselves help to make laws and elect lawmakers."

If the Declaration of Independence means "all people are created equal," this has clearly not been the case with women. They are expected to fulfill all their responsibilities while being denied one of their fundamental rights. If "no taxation without representation" was justification for the American Revolution, what does that tell women, who toil as hard as men, have

Museum of London/Photolibrary

A London cartoon from 1912 describes a number of important roles women hold while still being denied the right to vote.

The British Library/Photolibrary

According to the leaflet, Wyoming was the first state to allow women to vote in 1869. More than 40 years later, only 10 other states had extended the same right.

responsibilities equal or greater than those of men, who live with men under the same rules and laws of society, yet have no representation? Depriving women of the right to vote is both immoral, in that it denies women a fundamental right, and unjust, by not allowing them what is due them: the rights that coexist with responsibilities. If a woman is expected to take on those responsibilities, she must be accorded the rights due her, and one of those rights is the right to vote.

Perhaps someone will suggest that women are represented by their husbands or fathers. Would any man be willing to switch positions in this and regard it as fair were wives and daughters taken to represent accurately their views? Is it sensible, or fair, for half the population to hope that their views are represented by the other half? Might there not be a perspective on important political issues that women bring into consideration that would be otherwise ignored? Wouldn't political decisions be better informed, and thus be better decisions, if such an important perspective were taken into account? And who better to present the political perspectives women have than women?

The argument, then, is simple. Women are human beings, with rights and responsibilities. One of those rights, perhaps as fundamental as any, is the right to vote. Having deprived women of this right for so long doesn't mean it is fair, or just; it means that something unfair and unjust has gone on for far too long. One of the fundamental principles of a free and fair society is that its members deserve representation, and deserve to represent themselves. The only correct result, therefore, as a matter of the moral law and as a matter of justice, is to provide women with what they are due: their right to vote.

The Theories

The extraordinary thing about women is their virtue: their remarkable abilities to handle so many different things and to handle them well. They are caring, generous, nurturing, and practical; they are good friends, and, when their virtues are present in the appropriate way, they make good sisters, daughters, wives, and mothers.

Virtue ethics sees these virtues as precisely the things to emphasize for a virtuous women: never in their extremes, but always aiming at an appropriate and moderate degree, a Golden Mean. The virtue ethicist might then argue as follows: the virtues of a woman are best seen when displayed in the proper place and in the proper and appropriate way—in the home as a wife and mother, in the elementary school as a teacher, in the hospital as a nurse. These are roles women have excelled in for centuries, and society functions most efficiently and most productively when they continue to do so.

Tetra Images/Photolibrary

A virtue ethicist might argue that a woman's best virtues are seen in a woman's "proper" roles: as a wife and mother, for example.

On this same view, politics can often be contentious, ugly, confrontational, and even violent. Women do not do well in this kind of environment, and the virtues that women possess cannot be developed and improved, therefore, by engaging in politics. Women also lack the educational background and the general temperament for participating in politics. Giving women the vote will force them into an arena where their skills are inadequate, and will simultaneously prevent them from spending their time where they should be, and where their virtues are most evident. Any decision that has such disastrous moral results cannot be a good one, and thus the virtue ethicist would have to conclude that giving a woman the right to vote would be wrong, for her as well as for her society.

The deontologist, of course, disputes much of this characterization of women, and may well reject the idea that women have some set of "virtues" that are fundamentally distinct from those of men. Men aren't defined in terms of being a husband, a brother, a father. Why are women characterized solely in terms of their roles, rather than as free, independent, and creative human beings? Women may well be good wives and mothers, but that doesn't mean they can't be more than (or something other than) wives and mothers. Women may well be good teachers, but can't they also be good college professors? Women may well be good nurses, but can't they also be good doctors? Restricting a woman's educational opportunities, then criticizing her for a lack of education, is about as fair as putting a person in prison and criticizing her for not doing much traveling.

Michaela Begsteiger/Imagebroker RF/Photolibrary

A deontologist might argue for women's rights on the principle of fairness and equality.

The deontologist also has a traditional method to identify something as fundamentally unfair. If Bob is doing something unfair to Carolyn, Carolyn can simply ask Bob if he would be happy if that same unfair thing were done to him. Thus, more generally women can ask men the same thing: if men had the responsibilities that women do, would they object if they didn't possess the right to vote? The Golden Rule seems to provide a much stronger argument than the appeal to the Golden Mean.

In any case, the right to vote doesn't seem to the deontologist to be a right for men to possess, but a right for human beings to possess. As such, any woman who qualifies as a human being should possess the right to vote. To deny her that right is to treat her as less than a human being, to treat her as a means to an end, and thus to act unethically.

Some Conclusions

Ron Nickel/Design Pics Inc./Photolibrary

The right for women to vote is one that we and our children likely take for granted.

It is rather hard to imagine a politician today proposing that women not be allowed to vote: such a suggestion would be generally regarded as ridiculous. But it was a long, hard struggle; the 19th Amendment was passed 144 years after the Declaration of Independence, finally giving women a right we now take as one that requires little or no justification.

With the benefit of hindsight, we see that many of the arguments proposed were based on a conception of women (and men) that had a very long history, a conception that restricted women to specific roles in society. Critical scrutiny of this conception led to the realization that it functioned to prevent women from being full participants in their society. Even though women were regarded as sufficiently responsible to do many of the things society deemed extremely important, they were denied the rights that accompanied those responsibilities. From many ethical perspectives, denying women the right to vote was wrong for two reasons. First, it denied the rights that one acquires with responsibilities. As we have already seen, the right to possess a firearm brings with it a responsibility to handle that firearm safely and appropriately. Second, and more fundamental, denying women the right to vote was to deny them a right they possess as human beings. Thus, one is forced either to recognize their right to vote, or to argue, somehow, that they are somehow not human beings.

We also see from this discussion that ethical values and political values can frequently be in tension, and how one applies a specific theory in ethics may well determine the results of that application. For instance, imagine that we adopt a simple utilitarian perspective, and assume (safely enough) that allowing citizens to vote increases the happiness, or maximizes the utility, of those citizens. The clear result is that the greatest good for the greatest number is achieved by giving all eligible citizens the right to vote. But who is an "eligible citizen"? Is it all adults 18 and older? All adults 21 and older? Or should more restrictions be placed on who is eligible to vote, as has often been done in the past? Obviously enough, some people were not allowed to vote on the basis of race and sex (or gender); but other conditions have been imposed, such as being able to read and write, or owning property, to restrict the right to vote. Ethics provides us one way to examine such restrictions to see if they are justified on the basis of good, moral reasons, or, as seems often to have been the case, to allow those already in power to maintain their advantages. If we apply our utilitarian principle to a group, such as males, or whites, the greatest good for the greatest number of that group may well result in a situation that is quite unfair, were a larger group considered. So even taking a very basic utilitarian approach to a question may require us to think long and hard about what we mean by "the greatest number." In other words, when we consider the greatest good for the greatest number, we also have to ask: the greatest number of whom? And determining who belongs, and who doesn't belong, in the group in question, may not always be that easy.

Where Do We Go from Here?

Ethics can often seem like a sterile exercise, with little relevance for everyday life and the kinds of decisions we actually have to confront. Should I steal food to feed my starving family? I find the wallet of a person I know to be a drug dealer, and it has $1,000; what should I do with it? One very standard example in ethics asks this: if you were able to divert a train to kill one person, in order that the train did not kill five people, what would you do? It seems pretty clear that these kinds of examples are good to help us see what is at stake in applying and understanding ethical theory, even though we don't expect to be in the positions described here. Some might suggest that ethics, and philosophy in general, don't have a lot of to say that is relevant. But, as we've seen in the preceding historical example, ethical questions and scrutiny of the moral values of a society can, in fact, have a significant effect in changing a society.

This is not to say that all we need to do to address an unfair or immoral situation in our society is to pass out ethics textbooks and convince people to read the relevant pages. But familiarity with ethical theories, and familiarity with various ways of identifying things that are unfair, can at least help move the discussion along. Our values do not exist in some kind of vacuum, of course; they exist in a large, complex context of competing values, politics, and social structures such as educational institutions and religious viewpoints. Many other factors, no doubt, also play a role in understanding the ethical challenges we do, in fact, confront. But the more familiar we are with techniques in explaining and understanding those challenges, the better prepared we are to deal with them. This is, of course, not to guarantee that we will solve them, and we almost certainly won't solve them in a way that everyone finds satisfactory. But the better prepared we are to clarify the ethical problems we do have to deal with, the better prepared we are to address them and, in some cases, fix them.

The right for women to vote is a step toward equality, but it does signify equality in and of itself. There are many possible obstacles to overcome. Are there any that you can think of?

Of course, fixing—or at least improving—a specific case of injustice hardly means the matter is settled. One might think that giving women the right to vote was a step toward political equality, but it was only a step. Many other factors can still function as obstacles to that equality. Philosophers might suggest that the right to vote is a necessary condition for political equality, even though it is not at all a sufficient condition. In other words, without the right to vote, one cannot hope to gain that kind of equal participation in the political structures of one's society, but the right to vote doesn't, by itself, establish this participation. Many obstacles may still need to be overcome, and, presumably, this is an ongoing competition to determine the scope and limits of one's rights. But at least we can see that ethics can, in fact, contribute important things to the debate over such issues and can play a significant and productive role in how society addresses such questions.

Do Ethical Principles Change over Time?

Communities often define themselves as much by whom they exclude as whom they include; that is, to be a member of a community, or society, is often determined by establishing who does not belong. For centuries, the long history of racial exclusion in the United States prohibited African Americans from genuinely participating in society, obviously enough through the institution of slavery, but also through other means, such as requiring them to use separate facilities (waiting rooms, movie theatres, bathrooms, drinking fountains, etc.), preventing them from even registering to vote (let alone actually voting), forcing them to attend segregated schools from kindergarten through universities, and many other formal and informal ways of sending the message, "You don't really belong." Women were also prevented from voting, owning property, and being given credit in their own names, along with other more informal ways of excluding them from society. Native Americans, Jews, and others were similarly prevented from being full participants within what we now regard as their own society.

Workshop/Photolibrary

Less than 50 years ago, it was illegal in the United States for people of different races to marry. Ethicists would argue that it was not moral principles that changed, but society. Do you agree? What other examples can you think of in which this has been the case?

Does this indicate that the fundamental principles of morality changed? If so, that would seem to show that rather than being principles, they are the kinds of things that are not eternal and permanent, but simply ideas that gain sufficient support to be adopted in a given society. Many ethicists would argue, instead, that moral principles do not change; rather, society changes—often by expanding—those to whom those principles apply. Less than 50 years ago, it was illegal in a number of places in the United States for people of different races to marry; we generally now regard such "miscegenation laws" as discriminatory and ignorant. The principle of "rights" didn't change, in this case; rather, the idea of the right to marry was extended to be more inclusive. The Supreme Court, in 1967, declared it unconstitutional to prohibit people of different races to marry; since then, geneticists and other biologists have seemed to conclude that the very notion of "race" isn't a useful biological term at all. Thus, both the ethical principles, and the law, reflected the fact that it was wrong to exclude certain groups of people from exercising their rights, and thus the community expanded its conception of who belonged to that community.

These changes often don't come very easily; there can be a great deal of resistance to them, and even when laws are in place to prevent excluding groups from voting, buying a house, or marrying someone, those laws will often continue to be violated. A community, that is, may simply adopt an informal practice to prevent someone from doing something; in spite of a law prohibiting that practice, the majority of a given community may enforce it through peer pressure and other means. As the point may be put in legal terms, a law that is in force practically is a de facto law, in spite of it being illegal de jure, or against the official laws under which a community lives. If someone can successfully exclude African Americans from eating in his restaurant, that exclusion is in place as a de facto rule, even though illegal de jure.

Thus, even though ethical principles themselves may not change over time, we can see how they are applied does. A current debate in the United States concerns extending certain rights—to serve openly in the military, to marry—to homosexuals. The question here is not whether one's rights should be respected, but who should, and who should not, be included as part of the group that has such rights. Again, we see that ethics doesn't resolve such an issue, but it helps clarify what is at stake in the various resolutions that have been proposed. In any diverse community, the restrictions and expansions of rights, and the question of what kinds of things really are "rights," will continue to arise and be the source of debate. It should be clear, in any case, that ethics has a good deal to offer in identifying the terms of the debate, as well as determining what is at stake in these arguments.

2.5 The Workplace and Individual Rights

In various occupations, workers may be prohibited from exercising certain rights that, outside the workplace, cannot be restricted. This can lead to difficult conflicts between employer and employee, as well as among employees. Here we will look at some restrictions that may be imposed, to investigate what restrictions on rights employees can and cannot insist on. We will contrast virtue ethics here with a deontological perspective in order to present the two sides of the debate.

Restricting Employee Rights as a Condition of Employment

Here we will look at the issues that arise between an employer and an employee, in terms of what legitimate expectations an employer can have for his or her workers, and what the limits are to the conditions an employer can impose on employees.

The argument that the employer can restrict rights broadly

The management of a company, or corporation, brings with it many responsibilities. Management must, above all, see to it that the company runs smoothly and efficiently, to guarantee the best return on investment for stockholders and others who support it—and expect financial returns—from the company. In this context, the bottom line really is the bottom line. A company that fails to produce profits will, sooner or later, be unable to stay in business. It is the fundamental responsibility of management to see that the company remains profitable and, thus, successful.

Anything that interferes with meeting that responsibility is, consequently, something management must avoid. Some specific variables that a company can neither expect nor predict—a loss of access to raw materials or a change in the public's demand for a company's product—are, obviously, unavoidable. But those things that can be avoided, and which interfere with a company functioning smoothly and profitably, are precisely those things that a company must focus on to prevent (or at least minimize) them.

Employees, of course, have certain rights guaranteed to them, either by the Constitution, or by the laws that govern both employees and the company for which they work. Employees cannot be expected to work in conditions that make it likely that they will be injured or killed; they cannot be expected to work overtime without appropriate compensation; they cannot be terminated for refusing to do something illegal or for filing a justified claim (such as applying for worker's compensation).

Seth Joel Photography/Cultura RM/Photolibrary

Companies have to meet the fundamental responsibility of remaining profitable, but they must also guarantee certain rights to their employees, such as overtime compensation. Some would argue that companies can ensure these rights while enforcing certain necessary restrictions.

But, obviously enough, a number of rights can be restricted as a condition of employment. For instance, if Company A makes a beverage that has a secret and highly guarded recipe, the employees of Company A can have their right to free speech restricted by not allowing them to tell Company B (a competitor) what that recipe is. Any number of competitive advantages for corporations rely on such information, known as "proprietary information." It is completely reasonable for a company to require of its employees, and potential employees, to agree that they do not, in this case, have an unrestricted right of free speech. A federal agency, such as the CIA, clearly enough, can require secrecy from its employees as a condition of employment. An airline can require its pilots to undergo drug testing; a school system can require its employees to live within a certain area; many corporations require employees to act in ways that do not reflect poorly on the corporation, including behavior outside the workplace. In short, employers can insist on a wide range of restrictions that are both reasonable and justified as conditions of employment. Clearly enough, if a job candidate is unwilling to accept such restrictions, he or she is under no obligation to accept the position; if an employee finds such restrictions too burdensome, he or she is free to leave the corporation.

Many employees fall under the category of "at will employees," employees who may be terminated without cause. The details here can get a bit complex due to different laws in different states; however, in general, employees are "at will" if they are not working under a written contract, as might be the case for union members; they are working for the federal government; or they are employed in some other situation where an explicit contract is in force. Clearly it is in the employer's interest to have the company's workers happy, satisfied, and productive; a situation that employees perceive as unfair can interfere with that job satisfaction. At the same time, employees cannot insist on things that either violate the conditions of employment or prevent the company from operating smoothly and profitably.

Consider, for example, an employee we will call "Jim." Jim published in the local newspaper several articles that were sharply critical of some of the things done by the company for which he worked; he then reproduced these articles on his website. There may have been some merit to Jim's complaints, but airing those complaints in the way Jim did not only damaged the company's reputation and its standing in the community but also provided a weapon for its competitors to use against it. For both reasons, the company's profits fell, and Jim was fired. Were his rights violated? On the one hand, Jim was an "at will" employee, so the company wasn't obligated to justify his termination. But even if it were so obligated, it is clear that Jim did not have the right to do the damage to the company he did, nor to do it in the way he did. To prevent him from harming the company clearly outweighed whatever rights he might claim to free speech: his rights do not allow him to infringe upon the right of the company to be profitable, and thus harm not just the company as a whole, but also those who continue to work there. Here is a situation where one's right to free speech clearly can be restricted, and in the workplace, many such restrictions are legitimate and justified in order to protect the company's reputation, its profitability, and its responsibility to its stockholders.

The argument that the employer must restrict rights narrowly

Workers have rights that are guaranteed by the Constitution and by the various legal statutes that constitute "labor law." These rights—freedom of speech, religion, and so on—cannot be violated without showing that any such restrictions are absolutely necessary for the company to function. Simply because one is employed by a company, or is considering a job offer from a company, does not mean that he or she gives up those guaranteed rights.

There is no doubt that some conditions can be imposed upon workers; there is no "right" to be able to provide a competing company information that would be harmful to one's employer, and this is a legitimate condition of employment. It is also clear that requirements of national security and public safety may impose restrictions on some, relatively small, group of employees. Certain workers for the federal government may have the right to "free speech," but that right does not, for instance, extend to the right to give classified information to a foreign government. Given the potential consequences, airplane pilots do not have the right to operate planes while impaired, and courts have found it to be a legitimate condition of employment to require drug testing of pilots. As can be seen in such cases, the burden of proof is on the employer to demonstrate a legitimate and substantial need to restrict the freedom of speech and the right to privacy. Without satisfying that burden of proof, employers are in a position to violate their employees' rights unfairly and unjustly. An employer must show that any restrictions on employee rights are necessary; otherwise, "at will" employees reserve all rights guaranteed to them by the Constitution and the relevant federal and state laws. Consequently, the employer can only restrict employee rights in the narrowest circumstances.

Denkou Images/Photolibrary

Although some restrictions are necessary—particularly if they interfere with performance—they must be shown to be legitimate and needed, some would say.

What Would You Do?

You have been unemployed for several months and are desperate to find a job. You've been offered the job of being the representative of a local animal rights group. This group works to prohibit the wearing of fur, advocates vegetarianism, and seeks to ban the use of animals for the testing of perfumes, pharmaceuticals, and other products. The job is a very good one, but as a condition of employment the group requires that you not eat meat. After all, if you are seen shopping for steaks and pork chops, it would indicate the animal rights group is a bit hypocritical, in that you are paying for those steaks and chops with money the group provides. Yet you really like your occasional cheeseburger and barbecue.

FoodCollection/Photolibrary
Would you change your eating habits for a new job you need? Or would you hide your eating habits to satisfy your employer?

• Do you take the job?

• Is this a fair condition of employment to impose upon you?

• Are there limits to what an employer can require of employees, other than those that would require you to do something illegal?

Consider "Susan," who lives in a relatively small town, where jobs are hard to come by. She is interviewed for a job by a local nonprofit agency that lobbies government officials to impose very strict controls on the possession of weapons. Susan enjoys hunting with her husband and children and owns several shotguns. The agency offers her a job on the condition that she not own any guns, and that she get rid of any that she already owns. The agency insists that it would violate the image it seeks to project were its employees to own and use the same weapons it wishes to restrict. Can it demand that Susan agree to this condition? She was faced with either not taking the job and thus being put in considerable economic insecurity, or taking the job and seeing what she regards as her constitutional rights violated. The agency realizes that the community has a high unemployment rate, and thus there is considerable pressure on Susan to accept this condition. Susan could, of course, take the position and then, if fired, sue the agency. But that strategy would require hiring a lawyer and dealing with a lawsuit, which is both time-consuming and expensive. Susan, of course, doesn't have to take the job; that decision would preserve her rights—at the cost of being unemployed or making a great deal less money.

Here we see what might be a plausible reason for an employer to want to restrict the rights of its employees, and extend those restrictions outside of the workplace. It might be argued that without these restrictions, employees may act in ways that are detrimental to the employer and the company. But there also seems to be a considerable worry here that such conditions of employment go beyond what the company can legitimately demand and cannot be shown to lead, necessarily, to putting the company at a disadvantage in seeking to do what it wishes and needs to do. In short, these restrictions are unfair and cannot be appropriately required as a condition of employment.

Further concerns are raised here in the context of a tight job market, where economic insecurity and financial need may lead employees, and job candidates, to accept conditions for work that would otherwise be unfair. This may lead to a situation where employers have the potential to restrict rights even further, with the knowledge that it is difficult to leave a job and/or find another equivalent-paying job. This may lead not only to the potential abuse of employees' legitimate rights but also to a situation where workers are unhappy due to that abuse but are unable to leave because of significant restraints on employment opportunities. Employees should not be put in a position where they are faced with trading their legitimate rights for financial security, and thus any restrictions so imposed must meet a very high standard, showing that they are absolutely necessary for the company to function effectively.

Applying the Theories

As a legal entity, the corporation is recognized as a "person"—technically an "artificial person"—that possesses many of the rights people possess under the law. Using this idea, we can look at the corporation from the perspective of virtue ethics: What does it mean for a corporation, in this context, to be virtuous? Presumably we want corporations to act morally and as good, if artificial, "citizens"; virtue ethics seems to provide a way of characterizing what is then required of such corporate behavior.

The corporate "person" is under a number of constraints; however, it must, above all, maintain profitability. But recognizing that goal, it must also meet the legitimate needs of its employees, stockholders, and others who provide various kinds of support (financial and otherwise) to the company. This includes the community in which it is found, not just providing employment, but playing the role of good corporate citizen by supporting charities and perhaps other philanthropic work. It can be a difficult job to balance all of these obligations, while maintaining focus on the bottom line, but virtue ethics emphasizes precisely that kind of balance that may offer valuable guidance to the corporation.

Fancy/Photolibrary

Virtue ethics suggests the corporate citizen must somehow find a balance between its mission of profitability and satisfying employees, stockholders, and other vested interests.

For example, the company must seek a balance—a Golden Mean—between maintaining employee satisfaction, without distorting its fundamental mission. Thus, it must offer salaries and benefits that are competitive. If the wage-benefit package is too small, employees may desire to leave the corporation and it may be difficult to hire new workers. If the wage-benefit package is too generous, it may take too much away from the quarterly or annual profits. Just as this balance must be struck, a balance relative to employee rights; employee rights must be considered in the larger corporate context. These rights cannot be restricted in a way that is unfair to those workers, but legitimate restrictions must be maintained for the corporation to meets its fundamental goal: to be successful (specifically, in a for-profit company, profitable). Situations can arise where an employee may insist on a right that may well hinder the company in meeting its goals. In that case, those rights must be balanced against the needs of the corporation, and an appropriate balance must be identified and maintained.

To take a specific virtue, corporations should be honest, in dealing with both its employees and the community in which it is located. Obviously enough, there can be too little honesty—whether defrauding customers, skimming profits, lying on tax forms, or any number of the familiar examples of corporate behavior that are immoral, illegal, or both. Yet there can also be too much honesty, such as failing to protect proprietary information essential to a company's profits, or revealing marketing strategies to employees and, potentially, competitors, the distribution of which would put the company at a disadvantage. Neither too little honesty nor too much honesty is in the best interest of the company or, importantly, in the best interest of its employees. Virtue ethics, then, provides a way of seeing how to strike the balance here, whereby an appropriate amount of corporate honesty leads to the best results for the company, its employees, and its community.

The deontologist recognizes that companies, whether for-profit or not-for-profit, have a fundamental requirement: namely to carry out its mission. Specifically in the case of for-profit corporations, that mission is to make sufficient profit to stay in business and, preferably, continue to grow. Yet the corporation, even as an (artificial) person, must not violate certain rules: it must treat its employees, its community, and even its competitors, with respect. It must not follow or develop company policies that it would regard as fundamentally unfair were another company to have those same policies. The deontologist might explain this in terms of Kant's universalization test: If, for instance, company policy imposes certain restrictions on speech or behavior for its employees, could this policy be fairly imposed in all companies in the same context? The deontologist might also appeal to the Golden Rule here: If an employer were to impose a given set of restrictions on employees, would he or she be willing to work under the same set of restrictions?

Stockbrokerxtra Images/Photolibrary

Deontology recognizes that a company has a responsibility to carry out its mission of profitability and also examines whether certain restrictions can be applied fairly and universally on all companies in the same context.

We can look at how deontology can be applied here by looking at drug testing for airline pilots. The deontologist might well conclude that instituting such drug tests is precisely the kind of policy that could—even should—be put in place universally and in all similar contexts. Certainly, someone who imposes such drug tests may be quite confident that he or she would be willing to work under such a condition as well; hence, it seems to conform to the Golden Rule.

But there may be other situations where a company desires to restrict an employee's rights in ways that do not meet the universalization test or don't seem to satisfy the Golden Rule. Perhaps as a condition of employment, employees are told that they cannot join a union (or, in contrast, are told they must join the union). Although legal issues complicate the story, when observed from a moral standpoint, it is not clear that this restriction could be universalized: that no one could ever join a union (or that everyone must join a union) would seem to lead to the result that the very notion of a union becomes meaningless. And it seems quite possible that one who tells employees that they cannot join a union—or must join a union—might well be unwilling to work under those same conditions, indicating a conflict with the Golden Rule. Consequently, the corporate (artificial) citizen must, on the deontological view, treat rules in precisely the same way as real citizens must. Any restriction on employee rights that fails to satisfy the universalization test, or conflicts with applying the Golden Rule, thus risks the genuine possibility of being an unfair, unjust, and immoral restriction.

Some Conclusions

In considering the fundamental goal of a for-profit company or corporation, the virtue ethicist and the deontologist do not really disagree. Both recognize that such a company must make profit to remain in business and must impose certain conditions on its employees and potential employees to do so. The tension comes not so much in applying the specific theories as in determining where an employer's rights to impose such conditions are legitimate, and where they infringe on the rights of employees. It may seem easier to strike an appropriate balance between these two sets of rights in theory than it is in practice.

Consider a company that receives much of its business from contracts with the federal government. This company has spent years developing a close relationship with Senator Smith, who represents the state where the corporate headquarters are located. The members of the company's board of directors are particularly close with Senator Smith, and he has made it one of his highest priorities to see that the company receives favorable attention in the awarding of federal contracts. The company benefited by supporting Smith, and Smith benefited in turn. Currently, Senator Smith is now running for re-election, and the CEO of the company is the director of his campaign.

Ann is an employee of the company and a staunch opponent of Senator Smith. She has worked long hours outside of work for Senator Smith's opponent, and has contributed both time and money to Smith's opponent.

The issue here that arises is one of the limits to what the CEO of Ann's company can do, relative to Ann's political views. Can he ask her to remove a political sign from her office cubicle? Can he ask her to remove a bumper sticker from her car, because she parks in the company parking lot?

A fundraising picnic has been scheduled, organized by the CEO, for Senator Smith. Admission is $25, and it has been made abundantly clear to all employees that their attendance is expected. Clearly enough, the company cannot require this attendance, but Ann is convinced that her chances for promotion and salary increases will be harmed if she does not attend.

Here we have what seem to be competing rights: the right of the CEO to do what he thinks is in the best interest of the company (and, he might argue, therefore in the best interest of Ann herself), and Ann's right to participate in politics in the way she sees fit. Virtue ethics, deontology, or any of the other ethical theories we have at our disposal may offer some insight into how this conflict might be resolved, but it probably cannot provide a solution that is satisfactory to all involved. As we have seen before, ethics can offer a good bit of insight into the problem, by identifying what is at stake, and how the conflict itself might be most accurately characterized. Yet, as we have also seen, we may be expecting too much from any ethical theory if we think there is an easy procedure to follow that will result in the one correct answer.

Where Do We Go from Here?

It is, generally, to the advantage of both the employer and the employee that their company thrive: all are then better off. In addition to maintaining its own economic well-being, a successful corporation can offer the community a number of things that will make it better-off, such as support for the arts, schools, and general culture of the community. Not to be overlooked is what is also known as the "ripple" effect: a successful company will pay its workers the kind of wages that filter through the rest of the community. A well-paid worker who takes her family out to dinner thus helps those who work in the restaurant, and those workers in turn may have sufficient disposable income to buy things that support still others.

But conflicts do arise, between what an employer thinks is the right thing to do for the company, and what an employer thinks is right for the employer. We've seen a number of examples of this kind of conflict, and most of us are familiar with being asked to do things at work that can, at least potentially, generate these kinds of problems. The situation, of course, is made worse when unemployment is high and jobs are difficult to find. That situation makes most employees more reluctant to register objections, even if legitimate; many will prefer being employed to having their rights maintained while being unemployed. As a result, the employer has just a bit more leverage to impose conditions on employees, and on job candidates, that can become increasingly unfair to those employees.

Here we see the not-infrequent situation where real life confronts what ethics may tell us is the correct, or moral, or just thing to do. At what point does one refuse to violate one's moral code? If we are being harmed, or being treated unfairly, do we stand up for our moral principles, or do we simply take it, realizing the importance of remaining employed? Does it depend on how extreme the case is? Would we be willing to lie to keep our job? Would we be willing to ignore certain legal requirements to keep our job? Would we be willing to harm others, or at least risk harming others, to keep our job? Again, we find ourselves between two extremes: we may not be willing to sacrifice our job to stand up for a relatively insignificant moral infraction, but we may be absolutely unwilling to commit a crime in order to keep our job. Many issues in business ethics, as we have already seen, arise from trying to find the appropriate point between these two extremes. Ethics may help up us find it; however, it doesn't guarantee that we will find it, or that everyone will agree with our conception of the balance we do strike.

How Can Workplace Conflicts Be Resolved?

Fran is the boss, and Steve is one of her salaried employees. Fran has told Steve that instead of writing his reports at work he will have to write his reports at home on the weekends, due to some layoffs and increased pressure for Steve's reports from the stockholders. On Fran's view, Steve needs to "step up" and be a team player; on Steve's view, Fran is asking him to increase his workload while not increasing his salary; in other words, she is asking him to work for free. When Steve complains about this, Fran suggests that he should be willing to do this extra work for the good of the company. Steve, on the other hand, not only doesn't like working for free but realizes that this work will take away much of the time he gets to spend with his family.

This dispute can be resolved in a number of ways, and it might be helpful, after looking at some of them, to see which ones work best. It might also be a good idea to consider still other ways of settling the dispute, if possible, in a way that both parties are satisfied, if not entirely happy. Because this situation arises with some frequency in the workplace, both between employer and employee as well as between and among employees, it is an important issue to which some attention should be paid.

One might suggest that Steve schedule an appointment with Fran, and in a free and fair exchange, lay out his reasons for resisting doing this extra work. How Fran receives this information may well depend upon her management style. She may have adopted the style that insists what the boss says goes, and may not even be willing to schedule such a meeting with Steve. Or, perhaps, she simply goes through the motions of hearing his complaint, realizing that the result will not change, regardless of Steve's explanation. She may, on the other hand, be very open to dialogue and seek to come to some sort of resolution with Steve that allows him a bit more flexibility, thus keeping an employee relatively happy.

But what if Fran simply rejects Steve's suggestion of a meeting to resolve their differences? Informally, he might consider talking to other employees to see if they have similar experiences. If he does discover that this has happened, he could organize some of these employees in order to present what they regard as a legitimate complaint. Fran may be more willing to listen to a group, rather than an individual, and the group itself may wield a bit more strength than any individual employee could.

Of course, a more formal version of this kind of approach would be to approach the union, if available, or consider organizing one to represent the employees' interests. This is another strategy available to Steve. At the same time, corporations have been known not to look favorably on unions, or on those who seek to organize unions, and this approach may increase the tension between employer and employees, rather than alleviating it.

Steve, of course, always has the option of quitting his job. This solves the problem, but he may feel that the issue isn't sufficiently important to justify such a dramatic step. He also may be in a situation, often very common, where it is difficult to find another job, or another job as good; he may simply think that quitting is too risky. Some employers may, at the same time, take advantage of that situation to impose a few more demands on their workers.

Workplace conflicts are inevitable, of course. A deontologist might suggest a specific approach that will guarantee respect for all of those engaged in such disputes; a utilitarian may evaluate different resolutions in terms of what produces the greatest good for the greatest number. In any case, we see that ethics can provide some insight and guidance in looking critically at these kinds of conflicts, although rarely offering an easy solution satisfactory to everyone involved.

2.6 The Debate over Pornography

Arguments over pornography raise a number of ethical issues. Pornography is often regarded as a question of freedom of speech; however, more recently it has been harshly criticized for how it is produced and the images of women it endorses. Some, in contrast, regard the consumption of pornography as a "victimless crime," and, because it does not harm others, should not be restricted extensively.

The Issue: Pornography Should Be Highly Regulated

Here we will examine the two sides of the debate, looking at both the consumption and the production of pornography. We will utilize utilitarianism and emotivism to provide some theoretical analysis of the issue.

The argument against extensive regulation

Adults in the United States are allowed to do many things that others may condemn. They may smoke, drink to excess, fail to exercise, watch too much television, eat too much junk food, and do many other things that aren't "good" for them. Yet they are free to do so: as adults, they are allowed to do those things that the state cannot demonstrate pose a genuine threat to others. I cannot change the oil in my car and legally pour the old oil down the storm drain: that poses a threat to the environment and can harm others. I can, however, if I wish, have root beer, pickles, and pizza for breakfast every morning; it may not be a good or nutritious choice, but it is a choice I am free to make.

In the same way, adults are allowed to read and watch whatever they choose, unless the state can show a compelling reason to prevent them from doing so. For instance, in the United States, one can read books about bomb making and terrorism; one can see websites where overthrowing the government is advocated. One can find material that supports various kinds of hatreds against ethnic and religious minorities, as well as conspiracy theories blaming different groups for a remarkably wide range of things, including the U.S. government being responsible for the attacks on the World Trade Center on 9.11.2001. These materials are available because the First Amendment to the Constitution insists on freedom of speech; unless one can show a genuine threat, restrictions on speech are prohibited. Even though many people find such things distasteful—and much worse—the freedom to read and watch this material is guaranteed as a fundamental freedom in the United States.

Pornography, which is very difficult to define, is precisely this kind of material. Many find it extremely offensive. However, they have no right to dictate to those who wish to consume pornography that they cannot. Adults in the United States are free to read and view pornography; they can be prevented from doing so only if the state can show a compelling reason to restrict it.

Eric Audras/Photoalto/Photolibrary

Some would argue that adults should be allowed to make their own choices as long as they are not harming others.

Some restrictions have been imposed; producing child pornography is illegal because it harms children. Thus, the possession of child pornography is also illegal, in that its purchase supports an illegal activity. Access to pornography is limited to adults, just as are various other products, such as alcohol and tobacco; various other restrictions prevent those who do not wish to see it from being exposed to it. Thus, certain controls are imposed on bookstores; network television does not show material that is regarded as too indecent by those who run it, and cable television has various controls in place, such as parental controls and various payment requirements. These and other restrictions have been put in place to do two things: to prevent the involuntary exposure of pornography to those who wish to avoid it, and to allow those who wish to consume pornography access to it.

Image100/Photolibrary

Others would note that there are restrictions already in place to prevent involuntary exposure to pornography.

Some have argued that the production of pornography involves the exploitation and mistreatment of women; thus, consumers of pornography support an industry that harms women. This may be true, but it has little bearing on restricting the rights of adult access to pornography. Many people work in industries that involve serious threats in hazardous situations: coal miners, electricians, and farmers, among others. To argue that pornography should be highly regulated, or censored, because some people have been mistreated in its production is the same as arguing that restaurants should be closed because some restaurants have had health code violations.

Finally, if pornography is highly regulated, there is a genuine danger of a slippery slope appearing. Historically, some things now regarded as great literature, and great art, were characterized as pornography and banned. This isn't to say all pornography is great art; it is to say that when one group of people is allowed to determine what other adults may read and watch, there is always the risk that they will be willing to regulate or ban material that should not be. Furthermore, how does society choose who does the regulating, and whose standards should be followed? For good reason, the courts have consistently decided that when in doubt, free speech must be tolerated, and that any regulations on pornography must be minimal and shown to respond to what would otherwise be a substantial danger to the public.

The argument for extensive regulation

Love between two people, including its sexual expression, is one of the most cherished values human beings possess. Pornography damages this value by dehumanizing those who appear in it and reducing them to objects that become simply a means to satisfy some other person's crude desires. This coarsens relationships between people and reduces the dignity each human being deserves. Pornography thus makes it more difficult to treat others with respect, and thus should be strictly regulated; it may even, in some cases, be censored or banned.

There is a well-known and traditional way of arguing for the strict regulation of pornography. On this argument, we can argue that pornography is sexually explicit material designed to generate a specific kind of response in the viewer. It is obscene, degrades its subjects,

67

and harms the values of society. If most people in a society regard pornography as violating its standards, then the society is well within its rights to restrict or even ban pornography. Otherwise, the moral standards of the society are attacked and undermined by a minority, who have no legitimate right to reject the moral standards of the majority. Furthermore, it corrupts not just society as a whole but also the individual who consumes it. Adults are allowed to engage in some risky activities, but the state has a legitimate role in preventing them from harming others and harming themselves. Even though the state may allow

Corbis/Photolibrary

Some would argue that pornography can coarsen and even damage relationships.

people to make unhealthy choices, it strictly regulates them: alcohol and tobacco are highly regulated, for instance. The state can require people to wear seat belts and motorcycle helmets. These regulations prevent, or at least limit, the things adults can do; because pornography is harmful to the individual, the state has a legitimate right to regulate it just as it does any activity that may harm an individual, society as a whole, or—as in this case—both.

A second, more recent argument, against pornography distinguishes it from "erotica." Erotica is the artistic presentation of human love, including its sexual expression. In contrast, pornography involves the degradation of people, particularly women, and often employs violence—including rape—in their depiction. It may also include other acts designed to humiliate and dehumanize women, by presenting them as submissive victims who enjoy being mistreated. Adopting this conception of pornography, it is seen as doing substantial harm: not just to the women depicted but also to the more general way women are regarded in society as a whole. In this way, the dehumanizing of women is seen to be a general harm to women that makes legitimate the state's ability to regulate, restrict, and even ban pornography. In addition, the production of pornography also causes harm to those women involved in that production. These women are coerced, threatened, humiliated, and exploited in making pornography; as a genuine harm to these women, the state has not just the right but the obligation to prevent that harm.

Pornography coarsens and degrades the moral values of a society and harms the person consuming it. Pornography harms women, both by exploiting them in its production and in providing a consistently demeaning image of women for the consumer of pornography that also affects the way women are regarded more generally in society. The state has a legitimate role in preventing harm coming to its citizens, and because pornography harms people in the various ways described, the state has a legitimate role—in fact, an obligation—to restrict and regulate pornography.

Applying the Theories

The most prominent and influential utilitarian theorist was John Stuart Mill. In Mill's classic text *On Liberty,* he puts forth what is now known as the "harm principle":

the only purpose for which power may be rightfully exercised over any member of a civilized community, against his will, is to prevent harm to others. His own good, either physical or moral, is not sufficient warrant (Mill 1909).

In other words, Mill is saying that the state must not be allowed to prevent someone from doing something, even if it is harmful to that person. The only legitimate way the government can step in to prevent some activity is if it can be shown to harm others. Among social scientists, there are passionate debates and a great deal of controversy over pornography. Many have insisted that its harms are obvious; others have responded that those harms have been exaggerated. Mill's point, however, is that even if one grants that pornography harms those who consume it, one can only restrict it if it can be definitively demonstrated that it also harms others. From the perspective argued here, that harm to others has not been sufficiently demonstrated.

The British Library/Photolibrary

Utilitarian John Stuart Mill's harm principle argues that restrictions are justified only if the activity harms others. It is better for society members to be free, he would say.

How does Mill's harm principle relate to the traditional slogan of utilitarianism, that one should do what produces the greatest good for the greatest number? The connection isn't made as explicit as one might like by Mill, but it seems fairly clear how it is made. Society is better off if its members are freer, and best off if they have the greatest amount of freedom possible—as long as one person's freedom doesn't interfere with that of another person. Thus, what generates the greatest freedom for the citizens of a state, or society, is the moral thing to do, which also means that the fewer restrictions, the greater the freedom. The greatest good for the greatest number is thus produced by a state with the fewest restrictions on its citizens, of a state with the greatest amount of freedom. The greatest amount of freedom, on Mill's view, is achieved by following the harm principle. Therefore, the harm principle is essential to a state that produces the greatest good for the greatest number.

Clearly enough, applying the harm principle and utilitarianism supports the idea that restrictions and regulations of pornography must be imposed only if they can be shown to prevent harm being done to others. The presumption, then, is that only the kind of restrictions mentioned earlier—such as the prohibitions against child pornography—are legitimate interventions by the state. One might argue that in a given society, if a majority wishes to ban pornography, then that would presumably produce the greatest good for the greatest number. Thus, it would be both moral and just to ban it. Mill might respond to this by arguing that it is short-sighted to apply the utilitarian principle in this way. Rather, one should see that, in general, fewer restrictions on freedom generate the greatest good for the greatest number. Therefore, in general, one should always use the greatest caution

Brian Mitchell/Photolibrary

How would you handle your teen's computer usage and Internet access?

in imposing any restrictions, even though, in some cases, this may conflict with the views of the overwhelming majority of the community. In short, using the utilitarian principle in this general way, in combination with the harm principle, indicates that pornography should be not be extensively regulated, banned, or censored.

Supreme Court Justice Potter Stewart once famously said that he had given up trying to define obscenity; rather, he observed, "I know it when I see it." This is analogous to some treatments of obscenity—and because it can be regarded as obscene, to some treatments of pornography—offered by the ethical view of emotivism. We may not be able to define "obscenity" and "pornography" to everyone's satisfaction, and we may not be able to explain why it is wrong. But we are confident in our view that it is obscene, and that it is wrong, when we see it. The emotivist gives us an ethical theory supporting that response.

The emotivist does not try to give reasons, or facts, or evidence, or even arguments for a given evaluation, including moral evaluations. To say something is "bad" or "wrong" is really just an indication of one's attitude or response to it. For this reason, emotivism is known as a "non-cognitivist" position in ethics. Non-cognitivism denies that there are moral properties, or moral facts; in fact, it denies that certain kinds of claims are the kinds of things that can be true or false. You may like ice cream, want to listen to jazz, or hope to attend a football game. You express those attitudes by saying and doing thing that express your approval of them. In the same way, you may not like artichokes, don't want to listen to bluegrass music, and hope to avoid going shoe shopping. Here you express those attitudes by saying and doing things that express your disapproval of them.

Those who object to pornography may respond in the same way, agreeing with Potter Stewart that, insofar as it is obscene, they know it when they see it. One can express this attitude—this disapproval—in a number of ways. Importantly, though, the various expressions of this attitude in a social context can be designed to convince others that it is a reasonable, and even correct attitude, and that they should also express their own disapproval. In a community, if a sufficient number of people share a common emotivist response to something, that reaction can provide the basis for designing policy for the community. In other words, the emotivist not only may indicate his or her own attitude but is free to persuade others to adopt that same attitude. Ultimately, then, the emotivist may insist that in a given community, there is sufficient disapproval of pornography that the preferences of the members of that community should be respected, and thus pornography should be strictly regulated and, perhaps, censored or even banned.

Some Conclusions

In the case of pornography, we see a sharp conflict between those who argue for minimal restrictions on adults—including restrictions on access to pornography—and those who argue that substantial restrictions are legitimate. On the one hand, we see those who advocate minimal restrictions adopting a position that one might call libertarian: that the state has no right to interfere with adult behavior that cannot be shown to harm others. On the other hand, those who advocate greater restrictions see pornography as harming the values of society, coarsening interpersonal relationships, and flooding society—through books, magazines, TV, films, and the Internet—with degrading and obscene images. The issue seems to revolve around the notion of what, if any, harms are involved, and what the legitimate role of the state is in addressing any such harms.

Two other results can be identified as emerging from this debate. One is a causal claim that those who consume pornography—especially pornography that is particularly degrading to women and that includes violence—are more likely to carry out the kinds of things they see. A standard pornographic fantasy involves a woman who is forced to do something against her will, only to see her come to enjoy it. Is it more likely that one who repeatedly reads about or sees such images will act on those ideas? The argument is that seeing violence, for instance, in a film will cause one to act more violently; thus, it is legitimate to minimize exposure to those things that will tend to cause that violence. If pornography contains the violent treatment of women and can be shown to cause actual violence against women, doesn't the state have a legitimate right to restrict it? Others respond, of course, that no such causal connections have been shown, and that, in any case, there are plenty of other examples of violence of all kinds available to people. If such exposure to violence in, for instance, films is said to cause actual violence, then wouldn't that exposure also need to be highly regulated? On this view, basing an argument on an unsubstantiated causal claim may well lead to a slippery slope where any number of things could be restricted, banned, or censored, limiting the legitimate rights of free speech guaranteed by the First Amendment. This response has been criticized by some who see this not as a restriction on speech, but on action, in that the speech in question causes real behavior that does genuine harm to others.

Those who argue for more restrictions on pornography would make a causal claim: those who see violence are more likely to carry such acts out. Others say this is an unsubstantiated claim that could lead to more unreasonable restrictions.

The second result that has emerged in recent years is the emphasis on those who produce pornography. On this argument, pornographic films almost invariably involve coercing, threatening, and exploiting women (and perhaps men) in their production. Often such women do not really "choose" to work in this industry, but find themselves there due to financial need and the financial opportunities involved. Those who have focused on this aspect of pornography have argued that both physical and psychological intimidation is frequently involved in the production of pornography, and that it takes advantage of women who may be financially or psychologically vulnerable; thus, it does not really involve the kind of "free" or "autonomous" choice that should be respected. Those who have put forth this perspective also insist that the images of women found in pornography continue to reinforce very negative and oppressive conceptions of women, leading to that conception of women being pervasive in society. Given the size of the pornography industry in the United States, this argument insists that the kind of images of women found in pornography must have an effect on how women are perceived in other contexts, a result that is clearly harmful to women and to society in general.

Where Do We Go from Here?

Many important issues arise in this discussion; however, the one that has gotten a great deal of attention is the causal claim regarding violence in pornography. Does seeing violence committed against women cause actual violence against women? More important, does a person who sees this kind of violence, on a regular basis, become more likely to commit that violence? Social scientists continue to gather data on this issue, interpret that data, and debate the implications. But this is, of course, not limited simply to pornography.

Mike Kemp/Rubberball/Photolibrary

The debate over pornography can be broadened to include exposure to violence on television and other media. Should media be regulated more stringently, or should First Amendment rights and Mill's harm principle take precedent?

A standard claim in the literature on television violence is that the average child will have seen 8,000 murders on TV by the end of elementary school, and 200,000 acts of violence on TV by age eighteen. Many have argued that these kinds of numbers indicate a considerable worry about exposure to violence. Some argue that such exposure to violence causes those so exposed to be more violent. Others argue that even if such a causal claim cannot be established, such extensive exposure to violence makes it appear to be a common feature of life and thus more acceptable, futile to try to prevent, and even an acceptable solution to problems.

The availability of information—of all kinds—has dramatically increased, and access to that information is also widely available. Books, magazines, newspapers, films, television, and especially the Internet offer an almost unlimited amount of content. Those whose arguments are based on Mill's harm principle and the First Amendment insist that wide latitude be given to this content and people's access to it; to restrict it without showing conclusively that otherwise people will be harmed is not only to violate the First Amendment, but is, more generally, an illegitimate extension of the government's power over its citizens. In contrast, those who advocate more extensive regulation simply point to the levels of violence, the degradation of culture, and the negative images and values that seem to pervade society. Surely something should be done to indicate our disapproval of that situation? Furthermore, from this perspective, even though some controls may have been imposed on certain content, including pornography, to allow those who wish to avoid it from being so exposed, the pervasive nature of objectionable material makes it impossible to avoid. Thus, one must take extraordinary steps to avoid it, and this also requires more effort on the part of some parents to keep their children from being exposed to things that they regard as obscene, immoral, and wrong. On this view, one shouldn't be forced to make extraordinary efforts to avoid being confronted with indecent and objectionable material. Rather, one should have the legitimate expectation not to be so confronted; those who wish to consume pornography and similar material should have, minimally, the obligation to make an extra effort to do so.

Can the Majority Be Prevented from Acting Like a Tyrant?

Democracy is a pretty old idea, going back at least to ancient Athens. The idea, of course, is that people know best what they want and need, and democracies allow their views to be expressed in the fairest way. Whether a democracy is direct (where people vote directly on all issues) or representative (where people elect others to represent their views), the majority view will prevail; if more voters want a particular law passed, for instance, it will pass. Majority rule is at the heart of democratic theory; however, a worry also arises. The point was made by Socrates and Plato about the Athenian democracy and has ever since been an issue for the idea of democracy: What if the majority chooses in such a way that the rights of the minority are infringed? Is that fair? And are there ways of preventing it? This can, naturally, be a substantial issue when a group is evenly divided. Imagine a community voting on a specific law; 51 percent are in favor, and 49 percent oppose it. The minority, in this case, may find the law deeply offensive, but just over half of the people support the law and thus are able to impose it on almost half the community. Such circumstances have led to the common concern that in democracies, there may be a temptation for this kind of thing to happen, an objection commonly known as the tyranny of the majority.

A number of the individual rights we have looked at—if, of course, they are "rights"—can be seen as raising this issue. Certain constitutional protections exist; however, what if the majority of a community decides to ban the ownership of certain guns, or certain reading material, or certain expressions of religious belief. We are also

Walter Bibikow/Age Fotostock/Photolibrary

Democracy is supposed to represent the will of the majority, but what if the majority chooses something that tramples on the rights of a minority?

familiar with instances of this from American history; often African Americans were subject to various forms of abuse and injustice simply because they were in a minority and had little or no access to the machinery of political power.

In a famous case in the 1940s, some schoolchildren in West Virginia refused to stand for the Pledge of Allegiance. As Jehovah's Witnesses, they were forbidden to act in a way that, as they saw it, treated the American flag as a sacred object and thus, refused to say the Pledge. As is easy to imagine, this was a very unpopular view, particularly during the height of World War II. The Supreme Court found that these students were protected by the Constitution. Here the legal protections were provided, but it is fairly easy to see how such a view was regarded by the majority and to picture the various informal ways members of that community might have expressed their displeasure.

Socrates and Plato were particularly concerned that democracy—in this case, specifically, direct democracy—left decisions up to a majority that might well lack sufficient understanding to make those decisions correctly. As Socrates might put it, one goes to a doctor for medical care because the doctor is trained to be an expert in medicine. One goes to a car mechanic for repairs because the mechanic is trained to be an expert in automobile repair. Yet direct democracies allow the majority to decide issues that are considerably more important for society than auto repair: whether to go to war, what taxes should be in place and what tax revenue should be used for, what the standards should be for water, air, and food, and many other crucial issues. Does the majority of citizens have the expertise and knowledge to make these kinds of decisions?

Philip Gordon/Photolibrary

The interior of the Japanese Diet, the country's bicameral legislature. The National Diet favors a more proportional party representation in an attempt to address some of the problems with democracy.

Defenders of democracy have a variety of responses. One, generally attributed to Winston Churchill, is to acknowledge the flaws of democracy: "Democracy is the worst form of government except all those other forms that have been tried from time to time." That is, democracy has many flaws, just not as many as any other form of government. Others have argued for such things as "proportional representation"; countries such as the Netherlands, Japan, and Israel have adopted a parliamentary system with many different parties. In this situation, if 5 percent of the voters find a particular party most suitable, they will, at least in theory, be able to elect someone to represent their view. The representation, that is, is proportional to the various views within the society. Many democracies have taken this path, in contrast to the United States, where generally a two-party system is in place; one chooses whichever party is closer to one's own views. (The drawback of this approach is often expressed as one voting for "the lesser of two evils.") Some political theorists have advocated proportional representation and alternative ways of voting methods in the United States to address the problem of minority rights being represented. In any case, we see that in spite of certain constitutional protections, the question of individual rights, and particularly the threat to the rights of minorities within a system that gives political power to the majority, will continue to generate discussion and debate about the extent and limits of those individual rights.

Some Final Questions

1. In a society that decides things on the basis of majority rule, is there a danger that the majority might ignore the legitimate concerns of minorities? What steps can be taken to protect minority rights?
2. Granting women the right to vote was, no doubt, long overdue. What other rights, in looking back at U.S. history, took too long to grant? Can you suggest a reason why it was so difficult to achieve those rights?
3. One often hears the phrase "you can't legislate morality." What do you think that means? Do you think it is true? What kind of moral issues require us to make laws prohibiting certain kinds of behavior?

3

Social Rights and Responsibilities

Chapter Outline

In this chapter, we focus on those issues that affect society as a whole. Given that most of us are members of a society, they will also affect each of us directly or indirectly. We will, again, see how ethical theory can inform our understanding of moral problems, make the problems themselves more explicit, and help us attempt to resolve them.

3.1 The Death Penalty

The death penalty, as practiced in the United States, has been the source of political and religious controversy for many years. After looking at the arguments themselves, we will look at the issue from the perspective of deontological ethics. Here, perhaps surprisingly, one can use the deontological perspective to argue both sides of the issue, indicating that one simply can't apply a theory to an issue and expect the correct answer to result: it isn't like putting two numbers into a calculator and pressing the "addition" button.

The Issue: The Death Penalty Should Be Abolished

The death penalty, as practiced in the United States, raises questions both about its morality and its effectiveness. Here we will examine both sides of the death penalty debate to help clarify what is at stake.

The argument against abolishing the death penalty

Human beings have rights that no one can deprive them of, according to many political theorists. Perhaps the best-known version of this claim is that found in the Declaration of Independence: "We hold these truths to be self-evident, that all men are created equal, that they are endowed by their Creator with certain unalienable Rights." An unalienable right is one that a person can never have taken away, by another person or by a government. Thomas Jefferson offered as his examples of such rights "life, liberty, and the pursuit of happiness." Thus, to murder another person is to deprive that person of his or her life, and society has the obligation to punish that person in such a way that its commitment to this fundamental right is made clear. In other words, if a murderer is not punished harshly, it might seem that the government doesn't regard murder as the kind of crime that deserves the most serious punishment. Because the death penalty seems to be the most serious punishment available, the government has not just the right but the obligation to impose the death penalty on murderers. This way, the murderer is punished, and the commitment to the right to life is reaffirmed. For this reason, some have argued that the death penalty is a symbol of a society's respect for life, and of the humanity of the victim and the murderer.

Image Source /Photolibrary

Some would say that a murderer has given up his right to life by taking someone else's. Do you agree or disagree?

It may seem odd to think that the death penalty indicates respect for the murderer; how is a person shown respect by being executed? The point is that society can only function if all of the people who live in that society live by certain rules. It seems like a good rule for a society that its members not kill each other. If someone violates that rule, he or she strikes at the very heart of what makes that society possible. By murdering a member of society, a person shows that he or she doesn't really belong in that society; this person has forfeited the right to live among other people. We show our respect for the murderer's humanity by recognizing that he or she, at one point, possessed the same right to life as everyone else. By taking another's life, the murderer has given up that right. In that way, we recognize the dignity of the murderer by imposing the death penalty: we show what the murderer had, and what the murderer gave up, by taking away the right of another person, namely, the victim. Just as a murderer treats the victim as if that victim didn't deserve to live, society must insist that those who act in such a way forfeit their own right to live.

The Print Collector /Photolibrary

The death penalty is often associated with the electric chair, although other execution methods are also used today. This print depicts the execution of William Kemmler, the first man to be executed by electrocution. Kemmler allegedly "chopped a woman to bits with an axe." Three surges of current were needed.

Furthermore, when society reaffirms the sanctity of life by executing those who unjustly take a person's life, it also sends a message to others. If people see that the price to be paid for murdering someone is the loss of one's own life, then that will prevent at least some of those people from taking that step. The death penalty thus serves as a deterrent. When functioning efficiently, the deterrent effect of the death penalty will lead to fewer people committing such crimes.

The death penalty affirms the humanity of the victim and the murderer. It also sends a clear message to everyone else in society that the right to life is so fundamental that one who takes another's life will forfeit his or her own life. Finally, what other punishment might be appropriate for someone already in prison who kills someone? Therefore, the only moral response is not to abolish the death penalty, but to keep it.

The argument for abolishing the death penalty

There are a number of good and sufficient reasons to abolish the death penalty. It has been applied in a way that reflects racial, class, and ethnic bias; it is too expensive; innocent people have almost certainly been executed; it isn't effective at deterring future murders; its use is barbaric, and puts the United States in company with other countries whose values we often deplore; and many religious leaders and many religions reject the death penalty. But here we will focus on the moral question of executing a human being.

Killing another human being is wrong. Assuming Thomas Jefferson is correct, and certain rights cannot be taken away, then the right to life cannot be taken away. A murderer has, of course, violated one of the fundamental roles of society by violating another person's right to life. Does that justify the state in depriving the murderer of his or her life? If so, then the right to life can be taken away, which would mean it is not inalienable; if not, and the right to life is inalienable, then the state is violating the murderer's right to life. A right cannot be both inalienable and alienable; that is a contradiction, and such a claim cannot be true. Thus, the state has to determine if such a right to life can be taken away, and under what circumstances. But if killing a human being is wrong, and the death penalty is the intentional killing of a human being, then isn't it wrong? Or is the murderer, by having murdered, no longer a human being? Yet the United States recognizes that we cannot torture the murderer because that would violate the murderer's constitutional rights. So if the murderer has some rights, presumably he or she is a human being. We seem to have yet another contradiction, that the murderer is a human being and is not a human being.

Too often those in favor of the death penalty assume those who oppose it are "soft" on criminals, and almost act as if they are advocating that the murderer not be punished at all. Of course, this is a very inaccurate description of the argument put forth by those opposing the death penalty. Rather, they argue that life imprisonment without possibility of parole is a good substitute for the death penalty. This alternative punishment can be supported for several reasons. It removes the murderer from society, and thus serves the function of protecting the members of society from that threat. Life in prison—again, without the possibility of parole—is at least as much a deterrent as the death penalty: presumably, someone thinking about murdering another would think at least as long about the consequences of spending 30, 40, or 50 years in prison as he or she would about being executed; It avoids the potential problem we saw arise, when the state insists that killing a human being is wrong and demonstrates it by killing a human being. Finally, it avoids the potential of discovering that an innocent person has been executed; a mistake that, for obvious reasons, is difficult to fix.

Christian Schmidt/Cusp/Photolibrary

Some would argue that life imprisonment is just as much a deterrent as the death penalty and is preferable for a number of reasons. Do you agree or disagree?

In general terms, then, all human life has dignity and deserves respect. If that dignity and respect is part of what it means to be a human being, it cannot be taken away from someone, no matter how horrendous or evil the act a person does. In other words, the respect for human life is inalienable and can never be taken away from someone. Society shows its true respect for human life by abolishing the death penalty; as Sister Helen Prejean once said, we are all more than the worst we have ever done. Executing a person says otherwise.

The state has an obligation to capture and punish those who break its rules, even its most fundamental rules, such as not killing other members of society. But it can carry out that obligation without employing the death penalty, thus punishing those who deserve it while revealing its genuine commitment to the right to life and its respect for human dignity.

To put this into a more concrete example, James's ex-wife, Lisa, has remarried another man, Frank. James is extremely jealous, and, after careful planning, murders Frank. In spite of that planning, James is caught, convicted of first-degree murder, and sentenced to death. Would James have been deterred from murdering Frank if he "only" faced 50 years in prison, without the possibility of parole? Would he, or others like him, have only been deterred by the possibility that he be executed, while knowing that not all those so sentenced are, in fact, executed? Does society gain more respect for life and human dignity by seeing the legal system declare that James can never be anything other than a murderer, and that there is no other solution for someone like James than to execute him? Had James been wealthier, could he have been able to afford a better attorney, who might have been able to make sure James avoided the death penalty? If so, would that mean that the state regards James's human dignity as depending on the size of his bank account, not on who he is or what he did?

Society can protect itself, punish those who violate its rules, punish most harshly those who violate its most important rules, and maintain its commitment to the dignity of human life without resorting to the capital punishment. Therefore, the only moral response is to abolish the death penalty.

The Theories

As we have seen, deontology is an ethical view that insists the morality of an act be evaluated in terms of certain rules or obligations, and whether the act in question conforms to those rules. This distinguishes it from consequentialist views, such as utilitarianism, which evaluates the morality of an act in terms of its consequences or results. This is not to say that the deontologist thinks acts do not have consequences. It just means that those consequences don't play a role in evaluating whether the act was morally good, morally bad, morally praiseworthy, morally blameworthy, etc.

In considering the debate we have just seen, deontology presents a peculiar result, relative to the issue of the death penalty. The most famous deontologist, we know, is Immanuel Kant. Kant was a strong advocate of the death penalty and gave forceful arguments, based on his deontological views of ethics, in favor of the death penalty. But other deontologists have used the same basic ethical perspective to argue against the death penalty. In fact, if someone says, "I'm a deontologist," you really don't have enough information to predict whether that person is for or against the death penalty. This is a good reminder that ethics may help us understand moral questions better, but you can't simply "plug in" the problem and hope the theory "spits out" the right answer.

Kant's argument is very similar to the previous argument in favor of keeping the death penalty. Kant is pretty clear about this, stating that if someone murders another person, "he must die." This is known as **retributivism**—a theory of punishment that would have the one who does something wrong be punished proportionately to the wrong that is done. On Kant's view, this is a requirement of justice. The murderer, by violating another person's rights (in this case, to live), forfeits his or her own right to live. For Kant, and this particular way of applying deontological principles, reason demands that the murderer be executed. Kant believes this shows the state's commitment to the respect for human dignity. A

DEA Picture Library/De Agostini Editore/Photolibrary

An engraving of 18th-century German philosopher Immanuel Kant, who was a strong death penalty advocate and would have argued retributivism: a murderer must be punished in accordance to his crime.

bit more informally, Kant thinks that retributivism functions in a way similar to those punishments based on the Hebrew Bible's "an eye for an eye" principle of punishment. He believes that the only way people can see how fundamentally immoral it is to violate the rule against murder is to see that if one person kills another, the killer must give up his or her own life.

This is a pretty popular argument and makes sense to many people who insist that anyone who thinks he or she can kill another person should have to pay the ultimate price. After all, the Golden Rule would seem to say I shouldn't kill another person if I don't want another person to kill me. Anyone who rejects this lacks something essential and shouldn't be permitted to live. It is important, by the way, to see the role of deterrence in this argument. The utilitarian might argue that the death penalty deters other potential murderers, and that benefit produces the greatest good for the greatest number and is, therefore, morally correct. Kant seems to agree that capital punishment may well have a deterrent effect, but, in line with his deontological view, this consequence cannot play any role for justifying it. If anything, any deterrence effect the death penalty might have is just an added bonus.

Images.com/Photolibrary

Other deontologists agree with Kant that human dignity should be respected but extend that argument to the murderer as well: all humans have worth and should be treated with respect.

Other deontologists, interestingly enough, have argued for precisely the opposite conclusion. We have, more or less, seen the argument in the preceding debate, but we can now put it in the more precise, theoretical language of deontology.

Those who argue against the death penalty accept Kant's claim, that human beings possess dignity and share his insistence that human dignity should be respected. They reject, however, Kant's retributivism and focus on another of Kant's claims, that people should never be treated solely as a means to an end but should always be treated as ends in themselves. In other words, to treat another person as some kind of object, or in a way that doesn't recognize the worth of that person, is to treat that person as a means. For instance, if someone needs money, stealing from another person is to treat the victim as a means to the goal (getting money); such behavior is prohibited by Kant's own ethical principles.

The deontologist who rejects capital punishment regards that punishment as treating the human being as a means to an end (in this case, presumably, that end is justice). For this deontologist, then, even a murderer has some degree of humanity that must be respected. On this view, it is pretty clear we don't respect that human dignity by killing the human possessing it.

This result isn't entirely unusual, by the way. Two people who claim to be working from the same ethical perspective may resolve a given situation quite differently. They may, for instance, apply the theory in a different way, or they may describe the moral issue involved in ways that result in different analyses. There is a little of both going on here. But the sticking point seems to be what the status is of the murderer: Is he or she still a human being? Kant seems to argue that the murderer has forfeited that part of his or her human dignity that must be respected, by committing an act of murder. Those opposing this result seem to argue that even in committing murder, the murderer still possess human dignity, and that dignity cannot be violated. Making clear where we come down on this question—whether we are obligated to treat the murderer with any degree of respect—helps make much clearer what we conclude when we apply a deontological analysis to the question of the death penalty.

Some Conclusions

Probably the most obvious outcome of our discussion of the death penalty is that deontology doesn't really provide an obvious answer. We might be happier if everyone agreed that capital punishment is right, or that capital punishment is wrong. But, as we have seen, ethics just doesn't work that way. As we have also seen, however, this kind of theory can provide a bit more rigor to our understanding of the problem, and can help make clear—or at least clearer—what is at stake in the debate.

One could take our results and use them to recommend pursuing another approach. Unfortunately, utilitarians also don't agree on the death penalty. Even though they may accept the fundamental idea of doing what creates the greatest good for the greatest number, utilitarians disagree sharply on whether capital punishment does, or doesn't, do so.

We can also, however, add to our theoretical analysis to make our ethical points have a bit more substance. Some argue that there is a clear case that the death penalty has a deterrence effect. This evidence would not justify its use for the deontologist, but it might strengthen the overall case. Others, of course, argue that there is no demonstrated deterrence effect, and thus might reject that argument.

A traditional argument has also been that it is more cost-effective to execute people than to imprison them for life. Yet, as it turns out, on the current procedure used to impose capital punishment, it is more expensive to execute someone than to imprison that person for 40 years. Decreasing the numbers of appeals available to the convicted murder might lower this cost. But some argue that innocent people have already been executed, and that if there are fewer chances to appeal, it is likely that more innocent people will be executed. Some advocates of the death penalty regard this as a price society is willing to pay; however, others suggest that one who is in the position of being executed of a crime he or she did not commit might see things otherwise.

One interesting development in the discussion of the death penalty is the argument that a significant factor in determining whether someone found guilty of murder receives the death penalty is race—the race of the murder victim, not the race of the murderer. In a well-known analysis, legal theorist David Baldus argued that someone who murdered a white person was more than four times more likely to receive the death penalty than someone who murdered an African American. Although his results have found many critics and many supporters, one might supplement an argument against the death penalty by drawing on these results to show that the death penalty is not applied fairly. If it is applied unfairly, then it may be arbitrary enough to be rejected as "cruel and unusual," and prohibited by the Eighth Amendment of the U.S. Constitution. Of course, the deontologist might well wish to use this kind of argument to indicate that those subject to the death penalty are not being treated equally under the law and, as such, aren't given equal respect for their human dignity.

As is so often the case, we see that ethical theory can deepen our analysis and understanding of various ethical problems, although it rarely solves them. But theories can also be used in conjunction with other material and other reasons, to strengthen one's position.

Where Do We Go from Here?

What lessons can we draw from this debate? There seem to be many, but the one that seems to emerge above all is that this debate will continue. During the course of the debate among religious leaders, lawyers, philosophers, and others, the argument has gotten much more rigorous and much more sophisticated. The argument itself has helped make much clearer what is at stake. The debate also helps focus the issue better and allows us to see what kinds of evidence might make a position stronger and what kind of evidence might make a position weaker.

One implication drawn by some who write about capital punishment is to consider the use of the death penalty in the United States and in other countries. These authors argue that the countries that have abolished the death penalty—England, France, Germany, and Japan, for instance—are precisely the countries the United States tends to compare itself to in many other categories, such as level of education, health care, women's rights, economic development, and personal freedom. Yet the countries that employ the death penalty are generally those that the United States does not regard as sharing similar values, such countries as Iran, the Democratic Republic of Congo, North Korea, and Yemen. Of course, one might respond that the United States is different in very specific ways from Western Europe and Japan as well as from the Third World dictatorships. It is an interesting experiment to look at the commitment various countries make to human dignity and to what extent the United States shares that value. The deontologist won't solve the problem, as we have seen, but one might use this kind of comparison to make the analysis more complete.

What Is the Relationship Between Religion and the State?

Few beliefs are as personal, as significant, and as profound as spiritual beliefs are for religious people. The Bill of Rights recognizes this by prohibiting government interference with religion, whether by establishing a religion, indicating the preference for a religion, or preventing religious expression. Yet, historically, many examples have arisen where an individual's, or a group's, religious beliefs and practices are in conflict with the laws or community standards of the larger society. Polygamy and ritualistic drug use in certain Native American religious ceremonies have conflicted with the law; atheists have objected to what they regard as state endorsement of religion by such things as the phrase "In God We Trust" on legal currency; some religious people object equally to being prevented from being allowed to display, on public property, Nativity scenes—crèches—at Christmas. These are difficult issues to resolve, for they involve the conflict between personal expressions of faith and the obligation of the state to treat everyone fairly and in accordance with the Constitution.

A related issue has more recently been seen in some political races. Roman Catholic politicians have been told, or threatened, that they will not be allowed to take communion if they support, or continue to support, laws that make abortion legal. Such a politician may well be presented with the choice between religion and public service. The right to an abortion is, with certain restrictions, legal in the United States. A politician may well argue that he or she can do more good for the community by serving in a political capacity, and might even be more effective in curtailing the number of abortions performed by doing so. Can one remain a member of a church, in good standing, while serving in a position that supports views that contradict those of his or her church?

Some have taken considerably more extreme action on the basis of religious beliefs. For instance, some who are convinced that abortion is the taking of an innocent human life—that abortion is murder—have gone on to murder abortion providers themselves. Presumably, the position here is more or less utilitarian, proceeding on the idea that killing one abortion provider saves many more lives than not killing the abortion provider. From this perspective, the view seems to be that it is just to kill someone who the killer regards as a mass murderer (the abortionist). Yet clearly the state has an obligation to protect its citizens who are not violating the law; the abortion provider was not doing anything illegal.

Traditionally, society has rejected the idea of "taking the law into one's own hands," or what is sometimes called "vigilante justice." Given the anger and other passions involved, the law insists that justice is much better served, and thus society much better protected, by following standard, socially endorsed procedures, using trials, judges, juries, and the like.

As we saw earlier, some people regard the rules of society as so wrong that they feel compelled to leave that society. Generally, however, some degree of compromise has to be struck. Society is a collection of individuals; it grants and protects

What Would You Do?

Your next-door neighbor, whose son was killed fighting in Afghanistan, asks you to sign a petition against the building of an Islamic mosque and cultural center in town. You know three other neighbors whose children died fighting in Iraq and Afghanistan, but you also work with, and are good friends with, a Muslim woman whose son died fighting with the U.S. Marines in Iraq. Your neighbors regard the mosque as a painful reminder of the deaths of their children and as a symbol of Islam; your co-worker is an enthusiastic supporter of the building of the mosque and hopes that it will help non-Muslims understand and appreciate Islam.

• Do you sign the petition?

• If so, what would you tell your co-worker if she asks you why you did?

• If not, what do you tell your next-door neighbor when you decline to sign it?

Dave Harrigan/Ableimages/Photolibrary
Would you sign the petition? Why or why not?

those individuals their rights. At the same time, each individual plays a number of different roles in that society, and much of what makes up that individual is his or her various roles in society. If you stop and think about the various things that constitute your identity—as a parent or child (or both), in your occupation, with your friends, and in all your various interests and any organizations to which you belong—they all represent a part of who you are. Certainly religion plays an important role here for many people.

This issue leads to complex questions in social theory, revolving around the relationship that exists between an individual and society. Is society nothing more than a collection of individuals, many or most of whom have a number of competing interests? Or are individuals really abstractions from society; in other words, is society the fundamental notion from which we get our various self-conceptions through the vast array of networks within which we live? We won't be able to decide this issue here, of course, but it is worth thinking about that relationship. As we will see, many questions about individual rights will have as an important component the social context of those rights.

But even here, we can see that living in society requires a set of trade-offs; I have to accept certain kinds of things that I may find offensive and objectionable, just as others may find me—or at least some things I do—offensive and objectionable. In a certain way, of course, this resembles the Golden Rule in a social context: we all agree to tolerate certain ways of living, and we expect our way of living also to be tolerated.

When the limits of tolerance are reached, however, controversy arises, and religious beliefs—and a lack of religious beliefs—often seem to be at the forefront of many such controversies. Here, again, we have to do a balancing act, and ethics can help us determine what the appropriate balance is. In some cases, one simply cannot expect society to tolerate certain kinds of behaviors; in other cases, perhaps society's level of tolerance can be re-adjusted. Drawing the line between what should be and what should not be permitted is often very difficult, but it is clear that the study of ethics provides essential information in trying to decide where it should be drawn.

3.2 Ethical Issues in Doing Business with Other Countries

With the accelerated pace of globalization, corporations find themselves doing business in many different countries, and they confront laws and customs that may be very different than those in their home country. What kinds of issues arise here, between the moral views that conflict between a corporation and another country in which it wants to do business? We will look at some of these conflicts from the perspective of relativism and utilitarianism.

The Issue: Conflicts Between a Company and Its Host Country

If a company wishes to do business in another country, should it simply accept that country's laws and traditions? What if those laws and traditions fundamentally conflict with the company's own principles? Does it abandon its principles, should it choose not to do business in that country, or is there a third option available?

The argument for adopting the host country's laws and customs

American companies that wish to do business in another country have to recognize that the other country may well have very different views about all sorts of things. Simply put, some things viewed in the United States as "rights," and even as "inalienable rights," may not be looked at in the same way in other countries. Some nations prevent access to various kinds of information in books, films, or Internet content. Furthermore, some countries may have cultural standards—about the treatment of women, ethnic minorities, and religion—that are quite different from the standards that prevail in the United States.

A company that wishes to do business in another country can't expect that country to change. A company that wants to do business, and profit by being in that country, must be willing to make the necessary adjustments to its social values, cultural traditions, and laws. Such adjustments may be relatively modest: different foods, different dress, a differ- ent understanding of relations between men and women, often a different language, and, more generally, a different way of doing things. To do business in England, we couldn't very well object to driving on the side of the road opposite to the side we drive on in the United States. If we do business in Japan, we may have to get used to taking off our shoes when entering someone's house. If a company wishes to benefit from business in Kuwait, it will insist that its employees be familiar with the fact that it is illegal to drink alcohol and eat pork there. Some countries have less strict controls than the United States on what people can read, such as pornography, whereas other countries have much stricter controls.

Comstock/Photolibrary

Some would say that doing business in another country means accepting and adjusting to accommodate their values, customs, and laws. When have you had to adjust to other cultures, even within your own community?

Simply put, if a company wants to do business in another country, it has to recognize that it must play by that country's rules. Imagine, for instance, an Internet-based company that wants to do business in a country whose government censors the Internet and demands that it have access to the personal accounts of its citizens. This government doesn't want its citizens reading or watching material it regards as dangerous, whether as a threat to national security or simply because it might damage the moral values of the country. In this country, the government regards the ability to access citizens' Internet accounts and to keep track of what its citizens are reading and writing simply as part of the way it governs. In the United States, this perspective, of course, would be regarded as a gross violation of privacy and none of the government's business.

We may not like the way the other country operates, but that isn't really what is at issue. Rather, if we want to do business there, we have to accept the laws of that country. The company, that is, must make a decision to "trade off" its ethical and political concerns for the benefits of doing business in that other country. If the payoff is significant, and the company will make substantial profits, not to make this trade-off would be irrespon- sible. It would also not be doing what the shareholders demand, namely, a return on their investment.

These issues aren't always just legal questions, of course. Perhaps one wishes to do business in a country where women aren't allowed to work in offices with men. In this case, the company has to recognize that the cost of doing business is to not hire women to work in its

offices. Perhaps one wishes to do business in a country where standard practice is to take a three-hour lunch break in the middle of the day. Here the company, again, has to recognize that it will have to adjust to this practice, if it wishes to gain access to this country and the benefits it offers. And if this company refuses to take advantage of these benefits, this is an opportunity its competitors may well exploit and use against it.

Ale Ventura/Photoalto/Photolibrary

Some would argue that a company's primary obligation is to secure a profit, which means making the necessary allowances for cultural differences.

There will, undoubtedly, be minor adjustments that any company has to make, in adapting to a different set of laws and cultural standards, and there may be major adjustments as well. But the general point seems clear: a company that wishes to do business in another country has to do so on that country's terms. No one is forcing the company to do business there, but if that is the company's choice, the rules that are in effect are those of the host country. The company is certainly within its rights, after becoming informed of both the legal and cultural standards of the other country, to decide against doing business there. But it is acting irresponsibly if it fails to fulfill its fundamental mission—to return a profit on investment—by refusing to go along with the standards of the host country. Its business, of course, is business; it is not a company's role to try to change laws, or even cultural standards, not to its liking. To do what it should, in fulfilling its obligation as a business, it must accept the laws and standards of the host country.

The argument for resisting the host country's laws and customs

A company may be confronted with a stark choice: to violate its own moral principles to promote its business or to lose some business and remain faithful to its own ethical standards. This can often be a difficult choice, particularly if the business opportunity offers great benefits. But a company that sacrifices its own moral standards in order to improve its profit statement will, in the long run, be doing something that is to its disadvantage. A company benefits from its public image, as well, and any company that presents itself as willing to abandon its morals may come to be regarded as a company without principles. And a company without principles may see its image suffer and end up losing more than it gains. In short, a quality organization doesn't reject its own moral values when it enters a new business environment.

Without question, when doing business in a foreign country, a company must adjust to that new environment. From very small changes in what one eats (or doesn't), to how business itself is conducted, employees must be willing to be flexible and tolerant. At one end of the spectrum, these small changes simply introduce new variables to navigate in order to gain the advantages this opportunity makes available. But at the other end of the spectrum, legal and cultural traditions may require too much sacrifice for a company to make, even if this requires that some short-term profits be abandoned. It is one thing to get used to doing exercises with fellow employees early in the morning, before getting to the actual work of the day. It is something entirely different if a government official asks you to fire a quality employee because he or she is discovered to be a member of a religion that the government finds "unacceptable." Somewhere between these two extremes, a company has to ask itself what its fundamental values are, and whether it is willing to ignore those values in favor of its profits.

Consider the Internet company that prides itself on its openness and its respect for the privacy of those who use its service. Its customers have come to rely on it as having high moral standards and a significant commitment to human rights. A customer who uses this company's products can be confident that no one else will know what he or she is looking at on the Internet when using its search engine, and that any e-mail sent will not be read by anyone other than the intended recipient. Certainly this customer has always assumed, correctly, that no government will be allowed access to his or her account; privacy and confidentiality are hallmarks of this business, and its commitment to these values is a major reason for its success.

Photoalto/Photolibrary

A company doing business in another country obviously needs to be tolerant and flexible, but the company must also examine how much it is willing to ignore for the sake of profit.

Now imagine that this company is given the opportunity to expand into a foreign country, with rich opportunities for growth and substantial potential for large profits. This particular foreign country is run by an oppressive government known for putting political opponents into jail, and even executing them. It censors newspapers, magazines, films, and music, frequently prohibiting material from even crossing its borders. It also restricts access to the World Wide Web and keeps close track of what its citizens read on the web, as well as what its citizens attempt to read on the web.

There is a great deal of pressure, in a very competitive business environment, for the Internet company to begin operations in this foreign country. The potential for profit is enormous, and stockholders have indicated their desire for this expansion to be carried out. But the CEO refuses to do so. She realizes that being willing to operate under the oppressive and anti-democratic laws of this country may, in the short run, generate substantial profits. She also notes that much of the company's success has been accomplished because it has high moral standards and insists on functioning in accordance with its very well-known public commitment to an ethical code. She puts this decision in terms of a trade-off: should the company seek short-term gains, it may well risk the substantial long-term gains and the reputation for integrity it has acquired by operating ethically. The CEO determines that the long-term gains here outweigh the short-term benefits, and thus decides not to expand under the conditions imposed by the foreign government. Indeed, the CEO argues that by refusing to abandon its moral principles, the company sends a strong signal to this foreign government that it needs to change its oppressive policies in order to participate as a full partner in international business. From this perspective, the foreign government may come to realize that it is losing out by failing to respect the rights of its citizens, and that it is to its own economic advantage to promote greater freedom.

The Theories

Any business has to make a wide variety of decisions: whether to keep assets or sell them, how many people it needs to hire (or lay off), whether or not to sign a contract with this or that supplier, and what kind of growth and expansion it wishes to undertake. All such decisions are made for one specific reason: to return profits to the investors—frequently stockholders—who make the company possible. All decisions, therefore, must fundamentally be made with one factor in mind: Is this decision good for the company and its bottom line? Does it make the company more profitable or not?

The cultural relativist recognizes that different cultures have different standards. These may be informal traditions that a given culture, or country, has always followed; they may be more formal policies that are written into the country's laws. What a given culture regards as the right thing to do must be understood in terms of that culture. In short, its values are relative to the specific culture or society where those values are embraced.

The ethical relativist argues, then, that the traditions, policies, rules, standards, and laws of a country are to be accepted by those who decide to locate in that country in order to do business. As the old saying goes, "When in Rome, do as the Romans do." This doesn't mean that you necessarily agree with all the practices you see in the foreign land; then again, many of those citizens might question some of the values found in your own country. By agreeing to take advantage of the opportunities another country offers, a business must accept that country's practices. For they are the practices that country has determined are correct for that country.

Stockbrokerxtra Images/Photolibrary

A cultural relativist recognizes that different cultures have different standards. An ethical relativist argues that those operating in a different country need to accept the standards and laws of that country.

A business must attend to its business, and that is returning a profit on its investment. It is not part of its mission to evaluate the traditions and rules of its business environment, except in those cases that those traditions and rules interfere with it doing business. As long at that interference does not occur, a company has neither the obligation nor the right to criticize the way a country and its government operates. By expanding its business into a foreign culture, a company has implicitly accepted doing business under the terms of that foreign culture.

This does not mean there isn't a right or wrong way to do things. Rather, it means that right and wrong have to be looked at from the perspective of a specific society. Right in China may be very different than right in Sweden; it may even turn out that right in China is wrong in Sweden. If one is doing business in Sweden, one follows Swedish laws and customs; if one is doing business in China, one follows Chinese laws and customs. A company cannot state a set of rules and force another culture to adopt those rules; those rules, of course, are only right relative to that company's own culture.

Consequently, the ethical relativist rejects the idea of some general conception of right and wrong, good and bad, or acceptable and unacceptable business practices. Instead, the relativist insists that these terms be viewed in terms of the culture where one operates, and those companies that choose to do business in a given country should recognize that the rules in force are the rules adopted as correct for that given country.

A utilitarian may come to a different conclusion, however, based on a more general conception of what benefits are involved. The utilitarian may include in her calculation of the "greatest good for the greatest number" a broader conception of whose good should be considered. Some may insist that only the stockholders' demands need to be considered; thus, the utility calculation should be based on what produces the greatest good for the greatest number of stockholders. But a more expansive view, while still utilitarian, would include employees, suppliers, vendors, the company's community, and even potential customers. This second view bases its utility calculation on what is called a "stakeholder" account. A specific decision may affect a much larger number of people than just stockholders; for instance, if a company decides to relocate its business, the surrounding community's economy may suffer. Losing those jobs will have a ripple effect, in that those who worked in the community ate in restaurants and shopped at local stores; thus, those working in those restaurants and stores may suffer a negative effect as well. These decisions, then, ripple throughout a given community.

In terms of deciding whether to operate a business under laws and rules that a company finds to be unethical, this utilitarian calculation may consider the damage done to the company's reputation as part of that calculation. How valuable is a given company's image for being responsible and for being committed to strong ethical principles? This is a difficult question to answer with a specific number, but companies that have lost this reputation have been known to have spent a great deal of money trying to regain it; some, having lost it, have ended up going out of business altogether. So even though this value may be difficult to quantify, it is an important factor to consider.

Carol and Mike Werner/Index Stock Imagery/Photolibrary
A utilitarian would note that a company's decisions affect other people and thus would argue that broader interests must be considered.

Let's return to our Internet company's decision to operate in a country that violates what we might regard as its citizens' civil rights. The utilitarian calculation may well lead to the result that, on the stakeholder view, the greatest good for the greatest number, at least in the long run, is produced by being unwilling to operate in that country. Short-term profits may be sacrificed, but the reputation of the company is maintained, leading to a sustainable model for growth that will lead, again in the long run, to greater profits. In this way, then, the utilitarian might well argue that the ethical thing to do is to be unwilling to distort one's fundamental moral principles, simply to obtain short-term profits.

Some Conclusions

We can see that this issue can lead to some difficult decisions, but the company must try to strike a balance between ethical concerns and the bottom line. For those who think the ethical values of a company are crucial, these considerations may outweigh the potential benefits another country may offer. For those who focus chiefly on the company's profits—perhaps especially short-term profits—the benefits are simply too great, and any morally troubling issues cannot outweigh them.

The result of the discussion here seems to lead to a range of possible options; there may, of course, be others as well. First, as we have seen, one can simply ignore any and all moral violations in the host country. A company is there to do business, and such moral concerns don't factor in to the relevant business decisions. At the other extreme, a corporation may choose not to do business in a country at all, if that country's moral and legal policies are too objectionable.

At the same time, each of these options may have its own difficulties. Should a corporation be willing to expand to a country that employs slave labor? What if a foreign nation systematically oppresses ethnic and religious minorities? Are there limits to what is permissible here, or does the corporation simply turn a blind eye to such ethical violations? Furthermore, if a corporation ignores such violations and continues to do business there, can't it be seen to be supporting those violations? After all, this corporation will be employing citizens of the host country and paying taxes to the host government; couldn't that be considered support for a regime many may find morally reprehensible? Can all such objections be dismissed as irrelevant? Would that mean that it doesn't matter how the company makes its profits, it only matters that it makes profits?

On the other hand, a company may have to be willing to be sufficiently flexible to accept some differences to do business internationally; no country will operate completely the same as one's own. If a potentially lucrative market is ignored for relatively minor complaints the company might have about another country's laws and culture, the company would seem to be irresponsible in failing to step up to its obligations as a business. Perhaps Internet access is more tightly controlled than it is in the United States; if a corporation refused to do business there, would that be a sufficient reason? Or is this a situation where one might not be happy with the policy, but might find the policy not so objectionable as to prevent a corporation from doing business there? Of course, drawing the line between what can and cannot be tolerated is difficult and can be the source of serious disagreements within a given company.

Another position that has been adopted argues that a company that works within a country may have more success in getting morally objectionable policies changed. Thus, rather than boycotting a country and refusing to have any dealings with it, engaging with the country's business and political structure provides an opportunity to change it. A company can make known its objections, in this case, because it has access to the country's power structure. This is a policy sometimes called constructive engagement: by engaging in dialogue, a corporation has a better chance of making its constructive criticisms taken seriously and may have a better chance of getting morally objectionable policies changed. It may also have a better opportunity to demonstrate the economic benefits of changing specific policies and what the economic consequences may be of not changing them.

In contrast to this perspective, a company may make clear from the outset that it finds a country's legal or cultural standards too objectionable. This approach seeks to demonstrate to a country, or perhaps its government, that by not respecting human rights, for instance, it is losing valuable business. Sometimes this is known as the carrot-and-stick strategy. A corporation has a carrot: the financial advantages it offers to this country in terms of economic development. Its stick is the threat of withholding those advantages, making clear what the country is losing by maintaining its morally objectionable policies. To be a bit blunt, it is, more or less, a threat; the company is saying "change your policies or lose these opportunities." From the company's perspective, of course, it is to everyone's advantage for the foreign nation to change: its own people have greater economic opportunity as well as greater freedoms, and the corporation can reap its own rewards from doing business there.

BlueMoon Images/BlueMoon Stock/Photolibrary

Some also debate whether a company should try to effect change by working with the country or threatening to withhold its presence and the economic benefits that come with it.

There are, no doubt, other ways of thinking about how to resolve the ethical conflicts that may arise when doing business in a foreign country. It is also clear that some foreign governments are fundamentally interested in maintaining power and control, and may therefore not listen to either objections that come from outside companies working there or from promises (or threats) from companies that might be willing to work there, regardless of the economic benefits that could follow. At the same time, only a business model that wholly ignores, or even rejects, any conception of ethical principles will fail to raise objections to practices that violate basic human rights and fundamental conceptions of human dignity.

Where Do We Go from Here?

With the development of technology—faster airplanes, cell phones, the Internet, the World Wide Web, videoconferencing, and many others—the opportunities for international business have never been greater. This brings with it, of course, interactions between and among different cultures and the recognition of distinct traditions, laws, and business practices. Although the opportunities have never been more abundant, the exposure of these cultural differences becomes more pronounced with the growth of these opportunities. Can ethics help provide some guidance in navigating these differences?

One value promoted by the various ethical theories we have looked at seems to be tolerance. That is, a company that seeks to expand into another country must be willing to adapt to practices that are distinct from its own practices. There will be conflicts, of course. One culture may prohibit alcohol altogether, whereas another may regard it as standard operating procedure to discuss important business decisions during late-night drinking sessions. One culture may forbid, legally or informally, women from taking on a corporate leadership role, whereas another culture may regard it as extremely important to have a substantial number of women in corporate leadership roles. These cultural differences will have to be worked out, of course, if productive business is to be carried out. But the

Eric C. Westbrook/Index Stock Imagery/Photolibrary

With increased globalization and technological advances, exposure to cultural differences becomes more pronounced. An individual must be equipped with the tools to navigate through the shades of gray. How has globalization affected your life?

chances of success are greatly increased if the parties involved are willing to be flexible and tolerant of those cultural differences that may simply be different, rather than wrong or immoral.

That doesn't mean, necessarily, that "anything goes." Each corporation will have a set of different standards, and most corporations will recognize that some things are simply wrong, or sufficiently wrong as to be intolerable. An Internet company may refuse to do business on the condition that the government can access its customers' accounts; that may go beyond what this company can tolerate. On the other hand, it may conclude that this condition is acceptable. Corporations have obligations to satisfy stockholders' demands for a return on investment, but they have other obligations as well, including an obligation to have ethical principles and integrity. Ethics can offer a great deal in making clear what these obligations are and how to evaluate the many factors that are involved in making important business decisions. Ethics can also help clarify the fact that corporations do have an obligation to look beyond short-term profits, and that there is a value to a company for having a reputation of maintaining high ethical standards.

As globalization increases, and economies and markets become increasingly interdependent, these issues will arise more frequently. We also see that the rights of any individual corporation must be considered in the context of a much larger context: not just in terms of its competitors or even the host country, but the international context. Ethics may not be able to resolve these problems and certainly cannot offer solutions that will satisfy everyone involved. By clarifying the issues involved and bringing rigor to evaluating how those issues may be resolved, ethics makes a genuine contribution to making decisions in an international business environment.

Is There a Limit to Tolerance?

Tolerance seems to be a value that many insist is extremely important. Tolerance is not just prized in the context of business, or in the interactions between and among different cultures, but it seems to be important when dealing with others within one's own culture. In a diverse country like the United States, there are cultural, ethnic, religious, and other kinds of differences that make up the traditional conception of the United States as a melting pot that recognizes these differences while also affirming those things held in common. The well-known motto "E Pluribus Unum"—"Out of many, one"—recognizes this diversity as well.

But are there limits to tolerance? In its most radical version, relativism would seem to suggest that there are no such limits. One person's views may conflict sharply with another's, but the relativist argues that there is no way of resolving this conflict beyond recognizing that there is a conflict. What is true (and false) for one person is true (and false) for just that person; all another person can do is say that his or her truth (and falsity) is different. This extends, of course, to moral issues; the relativist insists that what is wrong for a person might not be wrong for another, but that there is no way of resolving this difference. So everything must be tolerated.

Some philosophers have argued that the position of radical relativism is incoherent, for a couple of different reasons. One argument against this kind of relativism is to see how people actually behave: Do they take things to be wrong just for them, or just for their culture, or do they act as if something is simply, flat-out, actually wrong? Many people worry about the inability of relativism to say that genocide and other evils that human beings commit are just "wrong" relative to an individual or a culture. Do we want to reserve a stronger way of condemning things such as rape, child abuse, slavery, and other acts traditionally regarded as evil?

> **What Would You Do?**
>
> You are the CEO of a company that does extensive business internationally. You have recently been informed that the host country will not allow Albert, who runs one of your most profitable subsidiaries, to return from his vacation because he is Jewish and recently visited Israel. You are also told that if he returns in spite of this ban, he will be arrested and deported, and there might also be negative economic repercussions for your company, such as some very lucrative contracts you have with the host country not being renewed.
>
> • Do you replace Albert with someone else?
>
> • Do you tell the host country that your company will leave if you are not allowed to retain Albert?
>
> • How do you come to the decision you make, and what factors do you regard as most important in determining your decision?

Another argument against unlimited tolerance is a bit more subtle, but it has been very influential. This argument might start by looking at simple mathematical claims; do we really want to say that for one person, "$2 + 3 = 5$" is true, but that for another it may not be true? At the level of being able to reason at all, are we committed to certain principles of logic that make our disagreements possible? Don't we have to agree on some principles in order to understand each other enough to recognize that we disagree? For instance, if two people differ about the legality of abortion, they may differ about whether a fetus is a human being. But both must seem to have to agree that the fetus cannot be a human being and, at the same time, not be a human being. They wouldn't be able to talk to each other, in this case, if they were willing to accept a contradiction of this form. It also seems to be the case that here both must have some basic idea of what each other's words mean; the radical relativist seems to be willing to say that words can mean just about anything. But if words can mean just about anything, how could people talk to each other and understand each other at all? This doesn't mean they completely understand each other, let alone agree with each other. Rather, the idea here is that they have to share a great deal in common, in the words they use, and the way they argue, just to be able to have a disagreement in the first place.

Some anthropologists have insisted that people often fail to realize that in discussing relativism, we may forget just how much we have in common. (Anthropologist Donald Brown has identified hundreds of such "human universals" found in every culture ever

Antenna/fStop/Photolibrary

Although we tend to focus on our differences, we probably have more in common than we realize or think.

encountered, including jokes, dreams, music, pronouns, and many more.) No matter how radically distinct two people's cultures may be, they agree on much more than they disagree. The disagreements are more interesting, of course, so we tend to focus on them. But imagine two people debating gun control. They may have very big differences, but they agree on many things that aren't even worth discussing. There is almost an unlimited number of things one could add to this list: guns don't make good hats, guns aren't good to eat, guns don't fly, and guns need ammunition, not to mention more general things like gravity or other laws of nature. When considering ethical disputes, we focus on the things over which we disagree. But this can lead us to forget that we have to share a great deal in common in order to have the disagreement to begin with. This, then, suggests that there are limits to tolerance, and that some notions must be maintained: that is, we can be tolerant of many things, but if we tolerate everything, we may lose the very ability to think, reason, and talk with each other.

3.3 An Historical Debate: The Internment of Japanese Americans in World War II

On December 7, 1941, Japanese warplanes attacked Pearl Harbor in Hawaii. About a year later—December 19, 1942—President Franklin D. Roosevelt signed Executive Order 9066, leading to the internment of approximately 120,000 Americans of Japanese descent, placing them in camps in California, Oregon, and other states. About two-thirds of those detained were American citizens.

The Issue: Should Japanese Americans Be Detained and Interned?

The Supreme Court heard two cases involving this internment, one of which—*Korematsu v. United States*—we will look at from the perspective of utilitarianism and deontology. Here again we will see how ethical theories can inform important decisions and have a real impact on people's lives.

The argument for detention and internment

A country at war cannot afford the luxury of respecting those "rights" that, at other times, may deserve some consideration. A nation, during wartime, has the fundamental goal of winning that war; all other considerations must be adjusted to this basic goal. For if the war

DEA Picture Library/De Agostini Editore/Photolibrary

The December 11, 1941, bombing of Pearl Harbor catapulted the United States into World War II and resulted in the internment of thousands of Japanese Americans.

Legacy Archive Hawaiian/Pacific Stock/Photolibrary

A World War II wartime poster. At the time, some argued that certain legal and moral principles needed to be looked at differently in times of war.

were to be lost, all those other rights would become meaningless. Abraham Lincoln, during the Civil War, suspended habeas corpus; thus American citizens could be detained and jailed without access to legal representation. Lincoln noted that the very existence of the United States was at stake, and during such an emergency, measures could be taken that were required to successfully prosecute the war. In general, legal and moral principles have to be looked at during wartime in a different way than they might be otherwise.

In a 1943 court case, Hirabayashi v. United States, the federal government argued that it was constitutional and just to impose curfews on and relocate Japanese Americans. The United States was at war with Japan, and it was thought likely that some of the people of Japanese descent might well be sympathetic to the Japanese cause. Thus, certain restrictions were imposed upon them, such as excluding them from areas important to the military. The Supreme Court, in hearing this case, determined that the military and the federal government should be given the "benefit of the doubt" in such cases. During wartime, as noted earlier, the military may require certain things that might not otherwise be permitted. The court determined that in this case, it was right to defer to the military authorities.

Drawing on the Hirabayashi case, Justice Hugo Black argued that the restrictions imposed on the movements of Japanese Americans were constitutional. Emergency wartime measures demanded that it was better to risk violating certain traditional rights than to put the security of the United States in jeopardy. As Black observed, the "properly constituted military authorities feared an invasion of our West Coast and felt constrained to take proper security measures" (Korematsu v. United States, 1944).

In a perfect world, all rights that one possesses should be protected; however, wartime emergencies are clearly not part of such a perfect world. The United States—represented by both the federal government and the military—were faced with the choice of protecting the rights of certain individuals or protecting the security of the United States as a whole. Deferring to the military during wartime, the Supreme Court argued, was a reasonable thing to do. The military saw the internment of Japanese Americans as an important step in maintaining the security of the United States, and the Supreme Court agreed. Therefore, it was both moral and just to intern people of Japanese descent while the United States was at war with the Japanese Empire.

The argument against detention and internment

The case against detention is obvious and straightforward and was seen as such by the Supreme Court justices who dissented from the majority opinion. Two basic reasons were brought forth to support the view that detention was unconstitutional.

First, to single out a group simply on the basis of its ethnicity is racist. The vast majority of Americans have ethnic ties to other nations and cultures, yet only Japanese Americans were detained and interned in camps. This suggests that Japanese Americans were treated arbitrarily and singled out on the basis of one, specific factor: their Japanese heritage. No arguments were provided indicating that Japanese Americans were more likely to be sympathetic to the enemies of the United States than members of other groups. Even though the United States was at war with Germany and Italy, as well as Japan, no German Americans or Italian Americans were detained solely on the basis of their ethnic background. As Associate Justice Frank Murphy observed in his dissent,

Richard Wong/Ambient Images/Photolibrary

A display at the Manzanar National Historic Site in California. Manzanar was one of the Japanese internment camps. The Japanese were singled out based on their appearance; no German Americans or Italian Americans were discriminated against although the United States was at war with Germany and Italy, too.

All residents of this nation are kin in some way by blood or culture to a foreign land. Yet they are primarily and necessarily a part of the new and distinct civilization of the United States. They must, accordingly, be treated at all times as the heirs of the American experiment, and as entitled to all the rights and freedoms guaranteed by the Constitution (*Korematsu v. United States*, 1944).

Associate Justice Robert Jackson provided the second reason for rejecting the constitutionality of detaining and interning Japanese Americans. Jackson's point was subtle, but worth considering. He argued that the military and federal government should be given the benefit of the doubt during wartime. But he also insisted that it was not the Court's role to endorse things as constitutional that were not. Jackson was particularly worried that if the court ruled such things as constitutional, the power so granted could be used when wartime emergencies were no longer in place. Jackson thus noted that there was a difference between the military deciding to intern Japanese Americans and the Supreme Court finding internment constitutional. As he put it,

once a judicial opinion rationalizes such an order to show that it conforms to the Constitution, or rather rationalizes the Constitution to show that the Constitution sanctions such an order, the Court for all time has validated the principle of racial discrimination in criminal procedure and of transplanting American citizens. The principle then lies about like a loaded weapon, ready for the hand of any authority that can bring forward a plausible claim of an urgent need (*Korematsu v. United States*, 1944).

The Theories

From a utilitarian perspective, the choice here might be described as one that takes into consideration the security of the United States. The greatest good for the greatest number of Japanese Americans may well be produced by not detaining and interning them, but that utility must be balanced against the utility of all Americans. Because the total population of Americans is so much greater, it is clear that the greatest good—the security of all Americans—outweighs the good of any smaller group. The assumption here, of course, is that the security of the United States required the internment of Japanese-Americans. On that assumption, to do what defends the United States will produce the greatest good for the greatest number, and thus internment would produce this result in contrast to not doing so. The utilitarian might also add that since Japanese Americans were also made more secure by this step, their own utility would be increased because the utility of all Americans would be maximized.

The deontologist, in contrast, might argue that the dignity and respect owed to human beings was consequently owed to Japanese Americans. To detain and intern them on the basis of ethnic identity—and not treating others in the same way—was to violate their rights and to use them solely as means to an end (the end being the security of the United States, again on the assumption that security required internment). It is a violation, then, of human dignity to treat people solely on the basis of their ethnicity, and the deontologist would reject as unethical the treatment of Japanese Americans. To put it in terms of the Golden Rule, the deontologist might ask if others would object to being interned in camps, and losing most or all of their property and possessions, solely on the basis of their ethnic backgrounds.

Carl Shaneff/Pacific Stock/Photolibrary

A list of the names of the dead at the *USS Arizona* memorial. A utilitarian might argue that the security of all Americans outweighed the good of any smaller group.

Some Conclusions

The approximately 120,000 Japanese Americans were interned in camps in various parts of the United States during most of the remainder of World War II. In January of 1945, the order to do so was rescinded. Those detained were given $25 and a train ticket; most Japanese Americans returned home, although some went to Japan. The Japanese surrendered in August 1945, and the last camp was closed in 1946. Many Japanese Americans lost a great deal of their private property, and due to that and to the internment itself, suffered

Richard Wong/Ambient Images/Photolibrary

A re-creation of a room at Manzanar.

psychological damage. A number of lawsuits were filed, and some financial settlements were reached, although only a fraction of what was asserted to have been lost. Manzanar, one of the relocation camps in central California, was designated a National Historic Site in 1992.

The Civil Liberties Act of 1988, signed by President Ronald Reagan, gave $20,000 to each of the surviving Japanese Americans who had been interned, amounting to a total of $1.2 billion. This act also explicitly included an apology, on behalf of the people of the United States, for the evacuation, relocation, and internment of Japanese-American citizens and permanent resident aliens.

Where Do We Go from Here?

In the Korematsu case, we see a number of issues that retain a good deal of contemporary relevance. We see that during wartime, there may be a compelling interest on the part of the state to restrict certain rights that would otherwise not be violated. We see that sometimes this compelling interest is not appropriately checked by careful consideration of the assumptions involved: in this case, whether Japanese Americans in fact posed a security threat simply on the basis of their ethnic background. We also see what John Stuart Mill recognized was a problem that confronted majority rule: the possibility that the majority could overturn or violate the rights of a minority. Mill insisted that conditions be imposed to prevent this "tyranny of the majority."

Finally, we see that ethical arguments, again, can make clear what the issues are, but it can't guarantee that the result will be the correct one, or one that all interested parties will find satisfactory. The arguments presented in the Supreme Court relied on certain assumptions, and certain applications of ethical theory. Given a more careful consideration, or perhaps just hindsight, we may come to realize that those assumptions themselves should be given critical scrutiny, and that more attention should be paid to whether a given ethical theory is applied correctly. As we've seen before, the rights of individuals often have to be understood within the context of the values of the larger society in which those individuals live.

Americans have become more aware, particularly in an increasingly diverse society, that there are risks involved in labeling large groups of people on the basis of their geographical origins, religion, ethnicity, and other characteristics. Because we've learned from mistakes in the past that acts taken on the basis of those characteristics can lead to serious violations of morality, ethics helps remind us that we must remain vigilant in treating individuals, and groups, with the respect they deserve.

What Is Patriotism?

The term "patriot" originates in the Greek word for "father." Just as a child had various duties owed to one's father, a citizen had duties owed to one's country. More generally, the relationship between the citizen and the state is captured by the analogy between a child and a parent that the term "patriot" draws on. Thus, we sometimes see one's country referred to as the "Fatherland": the land of one's father, and a country to which its citizens owe their loyalty.

Some regard patriotism as the unquestioning loyalty of a country's citizens to the leader and government of that country. In other words, to be a patriot is do whatever one's government tells one. Whether that idea is expressed as "My country right or wrong," or "America: Love it or Leave it," the attitude seems to be that criticism and challenges to governmental authority is somehow wrong, and quite possibly immoral.

Others have advocated, in contrast, a somewhat more complex relationship between a nation and its citizens. One may, indeed, have unswerving loyalty to one's country, but in this context "loyalty" also brings with it the responsibility to challenge the government when it is doing something unethical. In other words, loyalty does not mean uncritical obedience.

Sometimes this relationship is compared to that between a husband and wife. We can assume the wife loves the husband, and respects him, but this does not mean she does so uncritically. Rather, the truest sign of that love and respect is to inform her husband if he is doing something—perhaps unconsciously—that is wrong, or is causing a problem of which he might be unaware.

Jim West/Imagebroker.net/Photolibrary

Some think of patriotism as unquestioning loyalty. Others see challenging the government as part of being a patriot. Here, protesters voice their disagreement with 2010 health care legislation. What does patriotism mean to you?

Thus, one may love one's country, but that doesn't mean a true patriot never challenges what that country does. Particularly in a democratic society, what the country does it presumably does in the names of its citizens. In that sense, then, citizens must take responsibility for what is done in their names. And if a state is engaged in an activity that is immoral or unethical, it may be that the most genuine and most sincere patriotism is that which is willing to expose and discuss the state's moral failings. As Thomas Jefferson succinctly put it, "Dissent is the highest form of patriotism." On this view, then, the true patriot seeks the best country possible to live in, and that requires, on occasion, that the loyal citizen points out his or her country's flaws, so that it avoids moral errors and can improve.

3.4 The Environment and NIMBY: Not In My Backyard

Ethical issues that arise about the environment have, in recent years, received increasing attention from philosophers, among others. The Deepwater Horizon explosion in the Gulf of Mexico revealed, again, that such issues affect a large number of people. It also focused attention on corporate responsibility—in this case, British Petroleum—in doing business. The general question of the relationship between humans and their planet can become very complex, so we will focus here on one very specific issue: How do communities deal with the hazardous wastes that the community produces? A common expression heard in these discussions is "Not In My Backyard" (NIMBY). No one wants hazardous waste in his or her own neighborhood, but something has to be done with it. We will look at attempts to resolve this issue from the perspective of ethical egoism and utilitarianism.

Matthew White/Peter Arnold Images/Photolibrary

Oil washed up onto the beach at Grand Isle State Park, Louisiana, due to BP's broken deep-water well in mid-2010.

The Issue: What Should Be Done with Hazardous Waste?

Societies produce waste, and often produce hazardous waste, such as chemicals, solvents, and batteries. If we consume products that produce this kind of waste, we need to determine what is the fairest and the most effective way to deal with that waste.

Hazardous waste should be handled in the most economical way

All communities produce various kinds of by-products, some of which can be quite toxic. Whether it is individuals with old batteries or used motor oil, a dry cleaner or hospital, or a company manufacturing paint or chemicals, various kinds of wastes are produced. Of course, we need all these products, from the batteries and dry cleaners to the paint; our way of life is simply one that inevitably produces things that need to be taken care of safely. How can we handle these hazardous wastes in a way that best protects the environment, but without causing economic harm?

One obvious suggestion is that incinerators and storage facilities should be located as far away as possible from communities. This can help prevent some toxic chemicals from "leeching" into the water supply and doing other environmental damage; after all, no one wants dangerous chemicals in the water supply. Similarly, incinerators and landfills should be located where they pose the smallest risk to the environment. Preferably, sites will be available far enough away from a community that these risks are minimized.

Ideally, landfills and waste disposal sites need to be located far away from communities, but close enough that they're still useful.

Unfortunately, this ideal solution is not always available. Large communities produce a great deal of waste, both the hazardous kinds already mentioned but also significant amounts of basic, everyday household trash (which may also include some hazardous material). Landfills must be located close enough to the community to be useful to that community, and if the distance is too great, transportation and other associated costs become very high. Thus, a community may be confronted with the choice of locating a landfill closer to the community, or taking on substantial costs to dispose of the waste.

One should probably distinguish here between kinds of wastes produced and the measures that need to be taken to deal with the wastes involved. A nuclear power plant, for instance, may produce radioactive waste products that require specific treatment and storage for a long period of time. Traditionally, this kind of material has been the focus of specific government agencies such as the U.S. Nuclear Regulatory Commission. Of course, NIMBY is part of this discussion as well; many people are quite insistent that they do not want radioactive material stored near their communities. But this raises somewhat distinct issues than other kinds of hazardous waste.

How can communities deal with the kinds of hazardous materials found in ordinary household garbage? A brief list indicates some of the kinds of things that must be treated safely, but economically: thermometers, cell phones, light switches, antifreeze, insecticides, and many other household products contain a wide range of chemicals and other hazardous ingredients. The choice here isn't easy: it seems unlikely that we will quit using these kinds of products. Indeed, in both the United States and in developing economies, demand for these kinds of products will almost certainly increase. So we must determine a way to handle these materials safely and economically.

*Economists and others often speak in terms of **cost-benefit analysis**. That is, we weigh the costs of an activity against its benefits, and if the benefits outweigh those costs, then it seems to be an appropriate thing to do. Certain costs are involved in storing and otherwise handling hazardous wastes, and there are obvious benefits to do so safely and economically. If we assume that we cannot simply eliminate the wastes from the larger community, then clearly the cheapest place to handle them will be that place where the land is least expensive and where the economic impact of locating a landfill or incinerator is lowest. Consequently, given that we need to handle hazardous waste in one way or another, it seems clear that we should locate the appropriate facilities in places where the land is least expensive, and where locating these facilities will not damage the economic value of the land any more than necessary.*

Hazardous waste should be handled in the fairest way

We all engage in things that produce waste, and some of that waste is hazardous to human beings. The economic well-being of a community depends on a wide range of activities that inevitably will entail by-products that the community will have to dispose of, or store, in as safe a way as is possible. All share in the production of wastes, and all benefit from the activities that have such waste as their by-products. Who, then, should bear the burden of their disposal and storage by having an incinerator or landfill located in their neighborhood? Many will insist "Not in My Backyard," but such facilities will have to go in someone's backyard. The issue then becomes this: What is the fairest way to determine their location?

Because all share in the production of hazardous wastes, all should share in the burdens that accompany their storage and disposal. Those who live on the most inexpensive property do not produce more than their share of these by-products; it isn't fair for them to take on more than their share of the costs in their handling. The community generates this problem as a whole, thus the community should share in solving this problem, and should do so in the fairest and most equitable way possible.

A standard term in economics, relevant here, is the notion of **externalities**. *An externality is the effect of a decision—often an economic decision—on those who don't really have a say in the making of that decision. Here, one might think of the location of a hazardous waste site as generating externalities for those who live nearby. Perhaps there is a greater threat to the water supply in that area, or certain chemicals are released into the surrounding atmosphere. To take a specific example: consider a neighborhood that is close to a municipal solid waste incinerator. This incinerator increases the amount of lead in the local atmosphere, and may, therefore, increase the amount of lead in the bloodstream of the children in this neighborhood. Even a small amount of lead in the bloodstream has been indicated as a cause of learning disabilities and stunted growth among children. The children in this neighborhood pay a cost—elevated lead in the bloodstream—that is the responsibility of all of those who take advantage of the solid waste incinerator. Because these children are affected in a disproportionate way, this cost functions in this case as an externality. Put a bit more directly, these children seem to be taking on the burden of this incinerator that should be shared by the entire community.*

It's easier to ignore the issue of waste disposal if someone else is dealing with it.

We return here to the problem of NIMBY: no one wants an incinerator in his or her backyard, but it has to go somewhere. Is it fair to have the poorest neighborhoods take on this burden? Or is there a better solution, where the burden is shared more equally, and those neighborhoods that are already impoverished do not have the added disadvantage of the risks associated with storing and disposing of hazardous waste?

Sharing the burden here more equitably also may provide a set of improved incentives for minimizing toxic and hazardous waste. If a person is confident that he or she will not have to dispose of that waste, there may be less reason to worry about it. But if that person knows that some of it will end up in his or her own neighborhood, then there is a strong incentive to minimize it by recycling, reducing, and reusing that material. You might not worry about simply throwing away a computer if someone else, on the other side of town, takes on the risks associated with your action. As the saying goes, "out of sight, out of mind." But you might take extra caution in how it is disposed of—including its chemical compounds that can be toxic—if you are the one who will be exposed to the risks represented by those potentially toxic computer components.

We all engage in activities that generate hazardous waste. We should all, therefore, take responsibility for its safe disposal and for minimizing the production of hazardous waste. It is unfair to require those who live in impoverished neighborhoods to have this further burden placed upon them. Therefore, it is only fair that the community as a whole shares the responsibility for taking care of the hazardous waste that it produces.

The Theories

The ethical egoist's view is really encapsulated in the very idea of NIMBY—the egoist doesn't want a hazardous waste facility in his or her backyard, and that is clearly what he or she thinks is best. Therefore, acting of out self-interest, the egoist insists that it go elsewhere. Admittedly, the ethical egoist recognizes that "Not in My Backyard" is equivalent to saying "In Somebody Else's Backyard." But the egoist acts on the basis of what maximizes his or her own self-interest, and it is pretty clear that locating such a facility somewhere else is preferable to having it in one's own neighborhood.

> **What Would You Do?**
>
> You run a large company that produces batteries, and as a by-product your company also produces a number of heavy metals, such as cadmium, mercury, and lead, that must be dealt with. You have been disposing on them in a dedicated landfill that is inexpensive to use, but recent reliable studies indicate that some of these chemicals have been "leeching" into the water system, and may be causing birth defects and learning disorders in the community close to that landfill. It will cost quite a lot to dispose of these materials in a safer site, and your stockholders object that this cost is too great. You also know that the government may, eventually, require you to dispose of this material at the more expensive site, but that you can delay having to do so for at least 10 years through legal challenges, which are much cheaper than moving to the other site.
>
> - Do you decide to move, voluntarily, to the safer disposal site?
>
> - Do you decide to continue to use the less safe site until you are required to do so by law? How do you justify this decision?
>
> - How do you make this decision, and how do you balance your company's profits against the effects your hazardous waste has on the local community?

Ideally, the ethical egoist could engage in all sorts of consumption, without any concern whatsoever for the kinds of toxic by-products that might be produced. The best possible outcome for the egoist would be to enjoy the benefits and incur none of the risks. Rarely, however, is a person in this position. First, it is unusual for an individual to get to determine for a community how that community's resources are used; political decisions are generally made on a more democratic basis than this. Second, there is the much trickier problem of a situation where an entire community is made up of individual ethical

Aurelie and Morgan David de Lossy/Cultura/Photolibrary

The ethical egoist acts in his or her own self-interest. However, a likely response would be for the ethical egoist to attempt to simply minimize personal cost, risk, and responsibility when it comes to waste disposal. Can you think of a time when you've taken the ethical egoist position?

egoists, all acting to maximize their self-interest. Here we confront the extreme situation where no one wants to take on any of the burden of dealing with the hazardous waste, but everyone wants to do the kinds of things that help generate that very waste. Assuming a disposal site, for instance, must be located in someone's backyard, is it inevitable that some of these ethical egoists will believe their rights are being unjustifiably violated?

A more plausible response from the ethical egoist is to recognize that the ideal situation doesn't exist. We know that hazardous waste will be generated and that it will have to be disposed of, or stored, somehow. In this case, the egoist will be willing to pay certain costs—perhaps a small increase in taxes—in order to avoid the greater costs that might be incurred from having a waste facility located in the egoist's neighborhood. Here the egoist maximizes his or her self-interest by paying the lowest cost possible, relative to all others. Although the egoist will not be able to avoid entirely taking on some of the responsibility, he or she will be able to minimize costs, and risks, by insisting that hazardous waste sites be placed in locations that cost the least and present the smallest amount of harm, and risk, to the egoist. Of course, there may be other ways for the egoist to respond: perhaps self-interest is determined to be what is the best for the community, or perhaps the egoist maximizes his or her utility in yet another way. The point, however, is that whatever response the egoist offers, it will have to follow the fundamental principle of ethical egoism: to do what is in one's own self-interest.

The utilitarian, of course, looks at this decision from the perspective of this question: What produces the greatest good for the greatest number? The most obvious application of this principle may be to determine that no one group of people be forced to shoulder a burden that is out of proportion to their responsibility for generating that burden. In other words, since everyone helps in the production of hazardous waste, everyone should assume the burden for its disposal. The utilitarian might also argue that one should take on this responsibility in a way that is proportionate; one's responsibility for disposing of the hazardous waste is relative to the amount one produces. This may be a difficult calculation to make with any precision, but the general idea should be clear: sharing the benefits and sharing the costs produces the greatest good for the greatest number.

This may not be the only kind of response a utilitarian could offer, however. Perhaps locating hazardous waste facilities in a single section of the community makes the vast majority of that community better off; here a few would suffer but many would benefit. Even though this may generate the greatest good for the greatest number, it is also clear why utilitarians, and others, worry about majorities acting immorally. For here, the majority may decide that a minority should suffer, and be following the utilitarian principle. But, as J. S. Mill, himself a famous utilitarian, observed, this is to risk the "tyranny of the majority," and, potentially, to violate the rights of the minority in order to arrive at a result the majority would prefer.

One further result of the utilitarian approach to this question is to see the need for all the members of the community to participate in the decision-making process. This may prevent, in some cases, the majority from violating the rights of the minority. It will also ensure that all the voices of the community, and particularly those in the community most directly affected, will be heard.

The utilitarian, as we can see, doesn't provide an obvious answer to the problem of dealing with hazardous waste. It can be very difficult to determine what the greatest good is. It can be even more difficult to determine the greatest number affected by a decision: Is it those who live in the

Mike Kemp/Tetra Images/Photolibrary

A utilitarian might argue that no one group should be forced to shoulder the entire burden of waste disposal. However, a utilitarian might also argue that it is better that one goldfish suffer in polluted water than have all goldfish swim in a polluted bowl.

community as a whole? Can there be consequences for those outside the community—again raising the problem of externalities—that may be affected by the decision? But the advantage of the utilitarian approach is to force those making these decisions to define the benefits and costs of any specific decision. In this way, utilitarianism allows for a better decision-making process by making more explicit what is at stake in the results of that process.

Some Conclusions

The kind of question discussed here is, of course, one that is of great contemporary concern to communities and governments on all levels, from local municipal governments all the way to the federal government. One obvious result is that we see that our actions have consequences. If we wish to continue to manufacture and consume products that contain potentially dangerous chemical compounds, we must confront the problem of dealing with those by-products. These problems will continue to increase as demand grows for computers, cell phones, and other products that contain these materials. We also see that our own decisions may have far-reaching effects; I may not be risking anything by throwing batteries into my

Design Pics Inc./Photolibrary

As economic development continues, we will increasingly have to confront how we handle the resulting waste and pollution.

household trash, but somewhere down the line, the chemicals in those batteries could pose a serious health risk to others. These others may be in the next town, the next state, or even another country. Most ethical theorists, even ethical egoists, insist that these consequences must be taken into consideration in evaluating our behavior.

We also see that economic development brings with it increasing challenges to deal with environmental issues. Hazardous waste, acid rain, water and air pollution, and concerns about global climate change are just a few of the many problems that developed economies confront. With further development, more and more people will be affected by these problems and faced with the difficult issue of balancing economic development and potential environmental degradation. Even if we adopt a cost-benefit analysis as our approach, it is a difficult task to specify with precision what those costs are, and who will be required to pay them. It may not be that much easier to get a satisfactory grasp on what the benefits themselves are, and what time frame should be used for evaluating those benefits. Should we look to the near future, or much longer? And how does the choice of time frame affect our understanding of both costs and benefits?

We also see that individual rights, and choices, must be taken in a broader context. If someone wishes to preserve the "right" to dispose of toxic material in any way he or she sees fit, doesn't that interfere with the rights of others, and society at large, to be protected from the potential harm that material represents? A manufacturer cannot pollute local waterways without factoring the consequences for those downstream. In general, then, we see that individual rights are fundamentally connected with the rights of the larger society in which that individual lives. In the same way, a corporation is also a member of a larger community, and the rights and needs of that community cannot be fairly ignored.

Where Do We Go from Here?

It is clear that environmental ethics, the questions it explores, and the responses it provides will continue to receive a great deal of attention in the coming years. It is also clear that these questions will increasingly be looked at from an international perspective; one country's economic decisions often affect those in other countries. For instance, one country may choose to use a cheap energy source that generates extensive carbon emissions that may, in turn, affect a neighboring country (another externality). Thus, the use in America of high-sulfur coal may increase the likelihood of acid rain in Canada. What might Canada be able to do to minimize or eliminate this risk? More generally, with the rapid development of countries such as the People's Republic of China, India, and Brazil, with enormous populations and an increasing demand for development, the associated costs of that development will also continue to increase. And these issues will often have consequences far beyond the borders of any individual nation.

A central issue in this area is how to balance economic development with environmental protection. How can economic growth be sustained without doing substantial harm to the environment? Can we even reconcile the two goals of economic development and environmental protection, or are these two goals at cross-purposes? Given the increasing interdependence of the global economy, and the effects of one country's choice on another country, these potential sources of conflict will continue to deserve close scrutiny.

Again, we see that ethical theory can help clarify the advantages and disadvantages—both short-term and long-term—in generating a cost-benefit analysis. It can help identify what rights are involved and how to weigh and evaluate them. Individuals, organizations, corporations, and governments can, therefore, all find ethical theory informative and be productive in deciding how to strike the delicate balance between economic development and environmental protection.

How Are Good Environmental Policies Developed?

In the classic American movie *It's a Wonderful Life*, the lead character is shown what life would be like if he had never been born. It is an eye-opening experience for him, and he comes to realize that his life, and who he is, is fundamentally connected with many others. Not just his mother and wife and children, but his extended family and virtually all of the other members of his community. And, in turn, the influence he had on those people had important effects on those they influenced. The movie is a great demonstration of how interconnected we all are.

Paul Glendell/Still Pictures/Photolibrary

A key issue will be how to balance economic development with environmental protection. This street lamp in Cornwall, England, is powered by both a micro wind turbine and photovoltaic cells.

In looking at environmental policy, this is a good thing to keep in mind. What we do affects many others, often without our knowing it. The interconnections between any one person and all the others he or she encounters are too numerous to count, even if we were able to identify them. In the same way, a company's approach to the environment has long-lasting repercussions on those in a much larger area than just the immediate location of the company; those repercussions may even go well beyond neighboring countries and have an impact on the planet as a whole.

Environmental policy has to be formulated in such a way that it takes into account these effects and considers all those who may be affected by a given policy. At the same time, corporations have important responsibilities to provide a return on the stockholders' investments; that is, a for-profit company needs to turn a profit. A company must be able to balance this requirement to be profitable with the moral obligations it has to its community, however broadly we wish to interpret the notion of "community" here. Can these goals be reconciled? And if so, what role does the government play in formulating these policies in order to maintain a productive business climate while protecting the environment?

Most environmental ethicists argue that some consideration of those affected by corporate economic decisions and federal policies must be taken into account in making those decisions and formulating those policies. This doesn't mean, of course, that any individual, or community, has the right to veto what a corporation wishes to do or legislation a government body wishes to enact. But it does mean that their interests cannot be ignored. The famous political philosopher John Rawls described a procedure that might be useful here, one he called **reflective equilibrium**. This procedure allows for a wide variety of voices to be heard—in this case, the voices of the government, corporations, and the various members of the affected community—and taken into consideration in coming to a decision. Here, of course, that decision would be a specific corporate environmental policy or a piece of environmental legislation. Reflective equilibrium allows for a great deal of give and take and further allows for adjustments to be made to a specific decision based on the information provided by relevant parties. In this way, the most important information is included in the decision-making process. But it also allows for future adjustments to be made, if and when further relevant information becomes available.

Rawls's account, of course, describes an ideal situation, where all voices are heard and genuinely listened to, and all those involved—either by helping to make the decision or by being affected by it—are treated with mutual respect. This may not describe how policies are developed in the actual world of business and government, but it does offer a model that is worth considering. And, as such, it provides a way of including the insights of those not just drafting policies and laws but those who will have to live with those policies and laws.

3.5 A Debate: Should the Draft Be Reinstated?

In 1973, the United States ended compulsory military conscription—the draft—and instituted a policy of an all-volunteer army. Every now and then proposals to reinstitute the draft have been put forth, although they have not received much support. At the same time, many other countries have a policy of mandatory public service. Some have argued that an all-volunteer force has produced the finest military in the world; others have argued that this requires a minority of citizens to burden the responsibilities that should be shared by all. We will look at this debate from the perspective of utilitarianism and virtue ethics.

The Issue: The Draft Should Not Be Reinstated

The United States discontinued military conscription—the draft—in 1973, establishing an all-volunteer military force. On a regular basis, arguments have been offered for reinstating the draft, often citing for support that the burden of defending one's country should fall on all of its citizens.

The argument against reinstating the draft

> *The U.S. military is one of the finest fighting forces in the world. It has, unlike many other countries, maintained its fighting force on a voluntary basis. Rather than forcing people to join the military through conscription, or a draft, the military offers young men and women the choice to join. Given that one of the values the United States promotes is freedom, it only stands to reason that those representing the United States should be doing so on a voluntary basis.*

Wolfgang Siesing/Das Fotoarchiy/Photolibrary

The military offers incentives to its volunteers, including special training and education that can turn into valuable post-service career skills. This man is a machinist for the Navy. Do you know of others who were able to build on their knowledge because of their time in the military?

Radius Images/Photolibrary

A draft may force people into the military who don't want to be there, which may result in inferior, resistant soldiers. How would you respond if you were drafted?

There are a number of advantages to an all-volunteer force. First, and perhaps foremost, it means that those in the military want to be there. They choose that path, and see it as offering opportunities that might otherwise be unavailable. A soldier who makes this particular choice has a much different perspective on his or her role than does the soldier who is there unwillingly. It makes for a more cohesive and stronger fighting unit.

To attract the best recruits, the military in turn offers valuable incentives, including extensive training and the opportunity to attend college, that might not otherwise be possible financially. One can, of course, make the military itself a career. Others leave the service with significantly developed skills, in a wide range of areas—engineering, electronics, medicine, and even foreign languages—that are highly marketable. One also learns the value of hard work and discipline. In general, after joining the military, whether one stays or leaves after a certain period of time, he or she will have developed both important values and skills that enhance one's career opportunities.

In contrast, the draft by its very nature may force people who do not want to be in the military to be there. Most serve honorably, of course, but there will be a greater tendency for some to resist the military service they are ordered to perform. This can take many forms, from being an inferior soldier to deserting. Spending valuable resources on training those who may leave after the shortest required time is not an efficient use of resources. Furthermore, the cohesiveness of the unit is not helped, and may be harmed, by including those who are there only because they are forced to serve.

The all-volunteer force eliminates most of these problems by offering a desirable situation that produces not just good soldiers, but good citizens who are ready, when they leave the service, to make substantial contributions to society. This works best when the members of the military are there voluntarily, choosing the military as an option that makes sense for them, as well as for their country. It has been argued by some constitutional scholars that the draft violates the Thirteenth Amendment of the Constitution, which prohibits involuntary servitude. But even if the draft is constitutional, reinstating it would work against a smoothly operating military and would force those who do not want to be there to serve unwillingly. It would force the armed services to accept candidates that they might well not accept were the force constituted on an all-volunteer basis. An all-volunteer force avoids the many problems that are generated by a draft and leads to a more efficient and better fighting force. Therefore, the draft should not be reinstated.

The argument for reinstating the draft

The Preamble of the United States speaks of providing for the "common defense." We, the people, enjoy the freedoms, the rights, and the opportunities provided by our country. It is only fit that citizens also take on the responsibility of defending those same freedoms. The citizens of a nation have the obligation to defend that nation. That obligation should be shared by all, but historically it has not been. Rather, that burden has been carried, disproportionately, by those from lower socioeconomic groups and minorities. If citizens will not voluntarily carry out their responsibilities, it is the government's right to require them to do so.

In addition to the obligations citizens accept by living within a country, there are also a number of specific reasons to reinstate the draft. Relying solely on volunteers can stretch the military too thin. To have an effective military, it must have sufficient numbers to replace those who have served and left the service, as well as those who have been, tragically, killed and wounded defending their nation. If the number of available soldiers becomes too small, needed leaves become shortened beyond what the military itself recommends. The draft provides a more stable and sufficient population of those capable of serving.

Chuck Carlton/Index Stock Imagery/Photolibrary

Some wonder how voluntary military service really is, when sometimes those less privileged need the training and employment incentives to achieve career success.

A draft also ensures that all citizens share the burden of citizenship equally. The draft does not—or should not—distinguish between the wealthy and the poor or among different ethnic backgrounds. The privileged son should not expect his own obligation to defend the homeland to be provided by someone else, particularly someone who hasn't had similar advantages. Those privileges come at a cost, and those who benefit from them should be willing to serve to defend them. The draft eliminates class, racial, and ethnic distinctions in who does and who does not serve.

In addition, without the draft, it may be an open question how voluntary the service actually is. In an economy with high unemployment, some may not be able to find satisfactory employment except in the military. This means that those who are able to avoid service can do so simply because they can afford to. If one has few options, and none better than joining the military, it could be argued that this is not a wholly voluntary choice.

Tetra Images/Photolibrary

Some note that national service doesn't need to be related to the military and argue that all of us have an obligation to serve our country.

Finally, if the draft were reinstated, all citizens would be subject to the risks of war, and they would be keenly aware of the harms to which they would be exposed. This makes the decision to go to war one of great interest to all citizens and would require those citizens to engage in the political debate over this option. Furthermore, were the children of those making these crucial decisions also subject to the draft, and the risks it brings, they might also be extremely hesitant to commit the nation to a war unless absolutely necessary.

Many countries require its citizens to engage in compulsory national service, a requirement that often is, but does not have to be, satisfied by military service. This offers a way for those who for religious or other reasons wish to refuse to join the military an alternative, while still recognizing the obligation to serve one's country. This has served to demonstrate that all citizens belong to one nation, and share the burden of serving, and on occasion defending, that nation and its values.

A citizen has an obligation to defend the country that provides him or her with the rights and opportunities of that country. That obligation must be shared by all citizens and should not be left only to those who do so willingly, or do so out of economic necessity. Requiring military or alternative service to one's country is a crucial reminder that the nation shares the same goals and values, regardless of economic or ethnic background. Citizens should be happy to serve their country but, in any case, need to recognize the common obligations they share as citizens. Therefore, the draft should be reinstated.

The Theories

The utilitarian, of course, focuses on one basic principle: given a set of choices, one should choose what generates the greatest good (or maximizes utility) for the greatest number. As we have already seen, this principle does necessarily indicate what choice should be made, even after adopting the utilitarian perspective: different utilitarians can disagree, often quite sharply, about how the principle should be applied. Here, however, we can construct a utilitarian argument against reinstating the draft. (It might be good practice, however, to construct a utilitarian argument in favor of reinstating the draft.)

Society is made up of people with diverse backgrounds, skills, and ambitions. The best possible result is for all of these people to draw on what is productive in their background to develop their skills, and to learn new ones. In this way, they have increased opportunities, including a greater chance to realize their ambitions. But fundamental to this entire picture is the idea of doing what one wishes to; to prevent that is to deny a person his

Martin Barraud/OJO Images/Photolibrary

A utilitarian might argue that it is for the greater good that everyone should be free to choose his or her own path. What are some other ethical arguments that can be made?

or her freedom. Thus, the utilitarian will argue, in this case, that the only way for an individual citizen to maximize utility is to have the greatest amount of freedom possible; that freedom, in turn, makes possible the development of talents and the meeting of one's individual goals.

Clearly conscription, or forcing someone to sacrifice two or more years in military service is a denial of that freedom, unless there is no alternative. And, of course, there is an alternative: an all-volunteer military force. This preserves individual freedom and gives any citizen the ability to serve in the military and take advantage of the opportunities the military offers. To force someone to do this is to minimize individual freedom unnecessarily. Given that there is an obvious alternative, the all-volunteer force provides the greatest good for the greatest number. This becomes particularly obvious when freedom itself is factored in as an important, if not the most important, component of the good in question. No one can suggest that a policy of coercion—such as a military draft—maximizes a citizen's utility overall, if there is an available alternative. Thus, the draft doesn't provide as much freedom and opportunity as the all-volunteer military and, consequently, doesn't produce the greatest good for the greatest number. Rather, the all-volunteer force does maximize the utility of

Lelia G. Hendren/Photolibrary

Marines at the Iwo Jima Memorial. A virtue ethicist would emphasize the positive values the military represents.

the individual citizen, and thus all citizens who live in a given country. Therefore, the draft should not be reinstated, given that the alternative all-volunteer approach produces the greatest good for the greatest number.

The virtue ethicist recognizes the importance of freedom but also emphasizes certain virtues that are also necessary for a citizen to be, simply put, good. These virtues include such things as pride, an even temper, honesty, and courage. Those who have these virtues, among others (such as generosity), and have them in a harmonious balance with each other are much more likely to be the kinds of citizens who make positive contributions to society. Surely, any society will promote those things that increase the likelihood that its members will possess these virtues and understand their importance.

It seems clear that the military promotes many of those values endorsed by the virtue ethicist, as well as how these values must be in proportion. Undoubtedly, the military demonstrates the importance of, for instance, having an even temper; whether in combat or not, one who maintains

114

his or her temper in stressful situations will be more successful in and out of the military. Clearly the military emphasizes the importance of courage, but it also insists that too much courage—rash behavior—can be as harmful to the fighting unit as too little courage, or cowardice. The various virtues that have been highlighted by virtue ethics seem to be consistently those that are insisted upon in the military.

A society that emphasizes these virtues can rely on the military, or at least required national service, to promote these values and teach young adults their importance. These lessons are so important to a morally responsible society that all its citizens, not just those who volunteer for military service, must be made aware of them. Patriotism itself, of course, is a virtue, and pride in one's country, demonstrated by being willing to defend it, is an obligation that must be promoted. No more effective way of doing this exists than to require all citizens to enter military service, or an equivalent form of national service. Indeed, it should be regarded as a virtue itself to serve one's country. Thus the draft serves the purpose of guaranteeing that all of its citizens be exposed to the values of their nation, and be required to understand them. This makes each citizen aware of his or her moral obligations, and thus, in turn, makes the society—the collection of these individuals—one with higher moral standards and an increased ethical understanding of the central core of good citizenship. The draft effectively provides this and, thus, should be reinstated in order to establish these civic values.

Some Conclusions

There hasn't been a great deal of discussion of reinstating the draft, and most of those commenting on the issue agree that there is little popular or political support for doing so. That may make it seem as if debating the issue is a waste of time, but some valuable results emerge, from looking both at the arguments for and against reinstating the draft and at how ethicists might approach the problem.

Perhaps the most important result to consider is determining the obligations of a citizen. Is one to defend the country at any cost? Should all citizens agree, at least implicitly, with the oath sworn to by both those who enlist in the armed forces of the United States and the president, to defend their nation "against all enemies, foreign and domestic"? If citizens do incur such obligations as citizens, how are these values taught and maintained? Does the educational system do a sufficient job of emphasizing these values? If not, what other institutions are available to make sure all citizens understand and embrace them?

We also see emerge the question of whether or not national defense is a burden shared by only a part of those who benefit from it. Some who argue in favor of the draft have introduced the term **free-riding**. In economic theory, a free-rider is one who enjoys a benefit that he or she doesn't pay for. For example, a person who doesn't pay taxes, but still expects to enjoy the protection provided by the police, is a free-rider. Are those citizens who enjoy the freedoms and opportunities of their country free-riding on those who sacrifice their time and energy, and maybe even their health and lives, to defend those freedom and opportunities? Free-riding is generally thought to be unfair; if those who gain the benefits of a strong military aren't willing to make similar sacrifices, and thus free-ride, is this fair?

On the other hand, the insistence on the importance of freedom emerges as a result of this discussion, and those who advocate an all-volunteer force insist that those who defend freedom should do so freely. The military may well be a more cohesive and effective force if those who serve do so voluntarily. Some people may be particularly suited for military service, whereas others may not be very well-suited at all. An all-volunteer military can take advantage of this, and a voluntary force should thus lead to a situation where the military is a desirable option for many, and one that provides a great number of opportunities that may be otherwise unavailable. The law of supply and demand suggests that if a large number of people want a job that only a few of them can get, those hiring will be able to take only the most qualified. Clearly, if the military is a desirable career option, this law should hold as well, leading to a high-quality, productive, and effective fighting force.

Ethicists, of course, won't solve this debate with a simple, single answer that will satisfy everyone. Here again, we see that by raising this question, ethicists make clearer what is at stake: not just in terms of what is promoted by military service but what the relationship is between those who do serve and the larger society. Ethicists can also make clearer how we might attempt to resolve such a debate by making clearer what is at stake in each response, weighing the various conclusions put forth, and evaluating the evidence supporting—and failing to support—each of those conclusions. They may not solve the problems, but ethicists can do a great deal to make clearer what the problems are.

Where Do We Go from Here?

The U.S. Constitution is clear that the president serves as the commander in chief thus, the highest military authority in the land is a civilian, not a member of the military. This suggests that civilian oversight was seen to be very important to those who drafted the Constitution. But it may also imply that good citizens should be informed about the military and understand its role within society.

Some on one side of the political spectrum criticize those on the other side for having too little respect for members of the armed forces; after all, no greater sacrifice can be made than that made by those who are willing to risk their life in the defense of their country. In response, some insist that the United States spends too much money on defense. They claim that it is a military designed to defend against a one-time threat such as the Soviet Union and point out that the United States spends more on defense than the next 45 highest-spending countries in the world combined and 48 percent of the world's total military spending (International Institute for Strategic Studies, 2008).

These issues, of course, fuel very active and often hostile debates, but for our purposes, the argument over reinstating the draft leads to more general questions about the relationship between a country and its armed services. What, fundamentally, is that relationship? Are some citizens better equipped than others to shoulder the burden of national defense? Or should all citizens contribute, in whatever way they best can, to that effort? What are the genuine military threats a country faces, and how are these determined and evaluated? Who makes a society's crucial decisions about whether to go to war, and what level of economic support should the military receive? Should all citizens have both an obligation to understand these issues and make their views known to those who represent them?

Don Bishop/White/Photolibrary

What are your thoughts on the relationship between the individual and the society?

These questions, in turn, lead to an issue that continues to inform, in a fundamental way, all the questions we have been looking at and will continue to do so. What is the relationship between the individual and society? Is society nothing more than a collection of individuals, competing with each other and each seeking his or her self-interest? Or do individuals only understand themselves, at least in part, by the various roles they play in that society: as a parent, a child, a worker, a boss, an enlisted soldier, a commanding officer, among the many other social roles that identify all of us? Are there rights that pertain only to individuals, or do all discussions of rights involve a social dimension? That is, when people exercise certain rights, do they have to factor in the potential effects on others?

One simple example should make this clear. A person may have the right to drink to excess. That person, however, does not have the right to drive, for that would place others at risk, and thus their rights would be violated. Determining what rights, if any, do not bring with them questions of the larger social context is one we will continue to struggle with, and we will continue to see that drawing the line between the individual and society can become more difficult to draw the more carefully it is examined.

Do Those in the Military Risk Being Isolated in Society?

Particularly since the closing days of the Viet Nam conflict (the mid-1970s), both civilians and military personnel have expressed the concern that a division was beginning to be noticed between members of the armed services—particular the active personnel, rather than members of reserve forces—and the rest of society. The point was made earlier, with political scientist Samuel Huntington worrying in 1957 that the military has the outlook of an "estranged minority" (Huntington, 1957). These concerns have gotten increasing attention, again from both civilians and members of the military, particularly with the military operations in Iraq and Afghanistan. What, specifically, is the worry here?

The military has a very distinct role in society, and its members tend to live in isolation from the rest of the population for much of the time they serve, whether at a military installation in the United States, or while being deployed overseas. Those in the military and their families tend to interact largely with others who are also in the military, all of whom live under the specific kinds of rules required by the military. These members of the armed forces, on the view being considered here, develop distinctive ways of looking at things, whether it be economics or politics or even specific cultural values. Those outside the military may share this perspective, but often they do not; the viewpoint may in fact serve to divide the two groups. After all, a soldier who has served two tours in Afghanistan may well understand the situation in a way that is entirely different from those who have not; if this soldier tends to be surrounded with others who share that viewpoint,

Moodboard RF/Photolibrary

It is natural that soldiers will identify more with those who understand their experiences. Some worry that the military is at risk of being isolated from broader society.

an entire way of looking at Afghanistan, and its larger political context, is reinforced. Indeed, this soldier may be confident that those without the relevant experience have an inadequate understanding of that situation and are not sufficiently equipped to analyze or criticize it.

With an all-volunteer army, and with the increasing professionalization of the military as a career, questions have been raised whether those in the military are becoming a separate and distinct subgroup within the larger United States, with their own moral and cultural standards, and their own political and ethical viewpoints that can clash, often sharply, with the larger population as a whole.

The concern this raises must go in both directions for this view to have any merit. If those in the military are sufficiently isolated to develop distinct values from the rest of society, then those in each group will have difficulty understanding the viewpoint of those in the other group. Civilians do not understand the military way of life any more than members of the military understand the civilian way of life. Thus, it is worth worrying about if the current structure of the military, and how its members are recruited, does in fact increase the isolation of the military from other parts of society. If so, it may need to be asked further what can be done to minimize this effect. If not, it certainly is worth examining what is helping to prevent it. Fundamentally, it suggests examining the relationship between the military and the larger society—something perhaps not done enough by civilians or those in the military. For if the fear considered here is real, this kind of division could generate significant problems for that larger society. And, as Admiral Stanley Arthur observed about such a division, this is "not healthy in an armed force serving a democracy."

3.6 Where We Have Been and Where We Are Going

Naturally enough, we started out looking at ethics. After figuring a bit about what ethics is, and why one might study it, we moved on to some ethical theories. We saw the classical theories of utilitarianism, deontology, and virtue ethics, as well as some alternatives to those traditional theories: relativism, emotivism, and ethical egoism.

With a little theory under our belts, we turned to specific issues in ethics, particularly those that focus on individual rights: the right to bear arms and to have school prayer, as well the question of what rights employees retain in the workforce. We saw a historical debate about the right of women to vote and a contemporary debate over pornography. Even here we saw some difficulty in drawing a sharp distinction between individual rights, and the understanding of those rights in the larger context of society.

We then turned to rights that had a more explicit social component: questions about the death penalty, international business, and the environment. We also considered the historical issue of the internment of Japanese Americans during World War II and looked at a contemporary debate about reinstating the draft. Throughout these debates, we saw how ethical theory can be applied to these questions, and often saw how those theories can make our arguments more informed and more rigorous, even if they can solve the problem in a way everyone finds agreeable. But here the line between individual rights and society became still a bit less clear.

We will now look at ethical issues that confront, quite specifically, this relationship between an individual and society. We will try to clarify this relationship and understand what it means for an individual to have rights in relationship to others who live in that society, or even in another society. We will examine whether the very idea of a "victimless crime" makes sense, and how to determine where one person's rights begin to infringe on those of another person, or on the values of society as a whole. In addition to some specific case studies, we will again look at an ethical dispute from the past as well as a contemporary debate that has generated much controversy.

One important point should also begin to come into focus. When we discussed individual rights, they were examined from the perspective of the individual. But as we can see from this discussion, these rights affect a lot of people, enough to raise the question whether there are, really, individual rights at all. Is the context of rights always social? That is, can we really isolate the notion of an individual's right to do something (or be prevented from doing something) from the role that individual plays in society, and the role society itself plays in our understanding of such rights? As we go along, we will discover that a sharp line between the individual and society becomes increasingly difficult to draw.

It should be clear by now that ethics has a lot to offer, in articulating arguments, defending various positions, making debates clearer and more rigorous, and eliminating factors that aren't really relevant. But it may fall short of providing a solution everyone is happy to accept. So we can count on many of these ethical debates to continue.

Some Final Questions

1. Is the death penalty a kind of punishment that will always be justified, or might a society change its approach to punishment whereby it becomes regarded as either immoral, impractical, or ineffective? Explain.
2. What kinds of legal safeguards are there in the United States to prevent wholesale discrimination against a group of people on the basis of race, religion, or ethnicity? Can these legal safeguards prevent such groups of people from being treated unjustly? Explain.
3. What kind of steps might be taken to ensure that those who serve in the military feel part of the community for whom they risk their lives? What kind of steps might be taken to ensure that those who are not serving (or have not) served in the military can appreciate and understand the sacrifice and specific pressures on those who do serve?

4

Moodboard/Photolibrary

Rights and Responsibilities— Individual and Social

Chapter Outline

4.1 The Internet and Ethics

The Internet has become a basic feature of people's lives, changing many institutions—the media, education, entertainment, shopping—in fundamental ways. These fundamental changes have also affected how business is done and have raised a host of ethical issues with questions about privacy, the collection of information on personnel, and even free speech. Here we will look at some of these ethical challenges, contrasting utilitarianism and deontology to make clearer what these ethical issues are so that we can understand what has changed and what has remained the same in our digital era.

The Issue: The Individual Right to Privacy Should Be Restricted

Many people do a great deal of their work on a computer, and in recent years the question has arisen about how private that work should be. Should the employee assume that all work is private, should the employer have access to all such work, or should we strike a balance between these two extremes?

Employers have a wide range of rights to keep track of employees

The contractual relationship between an employer and an employee is clear and straightforward. An employer offers a job, with a salary and benefits, to an employee; in exchange, the employee does the job he or she was hired to do. Many such jobs require Internet access, and with that access comes a number of temptations. A variety of well-known social networking sites exist where one can chat with friends, take silly quizzes, play games, and engage in similar activities. Various other software packages offer instant chat opportunities, either through typing messages or talking on the phone using one's computer. One can browse an almost infinite range of stores in which to shop, one can play poker or chess or innumerable other games; one can read on-line blogs, newspapers, and magazines, or access virtually any kind of site to pursue whatever interests one may have.

Laura Doss/Fancy/Photolibrary

Those in favor of more Internet restrictions in the workplace argue that the employee is hired to do a job—and surfing the Web affects productivity. Have any of your employers blocked certain Websites? Did you feel like you were more productive as a result?

But, of course, the employee isn't hired to do any of these things; the employee is hired to do a job, and any time spent surfing the Internet in ways that are not job-related decreases the employee's productivity. While at work, the employer has every right to do what is necessary to maintain productivity, and thus has every right to limit or even prohibit access to those sites that distract employees from doing what they are hired to do. An employee may have the right to spend whatever time he or she wishes to on the Internet, but that right is not unrestricted; rather, the exercise of such a "right" doesn't extend to the workplace. The employer has an obligation to stockholders to return a profit on investment, and the time devoted to activities at work that are not work-related interferes with that return. Thus, the employer not only can restrict Internet access for employees but has an obligation to do so to carry out the fundamental obligation of running a profitable enterprise.

As we have seen, the employer can restrict or prohibit access to the Internet. At the same time, blocking Internet sites in a large-scale way can, at times, interfere with an employee gaining access to sites with legitimate purposes. Furthermore, those with sufficient computer skills may be able to get past many of the restrictions imposed. For this reason, the employer should also be able to monitor the activity of employees, keeping track of what those employees do while at work. Employees should be aware of this monitoring, of course, and it should be made clear, at the time of hiring, that such activity will be tracked. This will allow the employer to determine if any employees are wasting company time and to send a clear message to all employees to do what they were hired to do. An employee who knows he or she is being monitored is much less likely to submit to the temptation to surf the Internet, and thus much more likely to be a productive worker.

Radius Images/Photolibrary

It's been said that stricter Internet policies can help protect a company's reputation and proprietary information. What are some cases where information got out on the Internet and harmed a company?

Employers also have the right to restrict what employees can say on the Internet to the extent it interferes with the company's goal. Blogs and Web-sites that criticize or denigrate a company can harm the company's reputation, and make it more difficult to do business. A prospective client, for instance, who sees that some employees are unhappy with their company, may hesitate to do business or invest in that company. This can obviously harm the company, and thus it can prevent employees from participating in those activities that may be seen as producing such damage.

Given that the goal of the company, the employer, and the employees, is to maintain and develop a profitable business, a variety of practices should not only be allowed but be the kinds of things any responsible company must consider as part of its business practice. These practices can include restricting or prohibiting access to non-work-related Internet sites, monitoring employee activity on the Internet, and preventing employees from posting material that may be seen as harmful to the company's interests. Furthermore, it is obvious that some material available on the Internet can be quite offensive; viewing, for instance, sexually explicit or politically distasteful material could lead to a hostile work environment. An employer has the obligation to prevent, or at least minimize, such an environment, which provides another reason for limiting access to this material. All of these things, and others, are fully justified for a company that seeks to remain profitable.

Employers have a narrow range of rights to keep track of employees

Employers want their employees to be efficient and productive workers; both employers and employees share the same goal, to help develop a business that is profitable and stable. But, it is also clear that worker satisfaction is an important ingredient in this context.

Holger Winkler/Cusp/Photolibrary

Is tightening Internet access an insult to employees and an indication that the company doesn't trust them?

Employees who go to work enthusiastically, and who regard themselves as an important part of the company, are simply better employees. This means not only that they are satisfied with their jobs but that they are more productive, thus helping to provide an important component to the long-term health and profitability of the company.

An employer who tells employees that they cannot access certain sites treats those employees as if they cannot be trusted to do the job they were hired to do. Those employees who are expected to represent and promote a company that does not seem to regard them as capable of making responsible decisions may well regard this as an insult. Employees who are regarded as an important part of the company are more likely to feel invested in that company. Employees who are so invested are, in turn, much more likely to be efficient, creative, and productive employees who work harder to see the company succeed. Telling employees that they are not sufficiently responsible to do their own work, by limiting their access to Internet sites, sends a clear message to those employees and prevents them from regarding themselves as integral parts of the company. This lack of trust generates worker dissatisfaction and may prevent a company from being as profitable as it might be otherwise.

An employer who monitors employee Internet activity shows a similar lack of trust. In some cases, the work produced by a given employee may justify such monitoring. But to assume that all employees need to be watched again sends a clear message, telling those workers that the operating assumption is that they will, unless monitored, not do the work they were hired to do. A good employee should be assumed to be responsible and efficient, and assuming otherwise damages the conception that employee has of his or her role in the company, and perhaps of the company itself. Thus, employees should not monitor their workers, unless a clear reason, such as a lack of quality work or a lack of sufficient production, indicates a need for such monitoring. The respect that is thus given to employees will, in the long run, make for a more productive workforce.

Eric Audras/Photoalto/Photolibrary

Some say that workers who feel respected and part of a team are more likely to be productive.

The goal of a company, the employer, and the employees is to maintain and develop a profitable business. Having workers who regard themselves as important parts of the company, and who are trusted, respected, and considered responsible by their bosses, is crucial for developing a loyal, efficient, and productive workforce. Treating employees as if they cannot be trusted and assuming that they must therefore be prevented from accessing non-job-related Websites, monitoring their Internet usage, and violating their right to free speech leads to a work environment where workers feel alienated from the company. Such workers do not regard themselves as part of the corporate "team" and are therefore less likely to do their best to see that the business succeeds. Treating workers with respect is not only the right thing to do, but it promotes the kind of efficient and productive workforce that is crucial to long-term corporate success. Thus, those activities that indicate a lack of respect for employees should be used only as necessary and only within a specified and narrow range.

The Theories

The utilitarian, in evaluating a policy to determine whether or not it is ethical, must take into account all the various groups affected by the policy. That includes, obviously enough, employers and employees, but also stockholders, clients and potential clients, and investors and potential investors. Policies can have wide-ranging implications for the short- and long-term growth of the company, and these implications must be looked at very carefully in crafting corporate policy and in implementing that policy.

All the members of these groups share the same goal: a thriving, stable business that is profitable and that will continue to be profitable. Assuming that goal can be used to identify the utility involved, then whatever produces the greatest good or maximizes the utility of the greatest number will clearly be that which leads to short- and long-term profitability.

Those drafting corporate policy must keep this fundamental goal in mind. There are, of course, trade-offs; some minor restrictions on free speech or privacy may have to be sacrificed for the greater good of the company and those who depend on it. Perhaps in an ideal world a company would have no need to restrict Internet access, monitor employees, or prevent employees from saying what they think on a Website not directly controlled by the company. However, this is not an ideal world: companies must make sure that employees are not spending valuable time doing things that interfere with the basic goal of the company. Thus, to generate the greatest good for the greatest number, steps must be taken to ensure that employees do what they are hired to do.

bilderlounge/Photolibrary

A utilitarian might argue that restrictions are only reasonable to ensure that computer time is spent on company work.

Restricting Internet access is a reasonable step to make sure that time spent on the Internet is spent doing the company's work. Monitoring employees, either to make sure they are doing what they were hired to do or to make them aware that they were hired to do that work, makes workers more productive. Restricting what they can say outside of work, if it can be shown to harm the goals of the company, also benefits the company. Thus, these restrictions are justified in terms of maintaining a productive workforce, generating short- and long-term profits, and creating the greatest good for the greatest number. Therefore, such minor restrictions are both sensible from the company's financial

Marcus Mok/Asia Images RM/Photolibrary

A deontologist would argue that restricting Web access fails to treat humans with dignity.

What Would You Do?

You run a company selling a product over the phone. Mary is one of your most efficient and productive workers; she is always on time, rarely misses a day of work, has had several promotions, and is frequently cited as a model employee.

The stockholders have recently insisted that company-wide drug testing be instituted, and anyone who fails two such tests or refuses to take the test will be terminated.

Mary tells you that she is not willing to take the test. She explains that it is not because she is afraid of failing it but because she regards it as an invasion of her privacy. She sees it as an indication that the company does not trust her and does not regard her as a valued employee. She will seek employment elsewhere, possibly with your main competitor.

- How do you try to convince Mary to take the test?

- What kinds of reasons do you point to in trying to convince her?

- If she continues to refuse, do you terminate such a good employee or try to modify the company policy?

perspective and ethical because they maximize the utility of all those affected by corporate policy. Given that employees are themselves the beneficiaries of the company's success, they should recognize that putting such restrictions in place maximizes their utility. In this way, utilitarianism sees such policies as ethical and justified.

The deontologist, in contrast, asks a simple question: If you are an employee, how do you want to be treated? On the view of deontological ethics, one should treat others as one would want to be treated. Those who design and implement corporate policy may need to ask themselves whether the policy is designed in such a way that they would feel comfortable working under it themselves. It may indicate a problem if those who draft corporate policies hesitate to work under those policies they create. Employers, therefore, should have policies they would regard as just and fair were they employees.

Deontological ethics also emphasizes the respect and dignity owed to human beings simply because they are human beings. The deontologist may challenge the idea that respect for human dignity is demonstrated by treating employees as not sufficiently trustworthy to make their own decisions. Rather, being prevented from accessing the Worldwide Web, being monitored at work, and being prevented from speaking up outside of work treats workers as less than responsible, free adults capable of making the right decisions for themselves and for the corporation. In the language of the deontologist, this fails to treat employees as fully autonomous human beings. Any policy a company adopts that does not recognize its employees as fully autonomous is unjust. Hence, the restrictions discussed here, as limiting that autonomy, may be seen by the deontologist as unethical.

Deontologists will make one other, related, point in this regard. While recognizing that the company has a clear and specific goal—profitability—it is unethical to treat human beings solely as means to achieving that goal. Human beings deserve respect, and in the language of deontology, that requires that human beings be treated as "ends in themselves," not merely as means to an end. In short, they can't be regarded simply as objects to be used in order to achieve corporate ends, or goals; to do so is unethical. Thus, any policy that treats its employees as objects, used solely to achieve a company's goal of profitability, will violate a fundamental principle of ethics of treating human beings as deserving respect, having their human dignity recognized, and not being used solely as a means to the company's end.

Some Conclusions

As we can see, the goals of employers and the goals of employees may overlap: both have an interest, after all, in seeing the company succeed. Yet they may disagree on how that success should be achieved and what policies best promote it. We have seen one way of characterizing this conflict, On the one hand, the employer may regard as necessary certain Internet policies that some employees see as infringing on their rights and failing to give them due respect.

As we saw earlier, one way of dealing with such conflicts has been to adopt a strategy John Rawls called reflective equilibrium (1971). Rawls's account is elaborate and complex; nevertheless, here we can regard it as a way of understanding negotiations between groups with conflicting perspectives. The advantage of Rawls's approach is its insistence that all affected parties have the right to have their voices heard in such negotiations. Given that these parties share the same goal, it is also to their advantage to understand the views of each other as a way of promoting that goal. Even though there is obviously enough of a difference in the role and power of the employer relative to his or her employees, it may well be to the employer's advantage to do what is necessary to establish and maintain a satisfied and productive workforce. One result of this negotiation strategy may be to ensure that the respect employees deserve is factored into the way the company does business. This, then, would not only treat employees with respect, but may well result in a more productive, and thus more profitable, business.

A further financial advantage may accrue to a corporation that develops the reputation for being a business that is not only profitable but also well run. It is easy to see in the media various discussions along with lists of the "best companies to work for." Not only are these are companies successful, but their employees indicate a great deal of satisfaction with their jobs. This kind of reputation has obvious beneficial results: enthusiastic employees are more productive, good workers are easier to retain, high-quality employees are easier to recruit, and the profits and stability are attractive to both potential clients and potential investors. Thus, in the long run, the utilitarian's goal—maximizing utility—may best be met by also insisting that corporate policies follow the deontologist's insistence that employees be treated with respect.

Corbis/Photolibrary

A utilitarian might also argue that there are advantages to having a satisfied workforce. Would Internet access make a difference in how satisfied you were in your job?

Balancing the demands for a productive workforce with the ethical requirements of the deontologist may not always be easy, but it may indicate a goal that any profitable corporation, seeking long-term success, should take under consideration.

Where Do We Go from Here?

There has been friction between employers and employees probably about as long as there have been employers and employees. Technological developments may have changed the form in which these kinds of conflicts arise, but the conflicts themselves are nothing new. With the increasing importance of personal computers and Internet access, new challenges arise that successful and well-run companies will have to confront and, to be successful in the long term, resolve.

The famous Italian political theorist, Niccolò Machiavelli, once posed a significant question to political leaders: Is it better to be loved or to be feared? Many have seen this as an important question for those in business, as well. Does an employer have more success if employees fear the employer, or love the employer? Or, is there a third option here?

One might be tempted to think that a company is more successful if its employees fear their employer; the kind of work environment that may emerge in this case may ensure that workers do what they are hired to do, and the various kinds of restrictions on Internet access may be one more method to keep the workforce in check. At the same time, this kind of work environment may increase tensions between employer and employee and generate unpleasant—and potentially unproductive—results.

Movement Way/Imagebroker.net/Photolibrary

Italian philosopher Niccolò Machiavelli wrote in his famous treatise *The Prince* that it is better for a leader to be feared than loved if he or she cannot be both. How can this be applied in the work environment? If you're in a leadership position, how would you attempt to be both loved and feared by those you oversee?

On the other hand, one may be tempted to think that employees who love their employer work harder to help achieve his or her goals; a workforce in this environment may be more enthusiastic, more energetic, and generally happier, leading to better productivity. At the same time, there may be an increased tendency to take advantage of such an employer, leading to more time being spent on non-work-related activities and, thus, lower productivity.

Machiavelli suggests what is probably obvious: ideally, the good political leader (or good employer) will be both loved and feared. When appropriate, stern measures may be taken to produce the results a company seeks; but, when appropriate, making one's workplace an attractive place to work has genuine benefits, as well.

Again, balancing the private rights of the individual, and maintaining the respect owed to that individual, can be difficult to do in the context of a very competitive work environment. Here again, we see that traditional rights of privacy and free speech may not be wholly private when looked at from the larger perspective of society. Determining the legitimate boundaries of one's ability to exercise one's rights will continue to raise difficult ethical challenges. And the on-going development of new techniques for efficiently and pervasively monitoring employees' behavior, on and off the job, will continue to make this balancing act difficult to achieve.

How Are Workplace Relations Affected by the Economy?

As perhaps happens all too frequently, an employee will find his or her job situation intolerable: perhaps the workload becomes too great or too oppressive, the work environment may become too unpleasant, or it may just be that a co-worker makes it too uncomfortable to continue in the job situation. In such cases, the employee is free to quit and, presumably, seek employment elsewhere.

For a number of reasons, however, this may be easier said than done. Particularly important in this context is how competitive the job market is. In an economy where unemployment is low, or a worker has a particularly desirable skill, finding a new job may be relatively easy. In this case, demand is greater than supply. But often, supply is greater—and occasionally much greater—than demand. If unemployment is high, there are more workers competing for jobs than there are jobs available. A person who lacks specialized skills, or training, may discover that there are a large number of people who can also do whatever job he or she is qualified to do. In such cases, those seeking employment are much more likely to accept conditions of employment that might otherwise be regarded as onerous or reasons for rejecting a job. Furthermore, where the job market is very "tight," people are much less likely to quit their jobs even when their work environment becomes objectionable.

Consider John, a high school graduate working on an assembly line. John's job is a pretty good one—it pays a decent wage and, until recently, offered relatively generous benefits such as inexpensive health care insurance and a retirement package. But, due to a significant downturn in the economy, John's company has sharply reduced his benefits package; John's health insurance costs now take a much bigger percentage of his take-home pay. His company has also instituted a "two-tier" compensation structure. Workers who already work for the company continue to receive their traditional salary and the newly reduced benefits package. But new workers are hired at a lower base salary and an even lower employer contribution to their health insurance benefit.

John and his fellow co-workers have, as might be imagined, serious objections to these new company policies. But, unemployment in the area is high, and a large number of people, with equivalent or better skills, are willing to replace John. There are not a lot of jobs available in the area in which John lives, and there is a good deal of competition for the jobs that are available.

John weighs his options and recognizes that he is much better off keeping his current job than quitting and running the serious risk of not being able to find another. Furthermore, he realizes that even if he were to find another job, it would be unlikely to pay as well as his current job, and, given the competition for jobs, he may not have any better options. Thus, he stays in his current position.

Jim West/Imagebroker.net/Photolibrary

Detroit unemployed lined up in April 2010 to apply for 200 jobs at a new Meijer store. U.S. unemployment peaked in late 2009 in the wake of the economic crisis. Detroit was among the areas hardest hit. A weak economy can change both employers, and employees' perception on the job environment and workplace relations.

Here we see how the economic context can have a significant effect on the job environment. In a weak economy, there is considerably greater pressure to cut costs, and often labor costs are a prime candidate for such cuts. Employees, in this situation, have fewer options and thus may have to accept demands for increased productivity, lower salaries and benefits, or both. In contrast, in a booming economy, in an area where unemployment is low, or where one has a skill that is in great demand, an employee may have more options. In such cases, workers who find their jobs not offering enough in the way of compensation or in the quality of the work environment have the option of quitting and finding work elsewhere. In both cases, however, it is clear that the larger economic context can play a substantial role in determining what a worker may or may not be willing to accept.

Here again we see that individual rights must be understood within the larger social context. One may feel his or her rights are being violated, but the social setting—here, specifically, the economic conditions involved—may be an important factor in determining how to respond to such a perceived violation. One's opportunities may be expanded, or contracted, depending on the ease with which a new job, or better job, can be found. Factoring those economic conditions into such decisions clearly indicates that individual choices are fundamentally embedded in a much larger social context.

4.2 Terrorism, Privacy, and National Security

After the bombing of the Murrah Building in Oklahoma City, and even more urgently after the attack on the World Trade Center of September 11, 2001, a debate has emerged over how to balance the right to privacy and the need for the government to prevent further attacks. Some argue that the government has an obligation to protect its citizens, and that this obligation may require traditional rights to be violated. Others argue that the threat of terrorism does not provide the government the right to ignore important constitutional rights. We will look at this debate from the perspective of ethical relativism and utilitarianism.

The Issue: Restrictions on the Government Due to Terrorism

An open and free society brings with it certain risks, particularly in a time when terrorism is a serious and on-going threat. How can the right to privacy, and traditional American freedoms, be balanced with the requirements to protect citizens from potential terrorist attacks?

Rights may be restricted due to the threat of terrorism

Kordcom/age footstock/Photolibrary

The September 11, 2001, attacks on the World Trade Center propelled the debate on national security and privacy to the forefront of the nation's consciousness.

The fundamental obligation of any government is to protect its citizens and to provide security for them to carry out their ordinary activities. With the increased threat of terrorism, both from outside a country's borders and within, there is also an increased challenge to provide this security. Citizens, of course, have rights, but if they aren't safe from these threats, their rights mean very little. Hence the government must do what it determines is necessary to maintain the safety of its citizens.

Here, of course, we see that moral questions and legal questions are difficult to separate. The Constitution specifies various rights that the law is designed to maintain and protect, but, at the same time, these rights reflect important moral values the Constitution seeks to embody. Thus, we have the right to the free exercise of religion, and laws are designed to protect this right. The difficult issue that arises with modern-day terrorism is when a right, or a claim to a right, conflicts with what the government regards as necessary to fulfill its duty to protect its citizens. But, again, the role the government plays in providing security to its citizens is crucial; without that security, the ability to enjoy other rights may be irrelevant. As one obvious example: I may have the right to free speech, but if I'm not safe from being violently attacked for exercising that right, that would seem to mean that the right isn't worth all that much. After all, I probably would prefer to remain silent than to risk being hurt by speaking out.

Pixtal Images/Photolibrary

Some would be willing to give up certain rights for their security. What would you be willing to compromise to feel safe?

The government has difficult choices to make in this setting but must be driven by the one fundamental requirement noted previously: to protect its citizens. This may mean that rights need to be understood in this larger context and may need to be reevaluated in terms of what restrictions on rights may be necessary. Ideally, we may wish to assume that phone calls, e-mail, and other forms of communication are private. But should that desire prevent government from doing legitimate investigations, which may require accessing e-mail and listening to phone calls? Presumably, there are laws in place that permit this government "eavesdropping," but there may be a degree of urgency such that laws interfere with agencies gaining

Jochen Tack/Imagebroker.net/Photolibrary

Some would argue that we should not interfere with the government's duty to protect its citizens and that we should recognize that certain rights must be reinterpreted for us to remain safe.

important information. We should, therefore, defer to the government in such cases and give it the benefit of the doubt. After all, the various security agencies of the United States (the FBI, the CIA, and others) have access to highly classified information that may indicate that immediate action be taken. To deny the government the ability to take such action may interfere with its legitimate, and fundamental, duty to protect its citizens. Therefore, one should defer to the government in making such decision, and we should recognize that some "rights" may well need to be abridged, or at least re-interpreted, in order for us to remain safe.

Habeas corpus, for instance, is the requirement that an authority arresting a person show the reasons for that arrest. One simply cannot be put in jail without access to legal representation and to the courts. This is a legal doctrine, but it reflects a long-standing view that a person cannot be imprisoned indefinitely. During the Civil War, Abraham Lincoln suspended the right of habeas corpus in parts of the United States. Lincoln recognized that wartime threats required its suspension. Similarly, terrorism may require the government to broaden its abilities to read mail, tap phones, and access e-mail, from both citizens and non-citizens. It may need to use harsh interrogation techniques to discover crucial information that could not be obtained otherwise. It may need to detain suspicious people, perhaps indefinitely, and try them in a different legal setting than traditional civil courts. All of these may be extensions of government power, but these extensions are justified by the fundamental and overriding obligation of the government to protect its citizens.

Images.com/Photolibrary

Some make the case that rights are a fundamental part of our government and society. If we give up our rights, it becomes unclear what kind of state is being defended.

Rights may not be restricted due to the threat of terrorism

The government has an obligation to protect its citizens, but chief among the protections it provides are the rights of those citizens. To abridge those rights in the name of security is to violate the state's fundamental commitment to its citizens; it also risks changing the power and even the nature of the government to which its citizens owe their loyalty. The rights the government protects and the moral values those rights reflect are fundamental to our conception of that government. If those rights are abridged, do citizens owe their allegiance to that government, or owe it to the same degree? In short, if we give up rights in order to defend ourselves against a possible threat, haven't we given up too much? The state that is worth defending is the state that maintains and defends its citizens' rights; if those rights aren't sufficiently protected, then it isn't entirely clear what kind of state is being defended. Therefore, the rights of citizens cannot be restricted in the name of fighting terrorism.

*A standard logical mistake, or illegitimate form of reasoning, is known as the **slippery slope fallacy**. The slippery slope fallacy embraces the idea that if one begins down a path, even in a small way, it can then lead, eventually, to disastrous results. Thus, one might argue that if one allows one's children to stay up an hour past their bedtime, they will end up never going to bed; therefore, one should never allow one's children to stay up past their bedtimes. This, of course, is not necessarily the case; making an exception to a rule does not necessarily eliminate the rule entirely. At the same time, it is not clear that this is always a mistake in reasoning, as in the old saying "If you give them an inch, they will take a mile." Thus, it is worth considering whether allowing the government to abridge and restrict the rights of its citizens leads to results that are indefensible.*

We can certainly imagine persuasive arguments for a government being allowed to tap phones without a warrant. Perhaps it is an emergency, and important information may be lost otherwise. But if in this case warrantless wiretaps are allowed, then perhaps in the future the government will offer other reasons to do so. Eventually, the very notion of being able to talk on one's phone without fear of having the government listen to the conversation has vanished. By allowing some restrictions on rights—here the right to privacy in phone conversations—the threat of losing this right altogether arises. Many have argued the way to avoid such a potential result is to insist that rights not be abridged at all, adopting the view that if one gives the government an inch, the government will take a mile.

Moodboard RF/Photolibrary

The slippery slope argument is often considered a logical fallacy, but it is worth considering when it comes to whether a government can restrict rights. Can you think of a situation in which slippery slope would be a legitimate argument? An illegitimate argument?

This is not to deny that terrorism poses a genuine, and perhaps increasing, threat to the citizens the government is obligated to protect. One may argue—and as the courts have found—that in wartime emergencies there may well be overriding reasons to impose restrictions on rights, for the duration of the emergency. But fighting terrorism is not like fighting a traditional war: the enemy is not clearly identified, and it seems quite possible that terrorism may never be "defeated" in the way a traditional adversary in war may be defeated. Fighting terrorism, thus, may be much more similar to fighting a disease than to fighting a war. But if rights can be abridged due to the demands of a war, and the war on terrorism is never-ending, isn't this an argument for a permanent restriction on rights?

It can be very difficult to balance the rights of citizens and the need for security for those same citizens. Endless arguments have raged over what rights one might be willing to give up to feel secure. At the end of this line of reasoning, of course, is the totalitarian state, where one may have obtained a great deal of security, but the price paid for this security is the loss of virtually all of one's rights. Thus, those citizens who seek a government worthy of the name will give up their rights only in the most compelling circumstances, and try to strike a balance between security and the protection of those rights. Even though terrorism is a genuine threat, to abandon one's commitments to moral and legal rights in the face of that threat is to give up too much. As Benjamin Franklin once put it, "They who would give up an essential liberty for temporary security, deserve neither liberty nor security." Therefore, rights may not be restricted in the name of terrorism without a substantial indication of an imminent threat, and only with the guarantee that those rights will be fully restored when that imminent threat passes.

The Theories

Sinopictures/Photolibrary

A relativist recognizes that different cultures perceive issues of national security and rights differently. The Chinese government, for example, went head to head with Google in early 2010 over an Internet censorship dispute. Chinese officials argued they have a responsibility to protect against social conflict and other things that could undermine Chinese society and state.

Different cultures, societies, and countries have different conceptions of the balance between security and rights. Some cultures prefer a powerful central government, where there are relatively few rights but the level of security is very high. In these cultures, one may have no fear of walking anywhere, at any time of day or night. The trade-off is that in such cultures, one may not have as much freedom to express one's views, including the criticism of the government. In this case, then, rights have been restricted in favor of security. It should be noted, of course, that some people simply have such powerful central governments imposed upon them, and that little or no choice was involved. Other cultures may strike the balance in a different way; there is much greater freedom, in terms of citizens being allowed to say and do what they wish; but with that freedom may also come increased threats to security. After all, if citizens can go where they please and do as they wish, so can others, including potential terrorists. Curbing such freedoms in order to prevent terrorism will inevitably curb the freedoms of all.

The relativist sees this balancing of rights and security as an on-going discussion, where there is no one correct solution, but recognizes that the balance will be relative to the needs and desires of a given culture. With an increasing threat from terrorism, more emphasis may be placed on security, and relatively less weight placed on protecting rights. Fundamentally, there is no right or wrong answer here, simply an attempt to determine the degree of the threat and the appropriate response. That determination may also change over time, due to an increase (or decrease) in the threat involved. In the United States, with the increased threat posed by terrorism, it seems clear that one should increase the government's ability to deal with that threat, and this may well decrease some rights traditionally enjoyed by citizens. Other cultures and countries may decide to strike the balance in a different way. But for the relativist, it seems quite defensible to restrict those rights if they interfere with the government's ability to defend itself and the citizens it is required to defend.

The utilitarian, on one interpretation of utilitarianism, might well argue that the utility of all citizens is what is at stake, and that what is right, given the various options, is what produces the greatest good for all involved. Clearly, being attacked by terrorists is something to be prevented if at all possible. At the same time, the state that protects its citizens in terms of both their security and their rights will produce the best possible outcome. Restricting rights when unnecessary does not maximize the utility of the citizens of a given state, and often a state will increase its power over its citizens when given the opportunity.

The utilitarian recognizes that balancing security and the protection of rights can be difficult. At the same time, the utilitarian does not accept the conclusion that there isn't a correct and defensible position to adopt. Rather, identifying those rights that cannot be legitimately abridged, evaluating the significance of the threat to security that is involved, and weighing the utility of having those rights maintained while being secure to enjoy them are all part of the utility calculation. The utilitarian, on this view, then sees that only under extreme circumstances, and only as a temporary measure, can a citizen's rights be restricted. Otherwise, the rights that a citizen possesses are fundamental to that citizen's happiness, and thus should be fundamental to any determination of what will produce the greatest good for the greatest number. In this case, the presumption must be

Frances M. Roberts/Ambient Images/Photolibrary

A New York police officer checks a commuter's backpack at the Union Square subway station after a terrorist attack. A utilitarian might argue for some temporary restrictive measures to protect the broader population.

that rights are to be protected and can only be restricted under the most threatening and immediate circumstances, and only for as long as those circumstances permit. A vague claim of a potential threat to security cannot be used to justify a large-scale or on-going abridgement of the rights of citizens.

Some Conclusions

Terrorism is a serious, on-going, and possibly increasing threat to the security of citizens in the United States and elsewhere. Fighting that threat will continue to be a challenge to governments and the people they represent, and fundamental to that challenge will be determining how to balance the rights of citizens with the obligation to protect them from terrorist attacks.

In the United States, this challenge becomes more complex. As the Constitution indicates, the government obtains its power to govern from the consent of the people. Difficult debates arise, however, over what the limits are to that governmental power and what legitimate restrictions can be placed on the rights of citizens in order to prevent terrorist attacks. The relativist may insist that there is no right or wrong answer here and simply indicate that whatever solution is offered will be relative to the standards and values of a given society. In contrast, the utilitarian will insist that among the various possible solutions, that option (or, if equivalent, options) that generates the greatest good for the greatest number will be the correct solution. These ethical theories are in conflict about whether there is a right answer, but few would argue that determining what that right answer will be easy.

In any case, it is clear that ethical theory can provide some guidance—if not solutions—to this difficult challenge that confronts us. Are there rights that no government can, or should, restrict? Is any violation of rights justified if the threat from terrorism is sufficient? What kind of government does one defend if it is a government that is willing to deny its citizens fundamental rights? Can citizens be expected to care about rights if they are constantly confronted with serious threats to their own security?

Ethical theory can help make clear what is involved in trying to answer these difficult questions, and how we can go about formulating the questions themselves. As is often the case, making clear the questions can often be an important component in trying to provide answers to those questions. For instance, if the term "terrorism" is used too often, it may lose its strength in warning us of genuine threats to our security. But if rights are insisted on in an absolute fashion, we may be more vulnerable to attacks that could be prevented by a more moderate approach to what those rights involve. Ethics, then, helps us become clearer about what is at stake and provides clarity, rigor, and argumentation in helping us confront the challenge of terrorism we will continue to confront.

Where Do We Go from Here?

There is little doubt that terrorism will continue to be a threat for many years, if not a permanent feature in our lives. If it is such a permanent feature, citizens and governments alike will need to work to keep that threat to a minimum and to continue to work on maintaining a productive balance between security and the protection of fundamental rights. Here we again see that the notion of an individual right often must be understood within a much larger social and political context.

One approach that has been suggested, in order to combat terrorism, is to provide an alternative model to those who out of economic frustration and political powerlessness support terrorists, whether directly or indirectly. This requires, of course, a strong commitment to rights: legal rights, moral rights, and human rights. If this approach has merit, then those who now support terrorist activities may well see that a much better alternative exists. Those who work on behalf of such an alternative, where rights as well as one's safety are protected, instead of supporting terrorists, could deprive them of important support. This could, in turn, weaken—if not eliminate—terrorism as a continuing and significant threat.

On the other hand, various factors continue to contribute to the support for terrorism: poverty, desperation, frustration, and other things that convince people they have no alternative. Furthermore, new and troubling forms of terrorist activity threaten to emerge. Some have warned of "cyberterrorism," computer-based attacks on defense systems, water plants, power grids, and any system that is largely run by computer. Clearly, if feasible, an attack that could cripple the energy grid of a country is a serious threat. In this case, we can see how such concerns might generate discussions about what degree of privacy any of us should expect when using a computer. Yet again, the difficult balancing act is required to determine what, if any, restrictions on privacy are legitimate.

It would be nice, of course, if we could solve the problems raised by terrorism by applying an ethical theory and generating the one, correct result. Unfortunately, ethics doesn't really work that way. But by making our language clear and by determining what values are crucial to a state that protects its citizens' rights and provides security, we can increase our ability to understand and confront the challenge of terrorism. And, perhaps, that increased understanding will help us to construct a successful strategy in order to deal with that challenge.

Presselect/Photolibrary

Somali pirates head for the coast of Somalia. Some have blamed the rise in piracy off the Somali coast on poverty, which has driven some Somali men to seek more lucrative professions.

Does Democracy Work?

Democracy is an old idea, going back to the Ancient Greeks and Athens of 500 B.C.E. "Democracy" is itself a tricky word, and different people interpret it differently, but the general idea is that a democratic government acquires its ability to rule from the consent of the governed—the people—and can be replaced by those same people if found inadequate, or worse. People will differ on what countries really are democracies; some countries follow democratic policies but consider themselves republics, whereas other countries call themselves "democratic republics" when they are, in fact, oppressive and tyrannical regimes. So it is a good idea to look closely at what a country actually does when deciding whether it is an actual democracy. In any case, the idea of democracy is an old one, but it hasn't been, until somewhat recently, a particularly popular form of government. For most of the history of organized political states, democracies have been relatively rare.

Paul Katz/Index Stock Imagery/Photolibrary

A strong central government might be more effective at combating terrorism, but some would argue that giving up rights is too high a price to pay.

Earlier, we saw Socrates' and Plato's concern that a democracy was an inferior form of government. They objected that democracies tended to allow the majority to act in way that oppressed minorities, that it put uninformed people in charge of important decisions (rather than experts), and that politicians would appeal to voters on the basis of what those voters wanted rather than what they needed. After all, will a politician who announces that she will raise taxes, even if the tax increase is necessary, be successful?

When confronting the challenges of terrorism, one might also see an additional objection to democracy and the rights that traditionally accompany democratic forms of government. Wouldn't a strong central government be more effective at combating terrorism? A government that has little concern for rights and laws would have the ability to inspect all sources of information, whether within the country or coming into the country from elsewhere. Thus, all e-mails or phone calls could be accessed by a government agency; the government could censor publication of material it regarded as not helping the fight against terrorism (which might well include any criticism of the government). Such a government might not hesitate to imprison those it saw as potential dangers and might prevent those it so treated from having access to legal representation. It might, in short, be able to lock some people up and "throw away the key."

This kind of government may, in some sense, be more effective in combating terrorism, but many would argue that it is too high a price to pay. After all, the terrorists that attack democracies also attack a way of life, one that reflects important moral commitments. Fighting terrorists is, then, defending that way of life. But if a government is sufficiently oppressive in its fight against terrorism, it isn't clear what morals and values are being defended.

Democracy, as we can see, makes things messier, by not making decisions about how to fight terrorism easy. Rather, these decisions become more difficult because the rights of citizens must be taken into account and weighed against any need for restricting those rights. And the more diverse a society, the greater the number of views that must be taken into consideration. But if the morals and values of a democratic society are worth defending, then we are probably stuck with trying to negotiate the complex set of issues we've described here and to insist that citizens have the appropriate education and understanding to strike the right balance between rights and security in a democratic society.

4.3 An Historical Debate: The Dred Scott Decision

In 1857, a slave named Dred Scott sued to be free, based on the fact that he had lived in areas of the United States where slavery was illegal. The Supreme Court decided against Scott, returning him to his owners. Although this decision is widely regarded now as one of the Court's worst decisions, the decision wasn't very close: the Justices voted against Scott 7–2. Here we will look at this case from the perspective of deontology and utilitarianism, and we see not only how ethical theories can inform important decisions, but also how the assumptions of an argument can make an enormous difference. This case also makes clear the conflict that sometimes can arise between legal principles and moral principles.

The Issue: How Should the Court Have Found in the Dred Scott Decision?

Many historians now argue that in returning a former slave—Dred Scott—to his former master, the Supreme Court set in motion the inevitable collision over slavery. Looking at the arguments of that era gives us some valuable perspective on the continuing discussion of race in the United States.

Dred scott should not have been freed

In 1857, slavery was legal in the United States, and slaves were regarded as property of their owners. The moral question here must be kept distinct from the legal question; that is, this case is not intended to determine the morality of slavery. Rather, it is intended to

The Print Collector/Photolibrary

An 1860 wood engraving depicts slaves loading sacks of cotton onto a cart. Slaves were regarded as property and not as human beings at the time.

determine whether the owner was deprived of his property in a way that was illegitimate and unjustifiable. Clearly, Dred Scott was the property of his owner, John Sanford. Freeing Scott would have taken Sanford's property without due process, which violates the Fifth Amendment of the Constitution. That Amendment reads, in part, that no person can "be deprived of life, liberty, or property, without due process of law; nor shall private property be taken for public use, without just compensation."

Furthermore, as Chief Justice Roger Taney argued in his majority opinion, citizenship was not to be extended to anyone descended from Africans, whether free or slave. Taney observed that the Declaration of Independence made this clear: that the phrase "all men are created equal" didn't include everyone. Rather, as Taney wrote, "it is too clear for dispute, that the enslaved African race were not intended to be included, and formed no part of the people who framed and adopted this declaration" (Scott v. Sandford, 1856). He also notes that Africans and their descendants were excluded from those to whom the Constitution refers as "We the People." Rather, he observed,

> Negros had for more than a century before been regarded as beings of an inferior order, and altogether unfit to associate with the white race, either in social or political relations; and so far inferior, that they had no rights which the white man was bound to respect; and that the negro might justly and lawfully be reduced to slavery. . . . He was bought and sold, and treated as an ordinary article of merchandise and traffic, whenever a profit could be made by it. (Scott v. Sandford, 1856)

Given that Africans and their descendants were recognized as property and could not become citizens of the United States, and given that Dred Scott was the property of John Sanford, to free Scott would be to violate Sanford's rights. Therefore Scott was not to be freed and was to be returned to his owner.

Dred Scott should have been freed

It is clear that one cannot easily keep legal principles and moral principles distinct; the legal principles of a people codify the moral values and principles those people support. To describe a human being as property and to allow that assumption to go unchallenged violates logic and common sense. It is undeniable that Africans and their descendents are human beings. As such, human beings cannot be regarded as property, and thus no right is involved in recognizing that one person cannot own another. John Sanford therefore had no right to own Dred Scott, and freeing Dred Scott did not deprive him of property he held

Pixtal Images/Photolibrary

Many would argue that no human being should be kept as property.

The Print Collector/Photolibrary

This 1850s print depicts fugitive slaves fleeing to Delaware from Maryland using the Underground Railroad, a system abolitionists used to help escaped slaves.

legitimately. To conclude this would be similar to allowing a thief to keep what he had stolen, as if the thief had some right to his wrongly obtained gains.

Furthermore, at the time the U.S. Constitution was ratified, black males could vote in 10 out of the 13 newly formed states. Clearly, at that time they were regarded as citizens in these states. To deprive such people of their rights is arbitrary and unfair, and to violate their own right to due process. As Associate Justice John McLean wrote in his dissent, the arbitrary way in which citizenship was treated in this case meant that whether one was recognized as a citizen was "more a matter of taste than of law."

Obviously enough, in 1857 in the United States, there was considerable debate about the moral status of human beings, and whether they could be property. In hindsight, the issues appear clear-cut, but it is worth remembering that the 1863 Emancipation Proclamation freed slaves only in those states that had left the Union. (This debate—among others—would, of course, soon be settled by a Civil War.) But given that the claim that human beings can be property, owned and treated as any other property, offends our very notion of what a human being is, and the arbitrary nature in which Africans and their descendants were treated by the law, it is clear that Dred Scott was correct in claiming his freedom. The Court should have found in Scott's favor, given that Sanford had neither a moral right nor a sufficient legal right, to own Scott. Therefore, Dred Scott should have been freed.

The Theories

The deontologist insists that human dignity be respected, respecting the rights of the individual constitutes part of that respect. John Sanford, whose property was taken away from him, had the right to either due process or to be compensated for his loss. Freeing Dred Scott would have deprived him of his property with neither due process nor compensation. In so violating his rights, by freeing Scott, Sanford's rights would have been violated and his humanity would not be respected, as required by deontology. Indeed, Sanford could well have used a more informal version of the moral principle of the Golden Rule, and asked those who wished to free Scott whether they would be willing for their own property to be taken away from them. If not, then they have no justification for seizing, arbitrarily, Sanford's property.

The utilitarian, in contrast, raises the crucial question of who is included, and who is excluded, in calculating the good, or utility, involved. Do only those who own slaves, or approve of slavery, count when seeking the greatest good for the greatest number? Or must the utility of others, including Africans and their descendants, also be included in this calculation? Clearly, if one includes all those who are affected by this decision, slaves and those treated as second-class citizens will be able to show the genuine harm caused by being systematically oppressed. The utilitarian, arguing on behalf of freeing Dred Scott, insists that he is a human being, and thus his interests must also be taken into account. To return Scott to his owner may maximize the utility of those who own slaves. But the utilitarian includes Scott, and all those like him, in determining the right course of action. In doing so, it is abundantly clear that this larger group's good is what is at stake, and to generate the greatest good for the larger group, Scott must be freed.

Kristy-Anne Glubish/Design Pics Inc./Photolibrary

Proponents of either side can use ethical theories to their advantage. A deontologist might argue that the need to respect human dignity means the slaveholder's property rights must be respected. A utilitarian might include slaves in her argument for the "greater good" and thus advocate for their freedom. What are some counterarguments using the same or different theories?

Some Conclusions

The immediate result of the Dred Scott decision was to return Scott to slavery. (Scott was freed by his new owner—Sanford having been placed in an institution for the insane—some three months after the Supreme Court decision; he died in 1858.) More significantly for the history of the United States, the Dred Scott decision brought new attention to the issue of slavery. Those in favor of continuing slavery, and its expansion, hoped that it would be allowed in at least some of the new states entering the Union. Those objecting to slavery (abolitionists) feared that they were right, and saw the Taney opinion in Dred Scott as indicating he might well support the expansion of slavery. This debate divided the Democratic Party, and united Southern Democrats around this issue (among others) of extending slavery to Western territories. It united a new party as well, known as Republicans, and in 1860 they elected Abraham Lincoln to the presidency. Before Lincoln took office, seven states seceded from the Union; after the attack on Fort Sumter (April 12, 1861), four more states seceded. Thus, only four years after the Dred Scott decision was rendered, the Civil War began, and many historians regard that decision as an important factor in bringing it about.

Where Do We Go from Here?

Obviously enough, the debate over the Dred Scott decision depends on the crucial decision of whether or not to recognize a certain group of people—in this case, Africans and their descendants—as human beings. To reject this idea is to allow slave owners to justify owning slaves as property. It may now seem remarkable, but not so recognizing blacks (then, usually, "Negroes") was fairly easy to support with the Constitution, where in the now-infamous Article 1, Section 2, Paragraph 3, slaves were counted as "three-fifths" of a person. Many historians argue that this compromise simply delayed addressing the question of slavery, an issue that would have to be settled eventually.

We can also see here how crucial such an assumption can be in developing moral arguments, and how complex the relationship can be between moral claims and legal claims. On what now seems to be an almost universally accepted view, no person should be able to own another as property. Yet only 150 years ago, not only was this viewpoint not universally accepted, but it was widely rejected. This indicates that moral views can have a historical context, and that both moral assumptions, and the laws they can lead to, can change (or at least change for some). At the same time, in the subsequent 150 years, the United States has continued to struggle with the legacy of this history and seen the treatment of African Americans as second-class citizens who were often deprived of their moral and legal rights. Ethics allows us to focus on some of the crucial points of this debate and helps clarify what is at stake there. But even though ethics has helped make explicit what assumptions and arguments are at the center of the issue of race in America, it is also clear that the controversy will continue.

Can Property Rights Conflict with Other Rights?

As we have seen, the idea—once defended, even by the Supreme Court—that a human being could own another human being is no longer defensible. In this case, moral considerations were seen to outweigh strict legal considerations; looking back at a decision such as Dred Scott may cause us to wonder what exactly the Court could have been thinking to have come to the decision it did.

Richard B. Levine/Ambient Images/Photolibrary

New York City property owners, tenants, and elected officials gather on the steps of City Hall to protest eminent domain abuse.

But other kinds of claims to property rights continue to be very contentious, in both moral philosophy and the law. The debate often begins with the claim from the Fifth Amendment: Private property shall not "be taken for public use, without just compensation." The legal issues involved, as so often happens, overlap with the moral question: What is legitimate public use? What compensation qualifies as "just" or appropriate? Can a citizen refuse to accept compensation for his or her property if the citizen does not regard it as "just"? Can public use be seen as overriding the interest of the individual whose property is being taken?

A standard example of the kind of issue involved here is known as eminent domain, the right of a government to seize property—with or without the owner's consent—as long as just compensation is provided. A city, for instance, may determine that a public park is needed in a certain area and can require homeowners to vacate their homes in order to build the park. The city is required to compensate the homeowners, giving them fair market value for their property. Often, however, that compensation is seen as unfair and not sufficient to compensate the property owner for the costs involved (which may include items difficult to give a value to, such as the time and energy involved in moving, and one's attitude toward a home: How much, for instance, is it worth to someone to have to move from where they, and their parents, were born?).

We see in such cases, again, the conflict that may arise between legal statutes and the moral philosophy those statutes presumably seek to reflect. On the one hand, the right to own property, and more or less do with it as he or she pleases, seems to be a fundamental notion enshrined in the Declaration of Independence and Constitution. Furthermore, this was a right that was regarded as "unalienable" in the writings of those philosophers, such as John Locke, who were crucially influential in shaping the thinking of the Founding Fathers, such as Washington, Madison, Jefferson, Hamilton, and Monroe. At the same time, the government may have legitimate needs to "take" property for a greater common purpose: whether, as mentioned, for a public park or for a public highway, hospital, library, or military base. Presumably, the defense of an individual's property rights does not include a "veto" over such governmental needs. Just compensation is intended as a compromise between the individual's rights and governmental needs, but, as one might imagine, the two parties may not regard such compensation as equally "just."

It is probably obvious that such debates are of great interest to lawyers, but they are perhaps of even greater interest to ethicists. In this case, for instance, one might examine the issue from the perspective of utilitarianism. On one utilitarian interpretation, the greater good is served by the government being able to take a citizen's property in order to produce a good (such as a park or highway) that can be used by the larger community. Another utilitarian might argue, instead, that the greatest good for the greatest number is served by property rights being treated as fundamental, and that the community in fact is not well served by making it too easy for governments to practice eminent domain, or for compensation to be inadequate when it does. It is excellent practice to take such an issue and develop the argument for a specific conclusion: as we have seen, this probably won't settle the debate to everyone's satisfaction, but it will help those participating in the debate to focus on the crucial questions involved and to provide a strong theoretical basis for seeing what is at issue.

4.4 Product Liability and Corporate Responsibility

Corporations offer products to consumers, and consumers purchase and use those products. Many such products carry with them some degree of risk: small, in the case of, say, shoes, but much larger in many cases (such as pharmaceuticals or parachutes). Interesting questions arise over who carries the responsibility if using such a product, as intended, causes harm to the consumer. Ethics and the law recognize that both parties shoulder some of this responsibility; however, challenging issues emerge when the degree of that responsibility is considered. Here we will look at this issue from the perspective of utilitarianism and virtue ethics, seeing again the overlap between moral and legal problems, as well as the difficulty of isolating the right of the individual from the larger social context in which that individual lives.

The Issue: Who Is Ultimately Responsible for Consumer Harm?

When purchasing a product, what risks does the purchaser assume? Does the manufacturer have any responsibility to provide a safe product, and, if so, what is the extent of that responsibility? Is the manufacturer responsible for someone who uses the product incorrectly? As we will see, drawing the relevant distinctions here is not always easy.

Corporations should have a limited share of responsibility or consumer harm

Corporations that produce products for consumers adhere to an implicit contract with those consumers: the product, used as it is intended, should be safe. Thus, a car is produced by a company and sold to the buyer on the assumption that, driven correctly, the driver will not be put in harm's way simply by driving the car. Similarly with other products, whether they be power tools, over-the-counter medications, or food. No product can be guaranteed to be 100 percent safe, however. If one buys a chain saw and uses it appropriately, the manufacturer should do whatever is possible to make it safe. But there is some degree of risk involved in using a chain saw, no matter how carefully it is produced and no matter how carefully it is used. It is unreasonable to require the manufacturer to try to eliminate the very possibility of this risk, and equally unreasonable to hold that manufacturer liable if anything at all goes wrong and the person using the chain saw is hurt.

Mike Kemp/Tetra Images/Photolibrary

No product is 100 percent perfect or safe, and some would argue that it is unreasonable to hold corporations responsible if anything goes wrong.

Clearly, some corporations have been negligent in imposing sufficiently strict standards on their products. A famous example involves the Ford Pinto. Ford had discovered that the design of the Pinto increased the likelihood of an explosion if struck from the rear. Ford calculated that fixing that defect would cost it (in 1972 dollars) approximately $137 million ($11/car), and calculated that settling lawsuits for wrongful deaths at approximately $50 million ($200,000/death, estimating 180 deaths, plus costs for injuries sustained). Ford concluded on a cost-benefit analysis that it would make better business sense not to make the repairs. While fewer deaths resulted than Ford had predicted, internal memos were leaked indicating it had made these calculations. The lawsuits involved, and the damage to Ford's reputation, radically changed the cost-benefit analysis. In the end, then, Ford probably lost money and was widely regarded as doing something seriously unethical.

But this seems to be an exception rather than the rule. Most companies see it as both right and good business practice to offer products that are safe and work as advertised. Yet

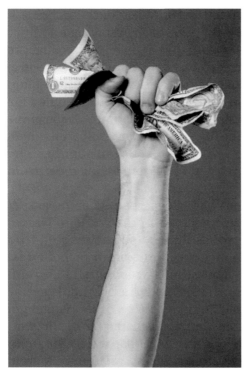

Roy Hsu/Uppercut Images RF/Photolibrary

Lawsuits filed by consumers are costly for manufacturers, and the costs of modifying products often get passed down to the consumer again.

lawsuits, frivolous and otherwise, filed by consumers dissatisfied with a product for one reason or another, are well-known. Tobacco companies and auto companies have been sued for billions for various reasons, and virtually any company that manufactures a product that could, under some circumstances, cause injury, has been sued. To avoid such lawsuits, manufacturers often have to add features to prevent injuries even when such injuries are unlikely, or are caused by the product being misused. These features, of course, cost the company a great deal to include, costs that are passed on to the consumer, thus raising the price for everyone.

This debate is most frequently discussed in a legal context, but as we have seen, laws are intended to capture in a basic sense what is right and wrong: what is, in other words, moral. To impose unreasonable requirements on a business, from a moral perspective, interferes with the right of a business to make and sell products and introduces distortions into the economic relationship between manufacturer and consumer. This interferes with the fundamental idea of the free market, making them less efficient, and thus affecting both the profits of the business and the right of the consumer to get the best deal.

The legal pressures these kinds of lawsuits place on corporations are extraordinary and add to the cost of doing business, a cost that is passed on to the consumer. Clearly, corporations must be responsible for producing goods that are safe and reliable. But they do not have the obligation, or probably the ability, to eliminate all injuries that can arise, whether the product is used in a way that it is not intended to be used, or simply because of human error or accident. To impose upon companies a burden that requires them to meet unreasonable standards is neither cost effective nor fair. Therefore, corporate responsibility must be held to a standard of liability that is reasonable.

Corporations should have a substantial share of responsibility for consumer harm

Consumers have every right to expect products that they purchase to work as advertised. Implicit in this right is the ability to assume that the product, if used correctly, will not cause injury to the user. Thus, if one uses a power tool, takes a medication, or eats in a restaurant, the consumer should be able to rely on doing so without being harmed.

Clearly enough, some consumers can be harmed by misusing a product. For instance, Homer Simpson is instructed by his computer to press "any key." His response, "Which one is the 'any' key?," indicates he is probably too incompetent to use a computer. More generally, one who does not follow the manufacturer's directions when using a product assumes the risk that misuse generates. Nor should we take seriously the consumer who watches a beer commercial on television and then sues the manufacturer when the apparent promise of young women accompanying drinking the advertised beer fails to be kept. These kinds of claims have given rise to the idea that the courts are overwhelmed with frivolous lawsuits.

The best-known frivolous law suit involved a woman and a cup of hot coffee from a major restaurant chain. As popularly presented, she spilled coffee on herself, and then sued the company for millions of dollars and won. A closer look at the case reveals that the restaurant chain knew its coffee was heated to the point that it would cause third-degree burns and had already reached out-of-court settlements in several similar cases. The woman had originally sued just to recover medical costs for the extensive and painful skin grafts that were required. However, it should be noted that she sued only after being repeatedly ignored by the corporation, and then being offered a sum of $800. The large figure she originally won was then reduced substantially on appeal.

Medicimage/Photolibrary

Consumers need to be able to rely on a product to work correctly if it is properly used. Some would argue that corporations need to be held responsible of any injury is caused.

As the Ford Pinto case indicates, corporations have to be held responsible for making decisions that are unethical and that put profit ahead of human suffering. Many such cases have become famous. The Dalkon Shield I.U.D. was shown to cause substantial harm to many of its users, and several medications (such as Fen-Phen and Vioxx) have also been demonstrated to cause severe health problems. These products were purchased in good faith, and used in accordance with the manufacturers' directions. In these, and many similar cases, the corporations were found not to have practiced sufficient testing and vigilance over the product before releasing it to the market, where consumers had no choice but to assume that it was safe.

To protect consumers' rights to safe food, medicine, and products, courts employ two different kinds of damages if a corporation is found to be negligent. **Compensatory damages** *are paid to make the victim "whole"—that is, to compensate the victim by replacing or remunerating what is lost.* **Punitive damages** *are sometimes awarded in order to indicate that the corporation acted in a way that was sufficiently negligent that compensatory damages aren't enough. Punitive damages, then, punish the guilty company, thus giving it a further warning, often by imposing a substantial fine.*

Product manufacturers, and those who purchase those products, have a mutual interest in seeing that those items offered on the market are safe. The consumer seeking a product has very little to go on when purchasing it, beyond the expectation that it is safe and that the corporation has acted in good faith. This means that the manufacturer has every obligation to meet the highest standard to ensure product safety, and that manufacturers who do not must be treated harshly. They have, after all, acted improperly and often have knowingly put otherwise unsuspecting consumers at risk. Therefore, corporations should be required to meet stringent standards of product safety and to share a substantial amount of responsibility for the products they offer.

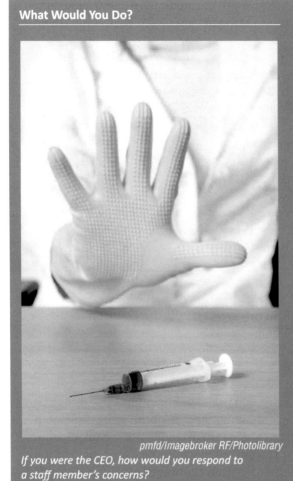

What Would You Do?

If you were the CEO, how would you respond to a staff member's concerns?

pmfd/Imagebroker RF/Photolibrary

You are the CEO of a major pharmaceutical company that has recently lost a considerable amount of its value; you have been hired to return it to profitability. Your newest product is a drug that, if successful, will prevent much of the risk of heart attack associated with diabetes. It will also be extraordinarily profitable.

The drug has been through several stages of animal and human tests and has been passed by the Food and Drug Administration. The stock value of your company has been increasing rapidly, and the drug is ready to be marketed.

One of your most-trusted scientists recently came to your office to express some serious concerns about some of the test data and the fact that this drug may have powerful side effects, including stroke, that haven't been sufficiently examined.

If you postpone marketing the drug to do these tests, it will delay the drug reaching the market by at least one year. This delay will also cause the value of the stock to plummet, and you may well be fired.

- Do you act on the basis of the FDA's approval, or take the scientist's concerns seriously?

- Do you order more tests?

- Do you delay the marketing of the drug?

- How do you justify your decision, whether to the stockholders or to the scientist?

The Theories

One might look at a free market, or set of free markets, from the perspective of utilitarianism, where all participate freely and equally. Thus, every person's happiness, or utility, is more or less equivalent to every other person's happiness or utility. In this case, then, the result that produces the greatest good for the greatest number will be that which promotes efficient and productive markets. Everything else being equal, those who sell goods and services want to get the highest price they can, those who purchase goods and services want to get the most they can for the least amount of money. Allowing these markets to operate with minimal interference permits both the greatest freedom for buyers and sellers, but also lets the market determine prices. If a seller's product is too expensive or inferior to a competitor's, his or her business will not flourish. This, of course, is the basic mechanism of free-market capitalism and has been seen to be remarkably good at creating wealth. Karl Marx, not a particularly sympathetic commentator, noted that capitalism

> has accomplished wonders far surpassing the Egyptian pyramids, Roman aqueducts, and Gothic cathedrals; it has conducted expeditions that put

in the shade all former Exoduses of nations and crusades (*The Communist Manifesto*, Part I).

Let us assume, then, that the free market, unencumbered by too much regulation or a concern about unreasonable lawsuits, is that system that produces the greatest wealth. We can also assume that such wealth can be an important part of one's utility. It follows that markets, allowed to operate freely, will produce the highest utility for all those participating in these markets, whether as producers or consumers. This means that restricting onerous and expensive regulations and preventing frivolous and otherwise unreasonable lawsuits lead to the greatest good for the greatest number. On this utilitarian perspective, the liability for any harms that come to a consumer should be kept to a reasonable level.

Even though this argument is presented within the context of economics, it is clear that it also has a significant moral dimension. If one begins with the idea that it is a basic right to be free, at least part of that freedom is to operate one's business in an efficient and profitable way. Similarly, consumers should be free and allowed to choose from the various options presented to them by the market. Too much interference, whether in the form of regulation or the threat of lawsuits, acts against these freedoms. Preventing one from being as free as possible is a violation of one's fundamental rights, and is thus prohibited on this moral theory. In sum, from the utilitarian perspective, the economic and the ethical results both point to the idea that businesses should be allowed to act responsibly but profitably, and thus not be prevented from doing so by the threat of unreasonable lawsuits.

Image100/Photolibrary

From a utilitarian perspective, consumers should have the freedom to choose just as corporations should have the freedom to do business without worrying about onerous regulation or lawsuits.

Virtue ethics insists that a person's virtues—whether honesty, courage, modesty, or the more complicated Aristotelian notion of temperance—reflect the character of that person. A complete set of virtues, balanced and in harmony, lead to what Aristotle called **arête**, which is often translated as "virtue" but might be better translated as "excellence." This excellence, combined with reason, leads to the highest good, or what Aristotle calls **eudaimonia** a term often now translated as "human flourishing."

These virtues should also hold for a corporation or a manufacturer. Fundamental to a company's ethical standards—what we might call corporate virtues—is responsibility. The manufacturer, in other words, must be responsible in offering safe products to consumers. A car, that is, should not injure the driver when operated as designed, and food shouldn't harm the consumer because of the way it is produced, packaged, or marketed. Furthermore, only the manufacturer of a given product knows if it has been adequately tested and if it is, in fact, safe to bring to the market. In contrast, the consumer must assume that the product in question is safe.

A for-profit corporation, obviously enough, must return a profit on investment to stay in business. At the same, a responsible corporation must consider factors other than profit alone. Consider a company that cuts corners on testing a pharmaceutical or gives an inaccurate representation of its testing data. This may be profitable, in that such tests can be very expensive. It may bring this product to market successfully, and thus "get away" with minimizing its testing costs. But it is, of course, acting irresponsibly and not bal-

ancing the public's right to safe drugs with its desire to turn a profit. Virtue ethics regards this as unethical behavior. An economist looking at this may add that in deciding to run the risks here, the company may bring a product to market and discover that eliminating some of the tests prevented the discovery of serious risks to consumers. This changes the cost-benefit analysis, of course; by minimizing costs, the potential for costs due to legitimate lawsuits from consumers increase. Furthermore, there can be significant, if difficult to calculate, damage to the company's reputation. From this perspective, doing the right or moral thing also makes the best business sense.

Tetra Images/Photolibrary

It can be tempting for companies to cut costs, but they need to ensure that they are not putting consumers (and themselves) at risk.

In a harsh competitive environment, there can be serious temptations to minimize costs in various ways. Succumbing to these temptations may well put consumers at risk, consumers who must operate on the assumption that the products they are purchasing are safe. To make this a good assumption, substantial regulations must be put in place to ensure the safety of consumer products. This means, further, that there must be enforcement mechanisms to guarantee that manufacturers follow both the law and standard moral procedures those laws are intended to reflect. Finally, there must be means to deal with companies that fail to follow these regulations, both by compensating victims and by punishing irresponsible corporate citizens. A well-run, ethically responsible corporation will follow these moral and legal codes and not regard liability requirements as a burden. Therefore, by instituting legal and moral guidelines for manufacturers, and punishments for those who fail to follow them, no burden is imposed on responsible corporations, and consumers can purchase products with the confidence that they are safe. This seems to be the idea behind most consumer protection law, but it should also be clear that such laws are intended to protect consumers' rights: specifically, the right to enter the market, voluntarily, with the assumption that the products we purchase function as indicated and in ways that, when used as directed, will not harm us.

Some Conclusions

Corporations want to be seen as responsible citizens; the best way to achieve this, of course, is to be a responsible corporate citizen. It is the moral thing to do, as we have seen from the perspective of both utilitarianism and virtue ethics. It is probably also the best business strategy, in that a company that produces unsafe products may suffer financially devastating lawsuits or develop a reputation that badly hurts their business. Companies have, in the past, gone out of business for both of these reasons.

Consumers, on the other hand, want to be confident that the food they eat, the pharmaceuticals they purchase, and the products they use, are safe. They have considerably less information about a given product than the manufacturer; thus, they have to be assured of this safety by regulations and laws and by the ability to sue a corporation that has caused them harm through no fault of their own.

At the same time, because companies want to turn a profit, they see onerous regulations and the threat of frivolous lawsuits as unjustified business costs. No company can prevent all possible injuries, no matter how hard they try or how high they have set their manufacturing standards. Too much regulatory interference can prevent companies from operating efficiently or can impose costs that, when passed on to the consumer, not only increase expenses and decrease profits but may make companies less competitive. Finally, if the risks of legal action become too high, companies may choose to play it safe, which could lead to less innovation and creativity and prevent the development of new products. This is a particularly important consideration in the development of new medicines.

Consumers, in turn, will seek the best bargain on the market, on the assumption that given an alternative, and everything else being equal, the least expensive product will be the rational choice. But this also assumes that all the products are equally safe, and if a product is less expensive because certain safeguards were ignored or preventive measures avoided, the consumer may well not be in a position to know that.

Both producers and consumers engaging in free markets agree that certain regulations are necessary, and that some such regulations are required so that markets not just be efficient but provide goods (and services) that are reliable and safe. Both producers and consumers, then, are in favor of "reasonable regulations." The sticking point comes when one person believes a regulation is justified and required, while another thinks that same regulation is onerous, burdensome, and unnecessary. Clearly, if the same regulation is seen by some as being reasonable and by others as unreasonable, resolving this problem can be difficult.

Ethics, along with the help of economics, can help clarify some of the issues in such disputes, although it is unlikely they will be resolved to everyone's satisfaction. The utilitarian may wish to broaden the notion of utility to include things other than quantifiable amounts of wealth. The virtue ethicist may argue that some policies that have been imposed have the relationship between profit and safety out of balance. Understanding the moral issues that underlie these economic and legal debates can help us focus on what legitimate regulations can be rightfully imposed on producers, and what kinds of penalties are justified for those companies that violate those regulations. Ethics can also require us to investigate what the consumer's obligations are in free-market exchanges. As we have seen before, questions of right and wrong are often reflected in the language of the law; here we may wish to reflect a bit more deeply on the ethical questions that help us clarify these legal conflicts.

Where Do We Go from Here?

Clearly, the debate over what are legitimate regulations and what are legitimate reasons for suing a company for alleged harm will continue. The debate itself, of course, is rather old. Scandals about food production, such as those described in Upton Sinclair's 1906 novel *The Jungle* led to the creation of the Food and Drug Administration. Thalidomide was introduced in the 1960s and was used widely not just to kill pain but to minimize the effects of morning sickness for pregnant women; it produced devastating and severe birth defects and generated widespread demands for more thorough and more systematic drug testing. Tobacco companies have been repeatedly sued and have been required to carry harsh warnings on cigarette packages. For the most part, both producers and consumers have regarded these kinds of regulatory interventions as justified and legitimate.

Martha Cooper/Peter Arnold Images/Photolibrary

An inspector with the U.S. Food and Drug Administration checks a shipment of coffee beans. Both producers and consumers generally regard the advent of the FDA and such regulatory intervention as a positive thing.

Yet there have also been consistent and widespread complaints that because government regulation has become so pervasive and lawsuits are such a commonplace threat businesses are prevented from doing what they should be doing: focusing on their business. Many companies hire employees who are responsible only for seeing that the company is in compliance with various regulations. Companies also frequently have legal staffs to avoid lawsuits or to handle those that arise. Thus, such regulations generate substantial costs. These costs, which are often passed on to the consumer, could be better spent on developing new products or improving current products. When a company has to pay a lawyer to defend it against a frivolous lawsuit, that expense is directly subtracted from revenue, thus diminishing profits for a reason that may have very little to do with the business itself.

In response, many have argued that the claim that frivolous lawsuits as a consistent and common feature of doing business in the United States has been greatly exaggerated. Many of the standard cases—the woman being burned by spilling hot coffee being the best known—appear quite different when the specific facts of the case are examined. Many other such lawsuits, clearly frivolous—one of the most famous being Roy L. Pearson, Jr., suing a dry cleaner for $67 million for losing his pants!—were often summarily dismissed. Furthermore, from this perspective, limiting the right to sue and limiting both compensatory and punitive damages may prevent individuals from receiving the full amount due them, as well as prevent courts, in particularly egregious cases, from punishing especially irresponsible corporate behavior.

What does seem to result from this dispute is the continuing need to carefully determine what are appropriate ways to protect consumers, without imposing an undue burden on business. As is so often the case, this delicate balancing act will continue to be the focus of ethical, legal, and political battles. But as we have also seen, a clear understanding of the moral issues involved helps a great deal in seeing what rights are involved, determining how we can evaluate the various and competing claims here, and understanding the ethical and political debates with which we will continue to struggle.

What Role Does the Warning "Let the Buyer Beware" Play?

An old Latin phrase, "caveat emptor," is still used with some frequency. It means "let the buyer beware." The basic idea behind this phrase is that the purchaser of a product should be aware that it is in the seller's economic interest to make a profit, and, on occasion, a product may be produced in a dishonest way to increase that profit. Thus, shortcuts may be taken in testing it, inferior materials may be used in making it, or it may promise results that it doesn't, or can't, really deliver. Most of us are familiar with this fact; we may shop with a bit of skepticism, allowing us to determine if the product is as characterized. Caveat emptor takes this skepticism just a bit further, indicating that the purchaser is responsible for any problems with the product. Presumably, this makes one a better informed consumer and gives us some motivation to be more careful shoppers. Someone who buys a car and discovers she is stuck with a "lemon," on this view, should have inspected the car more closely, done more research, or hired a mechanic to look at it. The buyer should beware of the possibility that products can be faulty, and that marketing claims may be a bit "optimistic."

A bit of healthy skepticism is probably a good idea, but consumers and manufacturers have recognized that caveat emptor, by itself, may lead from being a careful shopper to outright cynicism and the assumption that the seller may be trying to unload an inferior product. Consumers may not have the expertise or time to gain the needed knowledge to prevent this. But companies also recognize that it is to their economic advantage to gain the confidence of consumers and to gain a reputation for offering quality products. One traditional way of convincing customers to purchase a product is to offer a warranty; thus, if a product proves to be inadequate for one reason or another, the purchaser can return it for a replacement or to get her money back. In addition, for a "big ticket" item such as an automobile, the federal and state governments, have instituted "lemon laws," in order for those who discover they have been stuck with a car that fails to perform to advertised standards can return it. For the largest purchase most people make, a home, a number of safeguards—such as appraisals and required house inspections, and some sellers will even offer a short grace period during the process if one gets "cold feet"—are employed to avoid this kind of problem. In general, the more expensive the item, the less willing a consumer is to adopt caveat emptor without some kind of warranty or guarantee provided by the seller.

Classic free-market capitalism is often characterized as laissez-faire, French for "allow to do," indicating that the markets should be free of interference (generally by the government). On this view, caveat emptor is generally acceptable because competitors will eliminate a company that sells an inferior product. Once it becomes known that the product is inferior, few will buy it, and those who wish to purchase the product will get it from a competing company. In the end, the market will be efficient in rewarding those who offer a quality product and in driving those who do not out of business. But, as noted, companies recognize that consumers may not be willing to let the market work unfettered over time; after all, they may need the product now. Hence, manufacturers will see it in their interest to reassure their potential customers with warranties, guarantees, and other ways of showing that the manufacturer stands behind its product. The doctrine of caveat emptor provides an important perspective on how consumers make decisions, and what kind of moral (and economic) assumptions we make about telling the truth. It may also indicate what kind of expectations we have about being treated (and, of course, treating others) honestly.

Raygun/Cultura/Photolibrary

Some buyer skepticism is healthy, but it's in the company's best interest to offer a quality product. Also, free-market principles dictate that an inferior product will be eliminated from the market.

4.5 A Contemporary Debate: Immigration and the Borders

Traditionally—although with important exceptions—the United States has welcomed immigrants seeking a new start in life. In recent years, however, an intense debate has raged about securing the U.S. borders (particularly with Mexico), and the issue gained new attention with the attacks on the World Trade Center. Here we will present both sides of the debate from the perspective of utilitarianism, trying to clarify the issues and provide a more informed way of looking at them. An important result here will be that in determining the greatest good for the greatest number, defining the group whose interests are involved will make a significant difference.

The Issue: U.S. Border Control and Immigration

How a country controls its borders—who it lets in (and who it keeps out) and how it deals with those who come in illegally or without proper documentation—is a very controversial issue. Here we will look at some of the arguments that have been made recently on different sides of this issue.

The borders should be relatively open and immigrants welcome

Since 1886, the Statue of Liberty has beckoned those from abroad to seek opportunity in the United States, and features these lines from the poet Emma Lazarus:

Give me your tired, your poor,
Your huddled masses yearning to breathe free,
The wretched refuse of your teeming shore.
Send these, the homeless, tempest-tossed to me,
I lift my lamp beside the golden door!

Jon Feingersh/Blend Images RF/Photolibrary

With the exception of Native Americans, all Americans come from elsewhere. Some would argue that a relatively open U.S. border acknowledges the country's history as well as the economic and cultural benefits of having an immigrant population.

The story of America is, of course, the story of immigrants. With the exception of Native Americans, all Americans came from elsewhere: Europe, Asia, Africa, and South America, from all over the world, and for a wide range of reasons. Although those who came as slaves (and, often, indentured servants) did not come voluntarily, those who came willingly sought religious freedom, political freedom, and economic opportunity.

This has generally been regarded as being of great benefit for the cultural, political, and economic development of the United States. Immigrants have brought different traditions, from food to music (think "salsa," which can be both!), that have become part of the American landscape. Immigrants have been a creative and productive force, helping to generate the great "melting pot" that serves as the model for the United States and to create its powerful economy and a model for many countries around the world.

In this fashion, employers have benefited from the strong work ethic and creativity of immigrant workers and from the willingness of these workers to take on some of the most difficult and risky jobs a society needs to have done. From Welsh coal miners to Irish police officers to Chinese railroad workers to Mexican agricultural workers, these immigrants worked long hours, often in substandard and dangerous conditions, and frequently for less money than the native-born with whom, and for whom, they worked. This often culminated in the various kinds of success stories seen in America: a person willing to work hard, doing a job others don't wish to do, becoming a valued and productive member of American society, and testifying to its freedoms and opportunities.

Jim West/Imagebroker.net/Photolibrary

A U.S. Border Patrol agent stands by the fence separating Mexico and Arizona. Some advocates on both sides of the immigration policy debate agree that a country should be able to control who enters and expect immigrants to obey its laws.

In short, employers and workers have benefited from a system where workers take advantage of opportunities provided by doing important work that others won't do, or won't do on a given pay scale. If anything, these workers are being taken advantage of because, in general, they have been forced to leave their homes for jobs that are difficult, dangerous, and low paying. Furthermore, these workers pay significant amounts of taxes: income taxes, payroll taxes (FICA, Medicare), and, of course, consumption taxes (such as sales taxes).

This is not to say that borders should be entirely open and unguarded. All countries must be able to control who enters their borders and should expect those who enter to accept the laws and values of that country. Those who have come here seeking opportunity and have demonstrated their willingness to adopt the United States as their country by working hard, raising families, fighting in the armed services, and participating in their communities should be allowed to become full citizens of the United States. The process for citizenship should be accelerated for those who have indicated their desire to become citizens; they should not be discriminated against on the basis of their ethnic background; and they should be welcomed as valuable additions to the mosaic that is America.

The borders should be closed

No country can be safe if it fails to secure its borders. Indeed, even libertarians, who argue for a "minimal state" and as small a government as possible, insist that securing borders is one of the few tasks that a state is absolutely obligated to provide. Thus a government that fails to have strict controls at its border fails to carry out its responsibility, and fails to meet its most fundamental obligation.

The notion of an "open" border is ambiguous, in that such a term could refer to a set of possibilities ranging from being relatively easy to cross to being completely unguarded and porous. For purposes of this argument, an open border is simply one where there is insufficient control to keep out those people who try to enter illegally. As such, the United States' borders, particularly between the United States and Mexico, qualifies as open. This has generated a number of problems.

pmfd/Imagebroker.net/Photolibrary

Those in favor of a closed border would say that illegal immigrants are not only competition for U.S. jobs but are also a drain on resources and services.

Immigrants who come into the United States without proper documentation compete for jobs with those who are already in the job market, whether citizens or immigrants who have followed the proper procedures. Clearly enough, those who do obey immigration laws and are willing to enter the country legally should not have to compete with those who ignore those laws and enter illegally. Such competition is both unfair and, by rewarding those who break the law, provides an incentive for others to do so. In addition, a large pool of undocumented workers competing for jobs, which they are willing to do for lower wages, puts downward pressure on wages for all those competing for such jobs.

Taxpayers provide a large number of public services, from police and fire departments and public parks and libraries to schools and hospitals. These resources are expensive, and those who use these aren't asked if they are here legally or not. Hence, local, state, and federal governments incur substantial costs, and the amount of taxes paid by these immigrants is vastly less than the amount of services they use. Whether getting treated in a hospital emergency room, adding to increased class sizes in public schools, or placing greater demands on the police and criminal justice system, these increased costs must be paid for by an already burdened taxpayer.

There is also substantial evidence that some of those who enter the United States contribute to crime. This shouldn't be surprising, given that those who enter the United States illegally have already indicated their willingness to break the law. In addition to the more "traditional" crimes such as dealing in drugs, and the violence that often accompanies that activity, borders that are not sufficiently protected offer an opportunity for terrorists to enter the country. These are clearly threats to the security of a country, and require much closer supervision of the border.

Finally, while the United States has often been proud of its status as a melting pot, embracing those of many different ethnic, cultural, and religious backgrounds, the fundamental idea of the melting pot is for all to become part of one country, as the slogan "e pluribus unum—out of many, one" indicates. But if a large enough group of people enters the country without following legal procedures, they may well form a "critical mass," generating a culture within a culture. Such a group may feel more comfortable speaking its original language, following its own distinct cultural traditions, and in various other ways failing to become part of the greater society. In short, members of this group may well fail to assimilate into the United States as have past groups of immigrants and, thus, serve as a contrast to the tradition of America as the great melting pot where all feel part of a single, coherent society.

Demotix/Photolibrary

A man argues in favor of Arizona's new immigration law, known as SB 1070, which would require police officers to check a person's immigration status if they reasonably suspect the individual is an illegal immigrant. The bill gained momentum after an illegal immigrant trying to enter the country allegedly gunned down a rancher.

America should welcome those who are willing to follow the rules set down for immigration and for becoming citizens. It should not reward those who violate those rules, impose burdensome costs on taxpayers, and increase demands on the social services those taxpayers provide. To maintain security, a fundamental obligation of the government, the border should be strictly controlled, and those who have already entered the country illegally should be identified and returned to their native lands.

The Theories

The utilitarian seeks the greatest good for the greatest number, or to maximize the utility of all involved in a specific decision. Given various options, what should be done is that which produces this result. This raises a traditional difficulty, however: How does one determine the relevant group that is affected by a given decision? Using a utilitarian approach to the question of border control and immigration, we will be able to highlight the fact that how one characterizes the problem, and the relevant group, may produce contrasting results, even when the same ethical theory is utilized. Not only will this discussion show us that two utilitarians can disagree, but it will also reemphasize that solutions to problems often depend, in important ways, on how the problem itself is described.

On one application of utilitarianism, we should include not just the citizens and legal aliens of a given country but also those in other countries who seek to leave and those who remain. This, of course, is a much larger group, and extending the numbers involved will almost certainly change the utility calculation, and just as certainly make it more complex.

Clearly enough, the utility of those leaving an economically depressed condition to go where they can find employment, and possibly benefits, and take advantage of increased social services will be increased. Employers will, presumably, increase their utility by hiring workers, either to do jobs that are difficult to fill or at relatively lower wages. Another factor should not be minimized: those who come to another country and find employment often send money back home. These remittances can be substantial, and of course increase the utility of those who receive them. Finally, consumers will pay less for products because labor costs are lower. Thus, if wages are relatively low for agricultural workers, that savings is reflected in the cost of fruits and vegetables. In contrast, if wages are relatively high for those products, those costs are passed on to the consumer. Thus, the consumer's utility is increased by these products having lower prices.

Two issues complicate this utility calculation. First, it is difficult to determine what costs are imposed by undocumented workers on social services, and it is also difficult to determine with any precision how much in taxes these workers themselves pay. As the old saying goes, there are "lies, damned lies, and statistics," and currently the statistical information on costs and taxes is a source of great controversy within the debate on immigration. To generate an accurate utility calculation, reliable data are needed. Second, it seems clear that for low-wage and unskilled workers, a large pool of undocumented workers does depress wages. Thus, those who might otherwise make more money doing a job may lose out to someone willing to work for less. In this case, then, the utility of those workers would be lowered, and also must be factored into a general utilitarian analysis.

However, if the utilitarian perspective is taken broadly to include everyone affected directly and indirectly, it can be seen that the greatest good for the greatest number might well justify having relatively open borders and an accelerated route to citizenship for those who are already here. As we have seen, the calculations are complex; however, they do allow us to see how the choice of group involved will play a significant role in making those calculations. Understanding better what is involved here should also contribute to meeting some of the challenges immigration poses.

In contrast, a utilitarian may restrict the utility calculations to just those who live in the country hosting undocumented workers. Here some of the variables—such as the benefits

Thousands of Latino Americans protested in April 2010 before Arizona Gov. Jan Brewer said she would sign the controversial immigration bill, SB 1070. A utilitarian's position on immigration depends on whom he decides to include in his evaluation. What are the various positions a utilitarian could take?

of payments going to an immigrant's native land, and, for that matter, the utility of those gaining employment by violating immigration laws—are eliminated. It is more difficult to put a price on such intangible factors as the effect on citizens, and other legal residents, when they see their jobs taken by those who weren't willing to follow immigration law. The effects of depressed wages, however, are genuine and will certainly be relevant to the utility of those who either are unemployed or are required to work for lower pay. One may also have to consider the trade-off between lower consumer prices and these lower wages, specifically lower wages for legal residents. And while those who hire workers may regard their utility as increased due to lower labor costs, it is not clear that this increases the utility of society as a whole. Finally, the costs on social services—greater demands on health care, education, and police and fire protection—must also be factored in. Again, statistics may be found to support various results, but it should be clear enough that there is an argument that the increased costs, and the lower wages that result, from extensive illegal immigration do not produce the greatest good for the greatest number in a country with a large number of such immigrants. Thus, a utility calculation can surely be provided that will be found persuasive in demonstrating that a country that has tight border controls, and restricts immigration, will have a higher utility than it would otherwise. From this utilitarian perspective, we see the contrasting argument for a strict immigration policy.

Some Conclusions

If one result is clear from this debate, it is that profound disagreements erupt, almost immediately, over the question of immigration and border control. On the one hand, it is obvious that America has been greatly strengthened by the large and diverse groups of immigrants who settled here. Yet in a time of economic insecurity, immigrants may burden a system of social services and take jobs from citizens who need them. Both those who argue for a relatively open border and those who insist on strict border controls agree that there must be some degree of control; the dispute is rather what is an appropriate degree of control. The dispute also rages over how those who have already come here, as undocumented workers or illegal aliens, should be treated. Some argue for an accelerated path to citizenship for those who have shown the ability to work hard and contribute to their communities. Others insist that those here illegally should be deported, not just to punish them because they have violated the law but also to send a message to others who might be considering following this same path.

A further result is that we can see some of these issues can be greatly clarified by getting more accurate and precise information. For instance, what is the effect on wages if a substantial pool of workers is competing for a relatively small number of jobs? What are the economic costs to a country due to various social services being provided, and to what extent are those costs offset by the taxes paid by these immigrants? These and related economic questions continue to be analyzed to provide a fuller and more helpful evaluation of both the costs and the benefits involved.

We also see that it is, at times, difficult to separate economic issues from moral issues. For instance, does a person have a right to make a living to feed his or her family? Does this person then have a right to go where the work is to find such opportunities? If we are willing to recognize such a right, then what happens when this person's right interferes with another person's similar right? Here, importantly, we recognize that our economic analysis has an important moral factor, as can be seen in the term "economic injustice." Here the very notion of what is just or unjust is fundamentally an ethical issue; but much of our understanding of what is just or unjust, or right or wrong, will be informed by our economic understanding of the situation. Consequently, economics will tell us a good bit that is relevant to the moral issues involved, but at the same time, our ethics will have important information to add that allows us to evaluate economic decisions.

Cooperphoto/Flirt Collection/Photolibrary

There isn't really enough information to do a true cost-benefit analysis for the immigration question. Does competition for jobs drive up wages? Is the use of social services offset by taxes?

From this, we can see something that has arisen with some frequency in our discussion of moral problems: the in-principle difficulty of keeping individual rights distinct from questions of what is right for the greater community in which that individual lives. One may have a right to work, and flourish, but how that right is exercised must be understood, at least in part, by the effects it has on others. In this way, then, we can see that many ethical issues, even those about individual rights and responsibilities, can only be fully understood when their examination includes the social component, a component that, in any case, is often virtually impossible to eliminate.

Where Do We Go from Here?

There is little doubt that debates over immigration policy will continue and play an important role in both political campaigns and the development of American society. When economic insecurity increases, the issue is almost certainly bound to receive more attention, whether from those who identify illegal immigration as a cause of that insecurity or from those who insist that undocumented workers play an important role in providing economic vitality and strength. Furthermore, economic pressures often generate an increase of people leaving one country for better economic conditions elsewhere. Different people draw different conclusions from this: some suggest that improved economic conditions elsewhere will decrease the numbers of immigrants; others insist that bad economic conditions provide still more reason to prevent immigrants from entering the country.

Demotix/Photolibrary

The immigration debate can take on a nasty tone of nationalism. In this picture, an Arizona anti–illegal immigration protester voices support for Maricopa County Sheriff Joe Arpaio, a controversial figure known for his stance against illegal immigration. The protestor's board also references the 2009–2010 outbreak of H1N1, more commonly known as swine flu, which was first reported in Mexico.

A further implication is the renewed emphasis on nationalism. On the one hand, some have insisted on a specific conception of the United States that is challenged by large numbers of immigrants from different cultures and traditions. This can simply be the expression of a concern that a traditional picture of the United States is changing, or it can take a much sharper tone, descending into what might even be regarded as xenophobia, and an attitude of "us versus them." In contrast, others indicate that the fact that so many immigrants wish to enter the United States indicates that the American experiment is working, and that America is strengthened and energized by the new ideas and work ethic brought by immigrants. On this view, without denying that borders must be controlled to some degree, the desire for many people to enter the United States is an endorsement of its policies of freedom, and of the opportunities it offers.

The world and its economy (or economies) are becoming increasingly interdependent. With the development of much more rapid transportation, telecommunications, Internet business, and the various other technological innovations in recent years, we can no longer regard countries as individual units that are independent and self-reliant. Rather, virtually all developed and developing countries have important relationships with each other, in terms of its labor force, markets for its products, and as sources of raw materials. There seems to be little doubt that this globalization will continue, and probably accelerate, and this will make it more likely that the movement of people toward jobs (as in immigrants seeking work) and jobs toward people (as in outsourcing a workforce to another country) will become even more common. Ethics and economics have a great deal to inform us about these new developments, and, as we have seen, gaining an increased understanding of both components will be crucial in making quality decisions in both the short and the long term for all involved.

Do We Have Obligations to Other Countries?

In the twentieth-century, some social scientists (particularly economists and political scientists), mathematicians, biologists, and philosophers turned their attention to a field called game theory. This field didn't have much to do with traditional games, such as checkers or baseball. Rather, it examined how people and organizations interacted, and what kinds of strategies they adopted to attempt to win the game they were in. In certain ways, game theory brought a new level of rigor to traditional senses of negotiation and bargaining and also helped make clear both what assumptions one made in dealing with others and what were the best kinds of strategies one might adopt.

One well-known example of this involves the issue of nuclear weapons. After World War II, the United States and the Soviet Union had large stockpiles of such weapons, more than enough to destroy each other. During the Cold War, when tensions between the two countries ran high, the idea of mutually assured destruction was put forth. We can describe this simply with two countries, A and B. Both A and B have enough weapons to destroy each other. But if A were to attack B, B would still have enough weapons to destroy A. So while A's attack may be successful in destroying B, B promises that, if so attacked, it will also destroy A. Since no country wishes to be destroyed, it would never initiate an attack, for such an attack would result in the destruction of both countries. On this basic strategy, the Soviet Union and the United States maintained a large stockpile of nuclear weapons, yet never attacked each other. This is an example of what is now called game theory.

Academics have investigated many complicated games, with various numbers of people and involving people and organizations (such as businesses or countries) that may have different levels of information available to them. The various strategic results were often very technical, mathematical, and complex. But in 1981, a political scientist named Robert Axelrod published his results on these strategic interactions and indicated that what is possibly the simplest strategy of all was both the most effective and the most stable, a strategy known as tit-for-tat. Tit-for-tat indicates that when in a competitive environment, you should do what the other person (or organization) does. If the other person is nice, you should be nice; if the other person refuses to cooperate, you should refuse to cooperate. In a sense, Axelrod makes more precise a strategy most of us have recognized and used since we were children. If a person is cooperative, you cooperate with that person; if a person is not cooperative, you resist cooperating as well. Axelrod's account has spawned an enormous discussion, and its share of criticism; nevertheless, we can use his idea to look at two different ways countries can regard each other so that we might better understand how countries can treat each other ethically (Axelrod, 1984).

On one model, two countries simply regard themselves as competitors. Each country acts in its own self-interest, similar to the view we saw earlier described as ethical egoism. These two countries may practice the strategy of tit-for-tat, and end up cooperating or not. What will determine the results will depend on what each country regards as being in its own self-interest after watching the other country. This is, of course, a very traditional way of looking at international relations: every country is out solely for its own good, but because all the countries are aware of this, such selfishness is simply the fundamental assumption of how the game is played.

On another, somewhat more sophisticated and complex model, it is argued that such an egoistical approach fails to do justice to the fact that so many country's economies are fundamentally intertwined with each other. One way of seeing how this model is distinct from the other conception is to see that one country's self-interest can be, at least with some frequency, in the interest of another country. That is, rather than two countries regarding each other simply as competitors, there may be occasions where both realize that specific policies can be mutually beneficial. This perspective offers some possibilities that may be neglected or ignored in the more traditional picture.

Jon Feingersh/Blend Images RM/Photolibrary

Game theory examines how countries interact and relate to one another to stay on top. One of the simplest strategies, tit-for-tat, suggests that if one party cooperates or resists, the other will mirror the action.

This may be of relevance to the question of immigration. If, as many have urged, illegal immigration is a reaction to economic pressures, then alleviating that pressure may decrease the need for such immigration. As an example, if high unemployment in Mexico tends to make more people leave for the United States to find work, one way of dealing with this is to work on improving the Mexican economy. If Mexico's economy improves, there will be considerably less reason for people to leave to find work elsewhere. In this way, both the United States and Mexico see it as in their individual interests for the Mexican economy to improve. While this does not seem to conflict with the basis strategic thrust of tit-for-tat, it emphasizes the mutual benefits that can result when two interdependent countries recognize that their own self-interest may involve, or even require, promoting the self-interest of the other country.

Some Final Questions

1. Is society simply a collection of individuals, pursuing their own interests? Or do people understand who they are by the various roles they play in society, as the member of a family, a business, and a community? Explain.
2. Think of an activity that might be considered a "victimless" crime. Are there, in fact, some people who are affected, directly or indirectly, by this activity, who therefore might be considered "victims"? Explain.
3. If a company harms someone, intentionally or through negligence, is it enough for that company to pay compensation to that person? Or should a further message be sent, punishing the company by levying substantial fines to prevent such behavior in the future? Explain.

What Can Ethics Teach Us?

Chapter Outline

We have looked at a number of issues in ethics, as well as some of the different positions people have adopted on these issues, and applied several of the ethical theories that have been developed in order to strengthen the arguments involved.

It may seem that we have dealt with a large number of ethical issues—we have!—but there are, of course, many more that we haven't explored. After considering this material, however, you should be much better equipped to give each ethical question that arises at work, at home, and in everyday life the critical examination and informed scrutiny needed to make a right decision.

In the following sections, we will briefly examine some further topics that are relevant for the study of ethics. Some of these topics emerge from a more general consideration of moral questions; others reinforce some of the results we have already seen. One thing we will continue to see is that the relationship between individual rights and society will be important in determining the scope and limits of those rights.

5.1 Victimless Crimes

The term "victimless crime" has been used to characterize a number of activities that some people find morally objectionable but that generally are thought to be the kinds of things people engage in voluntarily. If I choose to do something that may harm me, but no one else, should I be prevented from doing so? Or, if two people voluntarily engage in behavior that doesn't seem to harm any others, is there any compelling reason not to allow them to do so? The claim is then made that if there really isn't a victim, then there really isn't a crime. It is worth considering this a bit more closely, to determine if there are such things as victimless crimes, and, in turn, what the issues here reveal about the relationship among individuals, their rights, and society.

Dick Enters/Imagebroker RF/Photolibrary

Smoking marijuana is often considered a victimless crime. Name some other examples of victimless crimes outside of the ones presented in this text.

Standard examples of crimes said to be victimless are such things as use of marijuana and other illicit drugs, prostitution, public intoxication, ticket scalping, and public nudity. Motorcycle helmet laws and seat belt laws are often pointed to as involving such restrictions on the rights of citizens. After all, if someone chooses not to wear a helmet when riding a motorcycle, that person seems willing to risk whatever harm may result.

Does this person have a right *not* to wear a helmet? If forced to do so, is that an illegitimate restriction of his or her right? In general, then, do people have the right to engage in activities, as individuals or with others, that may be either offensive to some, or even harmful to those who take part, as long as these activities are voluntary and consensual?

A Matter of Rights

Clearly enough, it seems wrong to violate another person's rights. If a thief hits Joe over the head and takes his wallet, Joe's rights—not to be hit over the head and to keep his property—have been violated. This is an example of the harm principle, where a person suffers some sort of harm. In contrast is the offense principle; if a house across the street from mine is painted a hideous color of neon orange, it may offend me. The question is whether it offends me, and my neighbors, enough to be regarded as a crime, or a violation of the rights of those who live in the neighborhood. This contrast isn't always easy to draw. If the same person who has chosen to paint her house neon orange insists on playing heavy metal music throughout the night at a very high volume, I may be able to point to an actual harm: namely, my inability to sleep and the problems that causes for me at work, for instance. But what if she insists on decorating her house with signs, flags, and pictures that question, in an obscene and blasphemous way, my religion, and the religion of most of my neighbors: Does an actual harm need to be shown, or can the offensiveness here be sufficient for me to prevent her from so decorating her house?

The question of voluntariness is an important factor here. I may find pornography offensive, but I also recognize that those who choose to view it do so voluntarily. I have little choice in seeing my neighbor's house; the offense in question is imposed upon me, against my will. Nor can I prevent my children from being exposed to this offensive display on a daily basis.

Dirk Westphal/Fancy/Photolibrary

You may dislike someone's appearance—or even be offended by it—but it's unlikely that your rights are being violated as a result. Or you might be offended by your neighbor's choice of house color, but it might not necessarily be considered a crime or a violation of your rights. Can you think of a situation where you were offended but it wasn't a crime?

Can a Crime Really Be Victimless?

Some have argued that, on closer inspection, there are really few, if any, victimless crimes. Even though prostitution is a standard example of an agreement entered into by consenting adults, commentators insist that it is naïve to see this as a genuinely voluntary agreement. Many, if not most, prostitutes engage in this activity due to economic necessity, or by being forced to by others, and many, if not most, prostitutes have reported being physically harmed by their customers. These customers also may create victims in that they cheat on their spouses, and society as a whole may regard prostitution as itself offensive. As we can see, the notion of victimless crime may depend on how we

Not all victimless crimes are as victimless as initially assumed. A prostitute, for example, may have no other means to feed her family. Can you think of other examples?

choose to identify the potential victims involved. Similarly, a person may choose not to wear a seat belt, but if he or she is injured because of that choice, costs are potentially incurred by those who pay for the ambulance and emergency care that can result. In these cases, others have various kinds of harms imposed, involuntarily, upon them; in that sense, they are, indirectly, victims of such crimes. If the consequences of such activities always have the potential for creating such victims, then it becomes less clear that there are victimless crimes, or at least as many as we may have originally thought.

Here again, we see that an individual's rights and freedoms may have to be understood within a social context. It may not always be easy to draw the line between where my rights stop and yours begin. But if the exercise of my freedoms, in pursuing my goals, interferes with the exercise of your freedoms, in pursuing your goals, it seems that we must at least attempt to draw that line. As we will now see, philosophers have argued for some time about how to understand this connection between individuals, and the effect these connections have on the society in which we live.

5.2 The Relationship Between Individual and Society

Even though the relationship between an individual—virtually all of whom live in communities with other individuals—and society as a whole is very complex, we can at least outline here a couple of different ways of looking at this relationship. These different approaches will then give us distinct perspectives on how to look at the moral rights people possess, helping us, in turn, make clear what is at stake in understanding moral problems.

Aristotle and the *Polis*

The first model of the relationship between individual and society may not be familiar, but it is quite ancient. Aristotle provides a clear statement of it in his *Politics*. He claims that "all humans are, by nature, political animals." As always with Aristotle, his language needs to be examined very closely. Here "by nature" indicates what might be called an "essential property," or a characteristic some thing must have in order to *be* that thing. For instance, a triangle has, by nature, three sides and three angles; without this essential property, a triangle wouldn't be a triangle. In the same way, Aristotle indicates that human beings by nature are "political animals"; in other words, if someone isn't a "political animal," he or she isn't really functioning as a human being. But what does "political animal" mean? (Aristotle, *Politics*, vol. I.1253a2)

The term "political animal," in contemporary terms, may suggest someone seriously involved in political activity: deal-making, campaigning, fundraising, and so on. This is not at all what Aristotle means. Rather, by "political" he means someone who lives in a *polis*, the term for Greek city-states, such as Athens, that structured the society of Aristotle's day. More generally, one is "political" in this sense if one lives with others in a community and, as a result, comes to depend on others and is depended upon by others. (The term translated as "animal" is *zoon*, from which English gets such words as "zoology"; thus, "animal" here is to be taken quite literally.) This aspect of dependence is crucial for this conception of society. Just as I depend on others to provide food, transportation, shelter, and many other things, others may depend upon me, for instance, to teach philosophy to their children, to buy that food, transportation, and shelter, and to pay my taxes. My activities, then, are deeply involved with the activities of the others in my community. Indeed, we may in some cases consider the planet as a whole to be our community: when I use electricity or gasoline, I am involved with those who produce coal or petroleum, and I may be affecting the climate of many of those around me. Multiplied by the number of people in the community, whether my immediate neighbors or all those living on the planet, these effects are pervasive and substantial.

Some thinkers have described our society as an interconnected community in which we are dependent on one another. How do your actions affect someone in your neighborhood? In a different country?

As the poet John Donne put it, some 18 centuries after Aristotle, "No man is an island, entire of itself; every man is a piece of the continent, a part of the main." For both Donne and Aristotle, the individual must be understood in social terms; the very notion of what a human being is will be informed by all the interpersonal relationships by which we identify ourselves. This isn't, perhaps, very surprising: consider how you identify yourself, and you will probably immediately think in terms of being a parent and/or a son or daughter, a brother or sister, a spouse, as well as in terms of the other relationships that provide your sense of self, be it religion, ethnicity, citizenship of a specific country, or all the other things human beings take to be important. On Aristotle's conception of society, we cannot eliminate these kinds of characteristics, for, to a large extent, they determine who we are.

Collection of Individuals

In contrast, a conception of society is provided by other thinkers who regard society as just a collection of individuals. Rather than beginning with society or the political community as a whole, this conception begins with the individual, and the sum-total of those individuals is what creates society. This model, naturally, emphasizes individual rights and responsibilities, and regards the rules and conventions of society as the result of agreements made among those individuals.

This model of society is perhaps more familiar than the previous one; it has had a great deal of importance in American ethical and political theory due to such important thinkers as John Locke, who in turn was an important influence on Thomas Jefferson and many of the Founding Fathers. The economist Adam Smith is perhaps the best representative of this view; for Smith, society is constituted by individuals pursuing their own interests. If I need a good or service, another person will find it in his or her self-interest to provide that good or service. We negotiate with each other, and, ideally, I will get what I want as will the other person. Society is constructed out of countless such exchanges, and these exchanges are predicated upon the idea that we all act in our own self-interest. As Smith famously observed, "It is not from the benevolence of the butcher, the brewer, or the baker that we expect our dinner, but from their regard to their own interest." In a certain sense, as we have seen, this kind of perspective is selfish, in that we are seeking our self-interest. Indeed, some writers have insisted that such selfishness is a "virtue," and generates the most efficient way resources can be utilized in order to create a prosperous society. In this context, "selfishness" is not necessarily the kind of greed that appears on canonical lists of the seven deadly sins; it is, rather, precisely the way rational human beings should act, and the way we should expect others to act toward us, at least within an economic context.

Seeking Balance

Of course, these two models are rarely seen in a pure form. No individual makes all of his or her decisions by determining the effect on the entire potential community affected; thus, it would seem a bit strange if, before going to the movies, I tried to calculate all the

Stockbrokerxtra Images/Photolibrary

Some see society as a collection of individuals rather than a cohesive whole. What view do you lean more toward?

ramifications that my plans for the evening would have on those involved (from the person making the popcorn to the actors in the film)! At the same time, society probably doesn't, and probably could not, function if everyone solely sought his or her own self-interest; should I really ask myself, when holding the door for someone following me into a building, "What's in it for me?"

These two perspectives do provide some insight into the relationship between individuals and society. On the one hand, the social context provides a great deal of information, often neglected, about individual activities and the potential harms they may cause, particularly when "community" is interpreted broadly. On the other hand, individuals, when taken as fundamental, and thus when society is treated as the aggregation of all those individuals and their competing interests, may regard some restrictions on their rights as unfair and oppressive. When looking at ethics, and the rights and responsibilities involved, it may be a good idea to look at the specific question from both perspectives to gain a fuller understanding of what is at issue.

Clearly, balancing the rights of the individual and of society will continue to be a source of argument and controversy.

5.3 Implications of a Global Society

As noted in the previous section, some activities we take part in can affect large groups of people—not just those in our town, state, or country, or even those in other countries or across the world. When we consider the cumulative effects of human activities, we may discover that what we do has significant implications for many others.

Economy

Increasingly, due to technological developments in communication, transportation, and other aspects of society that contribute to interdependence, areas of the world that once had very little interaction are now often quite interdependent. A car may be built in Tennessee, but the parts may come from Mexico, the engineering may have been done in India, some of the financing of the plant may have been provided by China. The cars themselves may be sold in Europe and run on gasoline from Venezuela. This interdependence can have both positive and negative consequences, depending on whose perspective one adopts. For instance, a person getting a job in Indonesia may welcome the opportunity to make a relatively decent wage, while the person losing that job because it is being outsourced to Indonesia may look at the situation in an entirely different way.

Environment

More than just economic relationships are involved in this global interdependence. Burning coal in the northern United States has been implicated in an increase of acid rain in Canada; the 1986 Chernobyl nuclear accident in the former Soviet Union had implications for agricultural production and consumption in Finland, Sweden, and even the United Kingdom. There seems to be increasing evidence that carbon emissions, from factories and automobiles, are having an effect on the planet's climate and that such effects will become more pronounced with increased carbon emissions that will occur with the industrial development of India and China. The destruction of large parts of the Brazilian rainforest, it has also been suggested, has had implications for people living in communities far from Brazil; in addition to its effects on global climate, losing some of

Roy Botterell/Flirt Collection/Photolibrary

Have you ever looked to see where your clothes are made? Clothing is one of many products that show how various countries depend on one another.

169

its rich ecological diversity may threaten certain options for the development of new plants and new pharmaceuticals.

Tracking the specific results of human behavior is hardly an exact science, but it is clear from these examples that economies and environments have components that are fundamentally interdependent between and among different countries. This interdependence, presumably, will increase with the growth of globalization, and thus is another factor that must be considered when evaluating moral behavior. If by my behavior I contribute to the pollution of a water system that affects others outside my immediate community, should I consider myself responsible, if only in my own small way, for having had a negative impact on those who depend on that water system?

Luiz C. Marigo/Peter Arnold Images/Photolibrary

Global interdependence can also include environmental actions. For example, deforestation and its effects on the water cycle in the Amazon rainforest can affect the climate as far away as North America.

As we have seen, different theories have been proposed to provide both rigor and systematicity to our investigations of moral problems. The deontologist requires that an act be done out of duty, or because it is right; the utilitarian will look at the consequences of a given act and, given the options available, will endorse the act that produces the greatest good for the greatest number. The increasing global dimension of our society doesn't alter the theory behind these responses any more than it fundamentally changes how we think of the role virtue plays in human flourishing. Nor does it necessarily alter the results we arrive at from such perspectives as ethical egoism, relativism, or emotivism. What it does require us to do is recognize that our perspective on who is involved in the human community may go well beyond our relatively narrow framework of ourselves or our family, town, or state. Rather, many of our decisions on what is right and wrong, particularly when multiplied by a large number of people making similar decisions, may have to factor in the much larger effects such decisions have on a planet that is becoming increasing interdependent and interrelated.

5.4 Learning from History

In earlier sections, we looked at various historical events, examining some of the moral, legal, and political issues involved. Thus, we explored the arguments that considered whether it was right for women to vote, right to inter Japanese Americans in camps against their will, and right to protect a person's right to property if that property was, in fact, a person (albeit a slave). The Spanish American philosopher George Santayana once famously observed, "Those who cannot remember the past are condemned to repeat it." Clearly enough, Santayana's remark is quite relevant for the kind of historical questions we have looked at. Even though we may have moved past an era where women cannot vote, citizens are rounded up solely on the basis of their ethnicity, and slavery is not regarded as morally abhorrent, similar questions will continue to arise. Seeing how ethical and legal arguments can be applied to historical questions can provide valuable insight into how our current debates can learn from earlier approaches (and mistakes) and can also continue to remind us not to forget this past and risk repeating it.

Returning briefly to the question of the Dred Scott decision, let us assume that even though the decision may have been technically justifiable in terms of property rights, it was immoral to allow one person to own another. Let us also assume that all members of our community generally share this view, and that the respect and dignity owed to all human beings prohibits chattel slavery. (These should be safe assumptions.) What can we learn from that history that is still relevant today?

What Makes Us Human?

Perhaps the most important lesson we can draw from the Dred Scott decision is the point already made: human beings deserve respect and deserve to be treated with dignity. But this immediately raises concerns about who is included in, and who is excluded from, the category of "human being." Slaves, at the time of the founding of the United States, were counted as "three-fifths" of a human being, a clear violation of this central claim of human dignity. We nevertheless continue to have debates about whether those at the extreme ends of the spectrum of human life "count" as human beings. For instance, does a person who has been declared to be in a persistent vegetative state, with no hope of recovery, retain rights? If so, what are those rights? Because this person cannot communicate, who serves as his or her representative? Do we have an obligation to keep this person alive, perpetually, or do we have an obligation to allow the person to die, presumably with dignity? Indeed, is a person whose brain shows no activity still a "person"? These are difficult questions, and the insight we can derive from such historical examples as we examined, as well as many other similar cases, can provide extremely useful information in trying to come to grips with these difficult moral questions.

Medicimage/Photolibrary

While it is clear that people of different ethnic backgrounds can claim their basic rights as human beings, what about people in a vegetative state or on life support?

At the other end of life, debate has raged, and continues to rage, over the status and "personhood" of the fetus. Some argue that the fetus is a human being, with inherent dignity, at conception. Others argue that, especially in its earliest stages—whether a zygote or a blastocyst—the fetus is a clump of cells. It thus does not deserve the same degree of respect owed to other parties involved, specifically the mother carrying it. Still others insist that that rights of the mother continue to outweigh those of a fetus in the third trimester, justifying late-term abortions if determined to be necessary or recommended by a physician. Yet others have attempted to identify different stages—such as quickening (being able to move on its own), sentience (being able to feel pain), or viability (being able to survive outside the womb)—wherein the fetus can be regarded as a human being. Clearly, this effort to characterize a fetus continues to be a profoundly controversial topic, but as we can see from history, much of this debate is informed by who is, and who isn't, regarded as "human," and what criteria we use to establish what is, and what isn't, human.

Beyond Humanity

Another lesson we can draw from history is that moral questions are not solely about human beings, but can also be about the environment in which humans live. It has been argued, for instance, that the devastation suffered by those who lived on Easter Island was due, in large part, to deforestation and other ways of treating the environment without regard to the consequences. It has also been argued that the catastrophic loss of life in the earthquake in Haiti was made considerably worse by the impact of extensive clear-cutting of forests, leading to extensive and dangerous landslides. From these, and many similar examples, we can see that how natural resources are used is highly relevant to our consideration of moral and ethical questions.

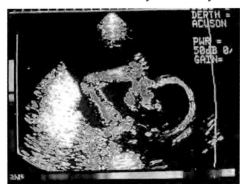
Howard Sochurek/Photolibrary

Abortion and anti-abortion advocates argue viciously over when a fetus is considered a human and allowed its own rights.

Photoalto/Photolibrary

Learning from history can also be applied to environmentalism—learning from our mistakes so our children don't inherit bigger problems.

Finally, we should not forget that historical examples can serve as important reminders that we are historical figures, and that what we do may have an enormous impact on future generations. Many ethicists insist that those future generations should be taken into account in evaluating moral decisions insofar as we have an obligation to those generations to leave a planet that is at least inhabitable and, preferably, sustainable. Whether seen from a religious or secular standpoint, this perspective claims that we are stewards of the planet, and to violate our obligations to take care of it not only violates the duties of such stewardship but also burdens future generations with obligations to which they obviously did not consent.

In short, we can learn a lot from looking at how ethical decisions have been made in the past, both in understanding the interaction among humans as well as human interaction with their environment. Mistakes that have been made in the past can be extremely helpful reminders that we must do our best not just to avoid such mistakes in the future but also to understand the kind of reasoning that led to these mistakes, in hopes of improving our abilities to, if not avoid all such errors, to at least minimize those we are bound to make.

5.5 Why Study Ethics?

As we saw earlier, Aristotle claimed that human beings, by nature, live in communities. He claimed, further, that a person separated from his or her community would be similar to a single, isolated checker piece. Just as a single checker piece isn't able to carry out its function (namely, participate with other pieces in a game of checkers), a single, isolated human being, not living in a community with others, is unable to live a genuine human life, which requires the interaction and interdependence a community, however small or large, provides. Whether we agree with Aristotle that living in a community is a necessary feature of human life, it does seem clear that the vast majority of us live in communities, and that we interact with others in wide range of ways. The question that relates politics and ethics, as well as relating the individual and society, is really this: What must human beings do in order to live together, and, especially, in order to flourish?

Fundamentally, the basic question of ethics—what is right and wrong?—also informs our ability to live with each other in communities. Although the question seems simple enough, as we have seen, from gun ownership through employees' rights to immigration, the answers can be bewilderingly complex. But we shouldn't forget, at the same time, that we all possess some basic conception of right and wrong. Psychologists, such as Jean Piaget and Lawrence Kohlberg, studied extensively the moral development of children and argued that children as young as four begin to develop a sense of morality (Kohlberg, 1984; Piaget, 1932). Others have even claimed that children are born with an innate sense of right and wrong. From the other direction, a traditional test of insanity is known in the law as the "M'Naghten rules," from an 1843 British court case. Simply put, the basic requirement, to determine if a person is sane, is whether that person can tell right from wrong. There are, naturally, ethical and legal issues involved in this determination, but the important philosophical implication should be clear: a fundamental indication of insanity is the inability to tell right from wrong. Indeed, we assume that those around us can draw this distinction, and we no doubt expect others to assume that about us. In general, whether from educational psychology, legal history, or plain common sense, our conception of the human being as rational is that human being's sense of morality.

Michaela Begsteiger/Imagebroker RF/Photolibrary

It is fundamental for us to be able to tell right from wrong to function properly in society.

Yet, as we have also seen, it is often not very easy to determine in a specific case the right thing to do. Whether trivial, such as deciding to lie to one's spouse about an upcoming surprise party, or tragic, such as determining what the appropriate treatment is for a person in a persistent vegetative state, we often confront ethical dilemmas, where no solution seems obviously correct.

Consider a very simple example. Steve is having supper with his family, and his son has recently gotten in trouble for lying to his mother. The phone rings, and Steve is confident that the person calling is the annoying neighbor who manages always to call at dinnertime and seems to talk forever. As his son goes to answer the phone, Steve considers whether he should have his son tell the neighbor that he isn't there. On the one hand, this would allow him to avoid talking to the neighbor and to continue enjoying his family dinner. But wouldn't it be a bit hypocritical, after having just lectured his son about why it was wrong to lie, to ask his son to lie?

Jose Luis Pelaez Inc./Blend Images RF/Photolibrary

Some believe that children at a very early age develop a sense of morality. Can you think of a time when you were a child or you were with a child that you observed that?

Philosophers and others have worried about these questions of right and wrong for a very long time and have for an equally long time suggested various answers. Some, such as Aristotle, focused on the character of the person and recommended a harmonious balance of virtues, such as temperance and courage. Appropriately done, the virtuous person will know what the right thing to do is, and will do the right thing. Since Aristotle's day, two other approaches have become popular. The utilitarian looks at the various options one confronts, and argues that the choice that leaves the largest group better off than any other option will be the right thing to do. In contrast, the deontologist will not take into consideration the consequences of the act, but will focus on the rule involved, and the reason a given act is done. An act that is the right thing to do in this case would, then, be that which treats others with the respect and dignity due to them, and would be the sort of thing that anyone in the same situation should always do.

Others, rather than trying to provide specific answers to ethical challenges, offer a different kind of approach. The ethical egoist insists that one should do what is in one's self-interest, whereas the ethical relativist argues that there is no "objective" sense of right or wrong and that different communities—and even different individuals—have their own sense of right and wrong. The emotivist takes an even more dismissive approach, claiming that when we call something "right" it just means we approve of it, and when we call something "wrong" it just means we don't.

As long as people live together in communities, questions will arise about doing the right thing and how we can identify what it is. We can see how important these questions are by considering how often, and how long, we spend talking to our children about them. The study of ethics offers the possibility of understanding the issues involved here with greater rigor and increased sophistication. Studying ethics allows us to dig a little deeper into the problem so that we can see what may be irrelevant to offering a solution to those problems. This, in turn, allows us to understand these questions and their solutions, with increased clarity, and to defend our answers with better reasons and better arguments. Through the study of ethics, we confront our moral challenges better equipped to understand them and to solve them. Thus, ethical questions will always confront us, and although we may not all agree on the solution, by studying ethics we are much better prepared to tackle the questions because we have developed the skills needed to understand them.

Some Final Questions

1. Some have argued that there really aren't such things as victimless crimes, pointing to the fact that innocent people may be harmed by those who participate in such activities as prostitution and drug use. Think of an activity that you would regard as *not* having such effects, and could truly be regarded as victimless. Is it possible that others might regard your example as still generating victims or cause others harm? Explain.

2. The current pace of development in technology, and transportation, indicates that human beings will continue to become increasingly interdependent. If this is the case, then many decisions one society makes may have consequences for those in many other societies. Think of such a decision that might generate a significant dispute *between* societies. What approach should such societies, or countries, adopt in order to resolve, or at least minimize, such disputes?

3. You are talking to a 12-year-old girl one day, either your child or the daughter of a good friend. She discovers that you are taking a course in ethics, and asks, sincerely, "Why should one study ethics?" How would you answer her?

Biographies

More details, and further bibliographical entries, can be located here:
http://www.encyclopedia.com/ssc/107185-philosophy-biographies.html.

Aristotle (384–322 BCE) Greek philosopher and scientist. Aristotle is one of the most important and influential thinkers in the history of Western philosophy. He wrote on virtually all fields known during his era and made original and significant contributions to logic, physics, biology, ethics, politics, and metaphysics, among others.

Axelrod, Robert (1943–) Professor of political science at the University of Michigan. Axelrod is best known for using game theory to explore how people cooperate with each other and how cooperative strategies change and evolve. His book *The Evolution of Cooperation* (1984) has been influential in political theory, economics, and many other disciplines in the humanities and social sciences.

Hume, David (1711–1776) Scottish philosopher and historian. Hume emphasized the senses and what results could be legitimately be drawn from the information they provided. He made important contributions to the theory of knowledge, ethics, the philosophy of religion, and the philosophy of art. Often regarded as a skeptic in his own day, he is now widely seen as possibly the greatest philosopher to have written in English.

Kant, Immanuel (1724–1804) German philosopher Kant is often regarded as the most influential philosopher of the modern era. He attempted to show the necessity of concepts to make judgments about information provided by the senses and is famous for having written the three great Critiques: *Critique of Pure Reason, Critique of Practical Reason*, and *Critique of Judgment*. He also made fundamental contributions to metaphysics, epistemology, ethics, philosophy of art, and philosophy of religion.

Locke, John (1632–1704) British philosopher and political theorist. Locke is best known for an early and lengthy defense of empiricism in *An Essay Concerning Human Understanding* and a defense of classical liberalism in his *Two Treatises of Government*. Locke's political theory had a profound influence on the thinking of those who founded the United States.

Machiavelli, Niccolò (1469–1572) Italian philosopher, writer, and political theorist. Machiavelli is best known for his book *The Prince*, which emphasizes realism and practical ways of gaining and maintaining power, by providing instruction to a political ruler.

Macintyre, Alasdair (1929–) Scottish philosopher who has lived and taught in the United States since 1969. Macintyre is best known for helping revive virtue ethics to make it part of the contemporary debate in ethics. He also has written influential work in political philosophy and in the history of philosophy.

Mill, John Stuart (1806–1873) British philosopher. Mill is best known for developing a sophisticated account of utilitarianism. He also made important contributions to economics and politics, and his *On Liberty* is widely regarded as a classic defense of freedom.

Plato (approx. 428 BCE–approx. 348 BCE) Greek philosopher; student of Socrates, teacher of Aristotle. Plato is regarded as without question one of the two or, at most, three important philosophers in the history of Western philosophy, making indispensable contributions to political theory, ethics, metaphysics, and philosophical inquiry itself.

Rawls, John (1921–2002) American political philosopher. Rawls is best known for his defense that justice should be understood in terms of fairness. Presenting his views systematically in *A Theory of Justice,* Rawls proposed that if people were to design a society in which they would live behind a "veil of ignorance," those things that lead to injustice (such as discrimination on the basis of sex, gender, race, class, and other things) would be eliminated or minimized. He is widely regarded as one of the most influential political thinkers of the twentieth century.

Williams, Bernard (1929–2003) British moral philosopher. Williams is perhaps best known for his criticisms of utilitarianism, willingness to recognize the complexity of moral questions, and the importance of history, politics, and culture for understanding philosophy. He also wrote a provocative account of Descartes's philosophy.

References

Alexrod, R. (1984). *The evolution of cooperation*. New York: Basic Books.

Aristotle, *History of animals*.

Aristotle, *Politics*, I.1253a2.

Department of Justice (2006). Crime in the United States, 2005. Retrieved from http://www.fbi.gov/ucr/05cius/offenses/expanded_information/data/shrtable_07.html.

Graduate Institute of International and Development Studies (2007). *Small arms survey 2007: Guns and the city.* Retrieved from http://www.smallarmssurvey.org/files/sas/publications/yearb2007.html.

Herbert, B. (2007, April 26). Hooked on Violence. *The New York Times.* Retrieved from http://select.nytimes.com/2007/04/26/opinion/26herbert.html.

Huntington, S. (1957). *The soldier and the state: The theory and politics of civil-military relations,* Cambridge, MA: Belknap Press of Harvard University Press.

International Institute for Strategic Studies (2008). The Military Balance. Retrieved from http://www.iiss.org/publications/military-balance/.

Kohlberg, L. (1984) *Essays on moral development: Vol. 2. The psychology of moral development.* San Francisco: Harper & Row.

Korematsu v. United States, 323 U.S. 214 (1944).

Loving v. Virginia, 388 U.S. 1 (1967).

MacIntrye, A. (1981). *After virtue*. Notre Dame, IN: University of Notre Dame Press.

Marx, K., & Engels, F. (1848/1967). *The communist manifesto.* New York: Pantheon.

Mill, J. S. (1909). *On liberty.* Harvard Classics Vol. 25. New York: P. F. Collier & Son.

Miller v. United States, 307 U.S. 174 (1939).

Piaget. J. (1932). *The moral judgment of the child.* Glencoe, IL: Free Press.

Rawls, J. *A theory of justice.* (1971). Cambridge, MA: Harvard University Press.

Scott v. Sandford, 60 U.S. 393 (1856).

Glossary

Act utilitarianism   applies to specific acts within the idea of utilitarianism, emphasizing that what is moral is what produces the greatest good for the greatest number. Contrast with *rule utilitarianism.*

Arête   is the term used by the ancient Greeks to refer to excellence; it is used to characterize what is good and just.

Argument   is a set of reasons (premises) put forth to support a claim or conclusion.

Compensatory damages   are the damages paid to the winner of a lawsuit to make that person "whole," or to provide compensation for losses, injuries, or harms suffered.

Conclusion   is a claim advanced as the result of a set of reasons; it indicates what an argument seeks to establish.

Cost-benefit analysis   evaluates a decision in terms of its advantages (benefits) and disadvantages (costs). Although it is often used in evaluating the economic impact of a decision, many argue that costs and benefits should not be understood only in terms of financial impact.

Deduction/deductive argument   describes the structure of a specific kind of argument; a valid deductive argument is one in which the conclusion must be accepted as true if the premises are accepted as true.

Deontology   is the study of moral obligation and necessity, finding the source of ethical correctness in the rules according to which one acts. It rejects utilizing the results or consequences of an act to evaluate an act as moral; thus, it is a non-consequentialist theory. It is regularly contrasted with the consequentialist theory of utilitarianism.

Dialectic   regards philosophical inquiry as carried out through discussion and debate, and necessarily takes into consideration one's opponent's views in formulating one's own position. With Hegel and Marx, "dialectic" came to have a very technical meaning, specific to their philosophical approach.

Emotivism   is the perspective on ethics that moral evaluations are merely expressions of approval and disapproval, and that ethics is constituted solely by these expressions.

Ethical egoism   is the view that all human behavior should be regarded as done in the self-interest of the individual person to satisfy that person's goals and desires.

Eudaimonia   is the term used by the ancient Greeks to indicate a justified state of happiness. Coming from the words meaning "good" and "spirit," it is often translated as "human flourishing," particularly to indicate that *eudaimonia* does not refer simply to pleasure but also to one's sound mental state.

Externalities   are those effects suffered (or, in some cases, enjoyed) by those who were not involved in the decision that resulted in those effects and whose interests were not considered in making that decision. A standard example is pollution: it may affect people in other countries, even though they had no input in the decision making and their views may not have been taken into account.

Free riding, in economics   expresses the idea of one who enjoys the benefits of society without paying for it, either by consuming more than one's share or paying less for what one consumes. An example would be a person who doesn't pay taxes but still benefits from police and fire protection.

Golden Mean   is the middle point between two extremes of too little or too much, particularly in the context of Aristotle's ethics. For Aristotle, all virtues must be possessed appropriately, not in an excessive or deficient way.

Induction/inductive argument   describes a specific type of argument that offers support for a conclusion in such a way that the conclusion is only probable; the degree of that support will indicate the inductive strength of the specific argument. Given the evidence, the better it supports the conclusion, the stronger the argument is said to be.

Intuition   is the immediate, spontaneous, or unreflective certainty about a certain claim. Rather than being supported by reason or argument, intuition does not rely on inferences for the conclusions it affirms.

Logic   is the systematic study of arguments—including inductive and deductive reasoning—to determine the correct rules of reasoning and when those rules are violated.

Premise   is a sentence put forth as a reason to accept a given conclusion.

Psychological egoism   is the view that people should do whatever maximizes their utility.

Punitive damages   are the damages paid, usually in addition to compensatory damages, to punish a person or company that has caused harm to another. These are designed to prevent behavior that might lead to similar harm in the future.

Reflective equilibrium is the point at which the parties in a dispute reach a conclusion, after reflecting on, and revising, the various positions each party holds. Reflective equilibrium incorporates the idea of discussion and an empathetic understanding of other positions, leading to potential revisions of the stances of each party in the discussion.

Relativism is the view that one's beliefs are conditioned by one's culture, society, and/or community. Rejecting absolute claims, all assertions must be evaluated in terms of the context in which they arise.

Retributivism is the theory that a fair punishment must have an appropriate and equal balance between the harm done and the punishment received for committing that harm.

Rule utilitarianism applies the basic principle of utilitarianism, that what is moral is what produces the greatest good for the greatest number, to develop general rules of moral behavior on the basis of that principle. Contrast with *act utilitarianism*.

Sentence is an assertion of something; it is sometimes characterized as expressing propositional content. Sentences are used to construct arguments, and on the assumption of bivalence are said to be either true or false.

Slippery slope fallacy is a mistake in reasoning that asserts a sequence of events will follow from a first; since the conclusion of that sequence is objectionable, this fallacy concludes that the beginning of the sequence is objectionable. An example would be that because many heroin addicts smoked marijuana, smoking marijuana leads to heroin addiction. (Since most heroin addicts also drank milk, a similar argument would suggest that the sequence leading to heroin addiction began with milk drinking.)

Sound/soundness is the property of a valid deductive argument, the premises of which are, in fact, accepted as true.

Utilitarianism is an ethical theory that determines the moral value of an act in terms of its results and if those results produce the greatest good for the greatest number. As a consequentialist theory, it is contrasted with non-consequentialist theories, such as deontology.

Virtue ethics is an ethical theory that evaluates the morality of the person doing a given act, rather than the act itself. Virtue ethics thus emphasizes that the various virtues and whether a person reflects those virtues in his or her actions are crucial to moral evaluation.